⊙ 普通高校专业英语教程系列

工商管理英语

司爱侠 陈红美 马飞 编著

清华大学出版社
北京

内 容 简 介

本书是针对工商管理专业学生编写的工商管理英语教材。本书内容切合行业实际，面向工作环境，力求切实提高读者实际使用行业英语的能力。

本书的每一单元由以下几部分组成：课文——包括管理基础理论、主要应用领域、常用方法和新颖观念；单词——给出课文中出现的新词，读者由此可以积累专业基础词汇；词组——给出课文中的常用词组；缩略语——给出课文中出现的且业内人士必须掌握的缩略语；注释——讲解课文中出现的难句，培养读者的阅读理解能力；习题——巩固所学知识；阅读材料——提供最新的行业资料，进一步扩大读者的视野。书后附有词汇总表，以便读者背记词汇或作为小词典使用。

本书既可作为高等院校工商管理类的专业英语教材，也可作为相关专业的培训教材，供工商管理从业人员自学使用。

版权所有，侵权必究。举报：010-62782989，beiqinquan@tup.tsinghua.edu.cn。

图书在版编目（CIP）数据

工商管理英语 / 司爱侠，陈红美，马飞编著. —北京：清华大学出版社，2016（2024.2重印）
（普通高校专业英语教程系列）
ISBN 978-7-302-45690-2

Ⅰ.①工… Ⅱ.①司… ②陈… ③马… Ⅲ.①工商行政管理—英语—高等学校—教材
Ⅳ.① F203.9

中国版本图书馆 CIP 数据核字（2016）第 277239 号

责任编辑：徐博文
封面设计：平　原
责任校对：王凤芝
责任印制：沈　露

出版发行：清华大学出版社
网　　址：https://www.tup.com.cn, https://www.wqxuetang.com
地　　址：北京清华大学学研大厦A座　　邮　编：100084
社 总 机：010-83470000　　邮　购：010-62786544
投稿与读者服务：010-62776969, c-service@tup.tsinghua.edu.cn
质量反馈：010-62772015, zhiliang@tup.tsinghua.edu.cn

印 装 者：三河市君旺印务有限公司
经　　销：全国新华书店
开　　本：185mm×260mm　　印　张：12　　字　数：292千字
版　　次：2016年11月第1版　　印　次：2024年2月第8次印刷
定　　价：65.00元

产品编号：070311-03

普通高校专业英语教程系列

编 委 会

主　编　司爱侠

编　者　宋德富　姜彦君　张强华　吕淑文
　　　　　马占青　古绪满　张美兰

前 言
Preface

工商管理业是我国从业人员较多的一个行业。该行业外资活跃、国际交往密切、竞争十分激烈。具备相关专业知识并精通外语的人员往往处于竞争的优势地位，成为行业中的佼佼者。职场对从业人员的专业英语水平要求很高，这有力地推动了从业人员学习专业英语的积极性。本书就是面向工商管理从业人员而编写的行业英语教材。

本书结合即将进入工商管理行业的学生情况、结合学生毕业后的就业环境、根据未来工作的实际要求，做了精心的加工。本书共有十个单元，每一个单元由以下几部分组成：课文（Text）——包括管理理论、主要领域、常用方法和新颖观念；单词（New Words）——给出课文中出现的新词，读者可以积累专业基础词汇；词组（Phrases）——给出课文中的常用词组；缩略语（Abbreviations）——给出课文中出现的且业内人士必须掌握的缩略语；注释（Notes）——讲解课文中出现的难句，培养读者的阅读理解能力；习题（Exercises）——巩固所学知识；阅读材料（Reading Material）——提供最新的行业资料，进一步扩大读者的视野。书后附有词汇总表，以便读者背记词汇或作为小词典使用。

读者在使用本书的过程中，如有任何问题都可以通过电子邮件与我们交流（邮箱地址：2qh3882355@163.com；cici2323@tom.com），也可通过出版社与我们联系。邮件标题请注明姓名及"工商管理英语（清华大学版）"。本书教学 PPT 和习题参考答案，读者可以从出版社官方网站下载。

本书既可作为高等院校工商管理类的专业英语教材，也可作为相关专业的培训教材，或供工商管理从业人员自学使用。

由于时间仓促，编者水平有限，书中难免有疏漏和不足之处，恳请广大读者和同行提出宝贵意见，以便再版时进行修正。

编者
2016 年 6 月

目 录
Contents

Unit 1

Text A	Management	1
Text B	Managerial Skills	10
Reading Material	Fayol's Principles of Management	15
参考译文	管理	18

Unit 2

Text A	Business Plan	21
Text B	Five Ps For Strategy	28
Reading Material	SWOT Analysis and Five Competitive Forces	32
参考译文	商业计划	34

Unit 3

Text A	Human Resource Management	37
Text B	The Nature of Motivation	45
Reading Material	Who Appraises Performance?	49
参考译文	人力资源管理	51

Unit 4

Text A	Marketing Management	53

Text B	Marketing Management Philosophies	60
Reading Material	Target Consumers	64
参考译文	市场营销管理	66

Unit 5

Text A	Operations Management	69
Text B	The Ever Changing World of Operations Management	77
Reading Material	Manufacturing and Services: Differences and Similarities	81
参考译文	运营管理	84

Unit 6

Text A	Logistic Management	87
Text B	Logistical Integration Objectives	93
Reading Material	Supply Chain Management	98
参考译文	物流管理	100

Unit 7

Text A	Total Quality Management	103
Text B	What is Six Sigma?	109
Reading Material	International Quality Standards	113
参考译文	全面质量管理	116

Unit 8

Text A	Project Management	119
Text B	Behavioral Aspect of Project Management	126
Reading Material	Project Management Tiers	129
参考译文	项目管理	132

Unit 9

Text A	Financial Management	135
Text B	Financial Accounting and Managerial Accounting	140
Reading Material	The Six Most Important Ideas in Finance	144
参考译文	财务管理	147

Unit 10

Text A	MIS	149
Text B	Components of Information System	154
Reading Material	Information Management and Society	158
参考译文	管理信息系统	161

附录	词汇总表	163

Unit 11

Text A	MIS	149
Text B	Components of Information System	154
Reading Material	Information Management and Society	158
参考译文	管理信息系统	161

Unit 1

Text A

Management

Management in businesses and organizations is the function that coordinates the efforts of people to accomplish goals and objectives by using available resources efficiently and effectively.

Management involves identifying the mission, objective, procedures, rules and manipulation of the human capital of an enterprise to contribute to the success of the enterprise. This implies effective communication, human motivation and some sort of successful progress or system outcome. As such, management is not the manipulation of a mechanism (machine or automated program), not the herding of animals, and can occur either in a legal or in an illegal enterprise or environment. Management does not need to be seen from enterprise point of view alone, because management is an essential function to improve one's life and relationships. Management is therefore everywhere and it has a wider range of application. Based on this, management must have humans, communication, and a positive enterprise endeavor. Plans, measurements, motivational psychological tools, goals, and economic measures (profit, etc.) may or may not be necessary components for them to be management. At first, one views management functionally, such as measuring quantity, adjusting plans, meeting goals. This applies even in situations where planning does not take place. From this perspective, Henri Fayol (1841–1925) considers management to consist of six functions: forecasting, planning, organizing, commanding, coordinating and controlling.

However, in the present era the concept of management is identified in the wide areas and its frontiers have been pushed to a broader range. Apart from profitable organizations even Non-Profit Organization (NPO) apply management concepts. The concept and its uses are not constrained. Management on the whole is the process of planning, organizing, staffing, leading and controlling.

1. Managerial Roles

In addition to the broad categories of management functions, managers in different levels of the hierarchy fill different managerial roles. These roles were categorized by researcher Henry Mintzberg, and they can be grouped into three major types: decisional, interpersonal, and informational.

1.1 Decisional Roles

Decisional roles require managers to plan strategy and utilize resources. There are four specific roles that are decisional. The entrepreneur role requires the manager to assign resources to develop innovative goods and services, or to expand a business. Most of these roles will be held by top-level managers, although middle managers may be given some ability to make such decisions. The disturbance handler corrects unanticipated problems facing the organization from the internal or external environment. Managers at all levels may take this role. For example, first-line managers may correct a problem halting the assembly line or a middle level manager may attempt to address the aftermath of a store robbery. Top managers are more likely to deal with major crises, such as requiring a recall of defective products. The third decisional role, that of resource allocator, involves determining which work units will get which resources. Top managers are likely to make large, overall budget decisions, while middle mangers may make more specific allocations. In some organizations, supervisory managers are responsible for determine allocation of salary raises to employees. Finally, the negotiator works with others, such as suppliers, distributors, or labor unions, to reach agreements regarding products and services. First-level managers may negotiate with employees on issues of salary increases or overtime hours, or they may work with other supervisory managers when needed resources must be shared. Middle managers also negotiate with other managers and are likely to work to secure preferred prices from suppliers and distributors. Top managers negotiate on larger issues, such as labor contracts, or even on mergers and acquisitions of other companies.

1.2 Interpersonal Roles

Interpersonal roles require managers to direct and supervise employees and the organization. The figurehead is typically a top of middle manager. This manager may communicate future organizational goals or ethical guidelines to employees at company meetings. A leader acts as an example for other employees to follow, gives commands and directions to subordinates, makes decisions, and mobilizes employee support. Managers must be leaders at all levels of the organization; often lower-level managers look to top management for this leadership example. In the role of liaison, a manager must coordinate the work of others in different work units, establish alliances between others, and work to share resources. This role is particularly critical for middle managers, who must often compete with other managers for important resources, yet must maintain successful working relationships with them for long time periods.

1.3 Informational Roles

Informational roles are those in which managers obtain and transmit information. These roles have changed dramatically as technology has improved. The monitor evaluates the performance of others and takes corrective action to improve that performance. Monitors also watch for changes in the environment and within the company that may affect individual and organizational performance. Monitoring occurs at all levels of management, although managers at higher levels of the organization are more likely to monitor external threats to the environment than middle or first-line managers. The role of disseminator requires that managers inform employees of changes that affect them and the organization. They also communicate the company's vision and purpose.

Managers at each level disseminate information to those below them, and much information of this nature trickles from the top down. Finally, a spokesperson communicates with the external environment, from advertising the company's goods and services to informing the community about the direction of the organization. The spokesperson for major announcements, such as a change in strategic direction, is likely to be a top manager. But, other more routine information may be provided by a manager at any level of a company. For example, a middle manager may give a press release to a local newspaper, or a supervisory manager may give a presentation at a community meeting.

2. Management Levels

Most organizations have three management levels: first-level, middle-level, and top-level managers. These managers are classified in a hierarchy of authority, and perform different tasks. In many organizations, the number of managers in every level resembles a pyramid. Each level is explained below in specifications of their different responsibilities and likely job titles.

2.1 Top

The top consists of the board of directors (including non-executive directors and executive directors), president, vice-president, CEOs and other members of the C-level executives. They are responsible for controlling and overseeing the entire organization. They set a tone at the top and develop strategic plans, company policies, and make decisions on the direction of the business. In addition, top-level managers play a significant role in the mobilization of outside resources and are accountable to the shareholders and general public.

The board of directors is typically primarily composed of non-executives who owe a fiduciary duty to shareholders and are not closely involved in the day-to-day activities of the organization, although this varies depending on the type (e.g., public versus private), size and culture of the organization. These directors are theoretically liable for breaches of that duty and typically insured under directors and officers liability insurance. The board sets corporate strategy, makes major decisions such as major acquisitions, and hires, evaluates, and fires the top-level manager (Chief Executive Officer or CEO) and the CEO typically hires other positions. However, board involvement in the hiring of other positions such as the Chief Financial Officer (CFO) has increased. In 2013, a survey of over 160 CEOs and directors of public and private companies found that the top weaknesses of CEOs were "mentoring skills" and "board engagement", and 10% of companies never evaluated the CEO. The board may also have certain employees (e.g., internal auditors) report to them or directly hire independent contractors; for example, the board (through the audit committee) typically selects the auditor.

Helpful skills of top management vary by the type of organization but typically include a broad understanding competition, world economies, and politics. In addition, the CEO is responsible for implementing and determining (within the board's framework) the broad policies of the organization. Executive management accomplishes the day-to-day details, including: instructions for preparation of department budgets, procedures, schedules; appointment of middle level executives such as department managers; coordination of departments; media and governmental relations; and shareholder communication.

2.2 Middle

It consists of general managers, branch managers and department managers. They are accountable to the top management for their department's function. They devote more time to organizational and directional functions. Their roles can be emphasized as executing organizational plans in conformance with the company's policies and the objectives of the top management, they define and discuss information and policies from top management to lower management, and most importantly they inspire and provide guidance to lower level managers towards better performance.

Middle management is the midway management of a categorized organization, being secondary to the senior management but above the deepest levels of operational members. An operational manager may be well-thought-out by middle management, or may be categorized as non-management operate, liable to the policy of the specific organization. Efficiency of the middle level is vital in any organization, since they bridge the gap between top level and bottom level staffs.

Their functions include:
- Design and implement effective group and inter-group work and information systems.
- Define and monitor group-level performance indicators.
- Diagnose and resolve problems within and among work groups.
- Design and implement reward systems that support cooperative behavior. They also make decision and share ideas with top managers.

2.3 Lower

It consists of supervisors, section leaders, foremen, etc. They focus on controlling and directing. They usually have the responsibility of assigning employees tasks, guiding and supervising employees on day-to-day activities, ensuring quality and quantity production, making recommendations, suggestions, and up channeling employee problems, etc. First-level managers are role models for employees that provide:
- Basic supervision
- Motivation
- Career planning
- Performance feedback

Unit 1

New Words

management ['mænidʒmənt] *n.* 管理，处理，经营

coordinate [kəu'ɔ:dinit] *vt.* 调整，整理

efficiently [i'fiʃəntli] *adv.* 有效率地，有效地

effectively [i'fektivli] *adv.* 有效地，有力地

mission ['miʃən] *n.* 使命，任务

rule [ru:l] *n.* 规则，准则，标准

manipulation [mə,nipju'leiʃən] *n.* 处理，操作，操纵

enterprise ['entəpraiz] *n.* 企业，事业，计划，事业心，进取心

imply [im'plai] *vt.* 暗示，意味

progress ['prəugres] *n.* 前进，进步

outcome ['autkʌm] *n.* 结果，成果

essential [i'senʃəl] *adj.* 本质的，实质的，基本的

relationship [ri'leiʃənʃip] *n.* 关系，关联

communication [kə,mju:ni'keiʃn] *n.* 沟通，传达

endeavor [in'devə] *n. & vi.* 尽力，努力

measurement ['meʒəmənt] *n.* 测量，度量

measure ['meʒə] *n.* 方法，测量，措施

profit ['prɔfit] *n.* 利润，益处，得益 *vi.* 得益，利用 *vt.* 有益于，有利于

adjusting [ə'dʒʌstiŋ] *n.* 调整，调制

situation [,sitju'eiʃən] *n.* 情形，境遇

perspective [pə'spektiv] *n.* 远景，前途，观点，看法，观察

control [kən'trəl] *n. & vt.* 控制，支配，管理

concept ['kɔnsept] *n.* 观念，概念

frontier ['frʌntjə] *n.* 国境，边疆，边境

constrained [kən'streind] *adj.* 被强迫的，拘泥的

staff [stɑ:f] *vt.* 在……工作；为……配备职员；任职于

hierarchy ['haiərɑ:ki] *n.* 层次，层级

role [rəul] *n.* 角色，任务

decision [di'siʒən] *n.* 决策，决定

interpersonal [,intə'pə:sənl] *adj.* 人与人之间的；人际的；涉及人与人之间的关系的

strategy ['strætidʒi] *n.* 策略，战略

assign [ə'sain] *vt.* 分配，指派

handler ['hændlə] *n.* 处理者，管理者

unapparent [,ʌnə'pærənt] *adj.* 不明显的，不清楚的，模糊的，不曾预料的

aftermath ['ɑ:ftəmæθ] *n.* 结果，后果

robbery ['rɔbəri] *n.* 抢掠，抢夺

supervisory [,sju:pə'vaizəri] *adj.* 管理的，监督的

responsible [ris'pɔnsəbl] *adj.* 有责任的，可靠的，可依赖的，负责的

determine [di'tə:min] *v.* 决定，确定

negotiator [ni'gəuʃieitə] *n.* 磋商者，交涉者，出售者，交易者

supplier [sə'plaiə] *n.* 供应商，厂商

negotiate [ni'gəuʃieit] *v.*（与某人）商议，谈判，磋商

share [ʃεə] *n.* 共享，参与，份额，参股 *vt.* 分享，均分，共有，分配

preferred [pri'fə:d] *v.* 提出，提升，建议；选择某事物

contract ['kɔntrækt] *n.* 合同 *v.* 订约

merger ['mə:dʒə] *n.* 合并，归并

figurehead ['figəhed] *n.* 名头，有名无实的领导

liaison [li(:)'eizɑ:n] *n.* 联络]

alliance [ə'laiəns] n. 联盟，联合
compete [kəm'pi:t] vi. 比赛，竞争
dramatically [drə'mætikəli] adv. 戏剧地，引人注目地
improve [im'pru:v] v. 改善，改进
monitor ['mɔnitə] n. 监管人员 vt. 监控
performance [pə'fɔ:məns] n. 履行，执行，成绩
threat [θret] n. 威胁
disseminator [di'semineitə] n. 传播者
vision ['viʒən] n. 愿景
disseminate [di'semineit] v. 散布，传播，宣传
trickle ['trikl] v. 滴流，使淌下；慢慢地移动
spokesperson ['spəukspə:sn] n. 发言人，代言人
announcement [ə'naunsmənt] n. 宣告，发表，一项公告
strategic [strə'ti:dʒik] adj. 战略的
routine [ru:'ti:n] n. 例行公事，常规，日常事务
presentation [,prezen'teiʃən] n. 报告，介绍，陈述
classify ['klæsifai] v. 分类
authority [ɔ:'θɔriti] n. 权力，职权
pyramid ['pirəmid] n. 金字塔 v.(使)成金字塔状，(使)渐增，(使)上涨
responsibility [ris,pɔnsə'biliti] n. 责任，职责
significant [sig'nifikənt] adj. 重大的，重要的
mobilization [,məubilai'zeiʃən] n. 动员

fiduciary [fi'dju:ʃəri] adj. 基于信用的，信托的，受信托的 n. 被信托者，受托人
duty ['dju:ti] n. 义务，责任，职责，职务
activity [æk'tiviti] n. 行动，行为
liable ['laiəbl] adj. 有责任的，有义务的
breach [bri:tʃ] n. 违背，破坏 vt. 打破，突破
auditor ['ɔ:ditə] n. 审计员，查账员
framework ['freimwə:k] n. 构架，框架，结构
accomplish [ə'kɔmpliʃ] vt. 完成，达到，实现
budget ['bʌdʒit] n. 预算 vi. 做预算，编入预算
schedule ['ʃedju:l; 'skedʒul] n. 时间表，进度表 v. 确定时间
coordination [kəu,ɔ:di'neiʃən] n. 协调，调和
emphasize ['emfəsaiz] vt. 强调，着重
define [di'fain] vt. 定义，详细说明
spire [in'spaiə] vt. 鼓舞，激发
guidance ['gaidəns] n. 指导，领导
operate ['ɔpəreit] v. 运营，运转，起作用
indicator ['indikeitə] n. 指标
diagnose ['daiəgnəuz] v. 诊断
behavior [bi'heivjə] n. 举止，行为
supervisor ['sju:pəvaizə] n. 主管，监督人，管理人
recommendation [,rekəmen'deiʃən] n. 劝告，建议
suggestion [sə'dʒestʃən] n. 提议，意见，暗示
career [kə'riə] n. 事业，生涯
diagnostic [,daiəg'nɔstik] adj. 诊断的

Unit 1

Phrases and Expressions

human capital 人力资本
contribute to 有助于，导致
from... point of view 从……的角度
view... as 把……看作
from this perspective 从这个角度看
be pushed to 被推到
be grouped into... 被分成……
disturbance handler 干扰处理者
first-line manager 初级管理者
middle level manager 中层经理
top manager 高层管理者，高管人员
resource allocator 资源分配者
be likely to 可能
inform sb. of 告知某人
board of directors 董事会
non-executive directors 非执行董事
be responsible for 负责
set a tone 定调子
develop strategic plans 制定战略计划

executive directors 执行董事
be accountable to sb. 对某人负责
fiduciary duty 受托责任，受信义务，信托义务
outside resource 外部资源
be involved in 涉及，参与
depending on 根据，依据
be liable for 负责，承担责任，对……有责任
directors and officers liability insurance 公司董事及高级职员责任保险
internal auditors 内审员
audit committee 审核委员会
branch manager 分公司经理
department manager 部门经理
in conformance with 与……一致
provide guidance to 指导
reward system 奖励制度
section leader 部门领导

Abbreviations

NPO (Non-Profit Organization) 非营利组织
CEO (Chief Executive Officer) 执行总裁，首席执行官
CFO (Chief Financial Officer) 首席财务官

Notes

1. Management in businesses and organizations is the function that coordinates the efforts of people to accomplish goals and objectives by using available resources efficiently and effectively.

　　本句中，that coordinates the efforts of people to accomplish goals and objectives by using available resources efficiently and effectively 是一个定语从句，修饰和限定 function。在该从句中，to accomplish goals and objectives 是一个动词不定式短语，作目的状语，by using available resources efficiently and effectively 是介词短语，作方式状语。

2 This role is particularly critical for middle managers, who must often compete with other managers for important resources, yet must maintain successful working relationships with them for long time periods.

本句中，who must often compete with other managers for important resources, yet must maintain successful working relationships with them for long time periods 是一个非限定性定语从句，对 middle managers 进行补充说明。在该从句中，compete with 的意思是"与……竞争"。

3 Monitoring occurs at all levels of management, although managers at higher levels of the organization are more likely to monitor external threats to the environment than middle or first-line managers.

本句中，although managers at higher levels of the organization are more likely to monitor external threats to the environment than middle or first-line managers 是一个让步状语从句。在该从句中，be likely to do sth. 的意思是"可能做某事，很有可能做某事"。

例如：He is likely to take over the company. 他可能要接管这家公司。

4 The board of directors is typically primarily composed of non-executives who owe a fiduciary duty to shareholders and are not closely involved in the day-to-day activities of the organization, although this varies depending on the type (e.g., public versus private), size and culture of the organization.

本句中，who owe a fiduciary duty to shareholders and are not closely involved in the day-to-day activities of the organization 是一个定语从句，修饰和限定 non-executives。although this varies depending on the type (e.g., public versus private), size and culture of the organization 是一个让步状语从句。

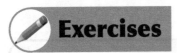

Exercises

EX. 1 根据课文内容，回答以下问题。

1. What does management involve?
2. What does management consist of according to Henri Fayol?
3. What are the three major types of management roles categorized by researcher Henry Mintzberg?
4. How many specific roles that are decisional? What are they?
5. How many management levels do most organizations have? What are they?
6. What does top level consist of?
7. What is the board of directors typically primarily composed of?

Unit 1

8. What does middle level consist of?
9. What are the functions of middle management?
10. What does lower management consist of? What are they usually responsible for?

EX. 2 把下列中文单词和词组译成英文，英文单词和词组译成中文。

1. 调整，整理 _____
2. 关系，关联 _____
3. 处理，操作，操纵 _____
4. 为……配备职员；任职于 _____
5. 决策，决定 _____
6. strategy _____
7. contract _____
8. supervisory _____
9. performance _____
10. profit _____
11. executive directors _____
12. top manager _____
13. human capital _____
14. internal auditors _____
15. branch manager _____

EX. 3 把下列句子翻译为中文。

1. A manager's job is complex and multidimensional, and requires a range of skills.
2. Conceptual skills are needed by all managers but are especially important for managers at the top.
3. One of the most important goals that organizations and their members try to achieve is to provide some kind of good or service that customers desire.
4. The outcome of leadership is highly motivated and committed organizational members.
5. The controlling function allows managers to evaluate how well they themselves are performing the other three functions of management and to take corrective action.
6. In reality, being a manager often involves acting emotionally and relying on gut feelings.
7. Organizations increase their efficiency when they reduce the quantity of resources they use to produce goods or services.
8. Today, companies can win or lose the competitive race depending on their speed—how fast they can bring new products to market—or their flexibility—how easily they can change the way they perform their activities to respond to the actions of their competitors.
9. Managers use conceptual, human, and technical skills to perform the four management

functions of planning, organizing, leading, and controlling in all organizations.
10. Quick, immediate reactions to situations rather than deliberate thought and reflection are an important aspect of managerial action.

EX. 4 把下面的短文翻译成中文。

Organization performance is a measure of how efficiently and effectively managers use resources to satisfy customers and achieve organizational goals. Organizational performance increases in direct proportion to increases in efficiency and effectiveness. Efficiency is a measure of how well or how productively resources are used to achieve a goal. Effectiveness is a measure of the appropriateness of the goals that managers have selected for the organization to pursue, and of the degree to which the organization achieves those goals.

Text B

Managerial Skills

Both education and experience enable mangers to recognize and develop the skills they need to put organizational resources to their best use. Michael Dell realized from the start that he lacked enough experience and technical expertise in marketing, finance, and planning to guide his company alone. Thus, he recruited experienced managers from other information technology companies, such as IBM and Hewlett-Packard, to help him build his company. Research has shown that education and experience help managers acquire three principal types of skills: conceptual, human, and technical. As you might expect, the level of these skills that managers need depends on their level in the managerial hierarchy. Typically planning and organizing require higher levels of conceptual skills, and leading and controlling require more human and technical skills.

1. Conceptual Skill

Conceptual skills are demonstrated in the ability to analyze and diagnose a situation and to distinguish between cause and effect. Top managers require the best conceptual skills because their primary responsibilities are planning and organizing. By all accounts, Jack Welch was chosen for his demanding job because of his ability to identify new opportunities and mobilize managers and other resources to take advantage of those opportunities.

Formal education and training are very important in helping managers develop conceptual skills. Business training at the undergraduate and graduate (MBA) levels provides many of the conceptual tools (theories and techniques in marketing, finance, and other areas) that managers need to perform their roles effectively. The study of management helps develop the skills that allow managers to understand the big picture confronting an organization. The ability to focus on the big picture lets managers see beyond the situation immediately at hand and consider choices while keeping in mind the organization's long-term goals.

Today, continuing management education and training, including training in advanced IT, is an integral step in building managerial skills because new theories and techniques are constantly being developed to improve organizational effectiveness. A quick scan through a magazine such as *Business Week* or *Fortune* reveals a host of seminars in topics such as advanced marketing, finance, leadership, and managing human resources that are offered to managers at many levels in the organization, from the most senior corporate executives to middle managers. Microsoft, IBM, Motorola, and many other organizations designate a portion of each manager's personal budget to be used at the manager's discretion to attend management development programs.

In addition, organizations may wish to develop a particular manager's abilities in a specific skill area—perhaps to learn an advanced component of departmental skills, such as international bond trading, or to learn the skills necessary to implement a new IT system. The organization thus pays for managers to attend specialized programs to develop these skills. Indeed, one signal that a manager is performing well is an organization's willingness to invest in that manager's skill development. Similarly, many non-managerial employees who are performing at a high level (because they have studied management) are often sent to intensive management training programs to develop their management skills and to prepare them for promotion to first-level management positions.

2. Human Skill

Human skills include the ability to understand, alter, lead, and control the behavior of other individuals and groups. The ability to communicate, to coordinate, and to motivate people and to mold individuals into a cohesive team distinguishes effective from ineffective managers. By all accounts, both Jack Welch and Michael Dell possess human skills.

Like conceptual skills, human skills can be learned through education and training, as well as developed through experience. Organizations increasingly utilize advanced programs in leadership skills and team leadership as they seek to capitalize on the advantages of self-managed teams. To manage interpersonal interactions effectively, each person in an organization needs to learn how to empathize with other people—to understand their viewpoints and the problems they face. One way to help managers understand their personal strengths and weaknesses is to have their superiors, peers, and subordinates provide feedback about their performance in the roles identified by Mintzberg. Thorough and direct feedback allows managers to develop their human skills.

3. Technical Skill

Technical skills are the job-specific knowledge and techniques required to perform an organizational role. Examples include a manager's specific manufacturing, accounting, marketing, and IT skills. Managers need a range of technical skills to be effective. The array of technical skills managers need depends on their positions in organization. The manager of a restaurant, for example, may need cooking skills to fill in for an absent cook, accounting and bookkeeping skills to keep track of receipts and costs and to administer the payroll, and aesthetic skills to keep the restaurant looking attractive for customers.

Effective managers need all three kinds of skills—conceptual, human, and technical. The absence of even one managerial skill can lead to failure. One of the biggest problems that people who start small businesses confront is their lack of appropriate conceptual and human skills. Someone who has the technical skills to start a new business does not necessarily know how to manage the venture successfully. Similarly, one of the biggest problems that scientists or engineers who switch careers from research to management confront is their lack of effective human skills. Management skills, roles, and functions are closely related, and wise managers or prospective managers are constantly in search of the latest educational contributions to help them develop the conceptual, human, and technical skills they need to function in today's changing and increasingly competitive global environment.

New Words

recognize ['rekəgnaiz] *vt.* 承认，认可；认出
realize ['riəlaiz] *vt.* 认识到，了解；实现，实行
technical ['teknikəl] *adj.* 技术的，技术上的，技巧方面的
marketing ['mɑ:kitiŋ] *n.* 行销，买卖
finance [fai'næns] *n.* 财政，金融；财政学
recruit [ri'kru:t] *vt.* 征募，使恢复，补充
acquire [ə'kwaiə] *vt.* 获得，学到
principal ['prinsəpəl] *adj.* 主要的，首要的
conceptual [kən'septjuəl] *adj.* 概念上的
diagnose ['daiəgnəuz] *v.* 诊断
distinguish [dis'tiŋgwiʃ] *v.* 区别，辨别
demanding [di'mɑ:ndiŋ] *adj.* 需要技能的；要求高的，过分要求的，苛求的

mobilize ['məubilaiz] *v.* 动员
opportunity [,ɔpə'tju:niti] *n.* 机会，时机
undergraduate [,ʌndə'grædjuit] *n.* (尚未取得学位的) 大学生
graduate ['grædjueit] *n.* (大学) 毕业生，研究生
provide [prə'vaid] *vt.* 供应，供给
theory ['θiəri] *n.* 理论，学说
confront [kən'frʌnt] *vt.* 使面临，对抗
scan [skæn] *v.* 细看，审视，浏览，扫描
reveal [ri'vi:l] *vt.* 展现，显示，揭示，暴露
seminar ['seminɑ:] *n.* 研究会，讨论发表会
senior ['si:njə] *adj.* 年长的，地位较高的，高级的

Unit 1

corporate ['kɔ:pərit] *adj.* 社团的，法人的，公司的

designate ['dezigneit] *vt.* 指明，指出，任命，指派

portion ['pɔ:ʃən] *n.* 一部分，一份

budget ['bʌdʒit] *n.* 预算 *vi.* 做预算，编入预算

discretion [dis'kreʃən] *n.* 判断力

attend [ə'tend] *vt.* 出席，参加；照顾，护理，注意

bond [bɔnd] *n.* 公债，债券，合同，联结

implement ['impliment] *vt.* 贯彻，实现

willingness ['wiliŋnis] *n.* 自动自发，积极肯干

invest [in'vest] *vt. & vi.* 投资

similarly ['similəli] *adv.* 同样地，类似于

intensive [in'tensiv] *adj.* 精深的，透彻的，强烈的

position [pə'ziʃən] *n.* 位置，职位

alter ['ɔ:ltə] *v.* 改变

communicate [kə'mju:nikeit] *v.* 沟通，通信

mold [məuld] *vt.* 浇铸，塑造

cohesive [kəu'hi:siv] *adj.* 有黏着力的，凝聚性的

possess [pə'zes] *vt.* 占有，拥有，持有

utilize [ju:'tilaiz] *vt.* 利用

seek [si:k] *v.* 寻找，探索，寻求

capitalize [kə'pitəlaiz] *vt.* 变成资本，以大写字母写

advantage [əd'vɑ:ntidʒ] *n.* 优势，有利条件，利益

interpersonal [,intə'pə:sənl] *adj.* 人与人之间的

empathize ['empəθaiz] *v.* 移情，神会

viewpoint ['vju:,pɔint] *n.* 观点，视点

peer [piə] *n.* 同等的人，贵族

subordinate [sə'bɔ:dinit] *n.* 下属 *adj.* 次要的，下级的

feedback ['fi:dbæk] *n.* 反馈

accounting [ə'kauntiŋ] *n.* 会计；会计学；清算账目

bookkeeping ['buk,ki:piŋ] *n.* 簿记

receipt [ri'si:t] *n.* 收条，收据

administer [əd'ministə] *v.* 管理；给予，执行

payroll ['peirəul] *n.* 薪水册，职工工资册，（公司）应付工资总额

aesthetic [i:s'θetik] *adj.* 美学的，审美的，有审美感的

attractive [ə'træktiv] *adj.* 吸引人的，有魅力的

absence ['æbsəns] *n.* 缺乏，没有；不在，缺席

venture ['ventʃə] *n.* 冒险，投机，风险

related [ri'leitid] *adj.* 相关的，有关系的

prospective [prə'spektiv] *adj.* 未来的；盼望中的，预期的

constantly ['kɔnstəntli] *adv.* 经常地，不断地，坚持不懈地

contribution [,kɔntri'bju:ʃən] *n.* 文献；贡献，捐赠

global ['gləub(ə)l] *adj.* 全球的，全世界的

environment [in'vaiərənmənt] *n.* 环境，周围环境

Phrases and Expressions

conceptual skill 概念技能
technical skill 技术技能
human skill 人际技能
cause and effect 因果
by all accounts 据大家所说
focus on 注视，关注
big picture 总体局势
at hand 在手边，在附近，即将到来
keep in mind 谨记
Business Week 《商业周刊》

a host of 许多，一大群
a portion of 一部分
at sb.'s discretion 由……随意决定
in addition 另外
capitalize on 利用
empathize with 同情
keep track of 明了，了解；记录，保持联系；跟踪
lead to 导致
in search of 寻找，追求

Abbreviations

MBA (Master of Business Administration) 工商管理硕士

Exercises

EX. 5 根据文章所提供的信息判断正误。

1. Michael Dell didn't realize from the start that he lacked enough experience and technical expertise in marketing, finance, and planning to guide his company alone.
2. Research has shown that education and experience help managers acquire three principal types of skills. They are conceptual, human, and technical skills.
3. Typically planning and organizing require higher levels of human and technical skills, and leading and controlling require more conceptual skills.
4. Formal education is the only important way to help managers develop conceptual skills.
5. Top managers require the best conceptual skills because their primary responsibilities are planning and organizing.
6. A manager who has the ability to communicate, to coordinate, and to motivate people and to mold individuals into a cohesive team is more effective than those who don't.
7. Human skills can be developed only through experience.

8. Thorough and direct feedback allows managers to develop their conceptual skills.
9. The array of technical skills managers need does not necessarily depend on their positions in organization.
10. One of the biggest problems that people who start small businesses confront is their lack of appropriate conceptual and human skills.

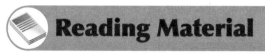

Text	Notes
Fayol's Principles of Management	
Henry Fayol (1841-1925) identified 14 principles that he believed essential to increase the efficiency of the management process. These principles remain the bedrock[1] on which much of the recent management theory and research are based.	[1] *n.* 根底，基础
1. Division of labor[2]	[2] 劳动分工
Fayol was among the first to point out the downside of too much specialization: boredom—a state of mind likely to cause a fall in product quality, worker initiative, and flexibility. As a result, Fayol advocated[3] that workers be given more job duties to perform or be encouraged to assume[4] more responsibility for work outcomes, a principle increasingly applied today in organizations that empower their workers.	[3] *vt.* 提倡，鼓吹 [4] *vt.* 承担
2. Authority and responsibility	
Like Weber, Fayol emphasized the importance of authority and responsibility. Fayol, however, went beyond Weber's formal authority, which derives[5] from a manager's position in the hierarchy, to recognize the informal authority that derives from personal expertise, technical knowledge, moral worth, and ability to lead and to generate commitment[6] from subordinates.	[5] *vt.* 得自，起源 [6] *n.* 承诺，约定
3. Unity of command[7]	[7] 统一指挥
The principle of unity of command specifies that an employee should receive orders from, and report to, only one superior. Fayol believed that dual command, the reporting relationship that exists when two supervisors give orders to the same subordinate, should be avoided except in exceptional[8] circumstances. Dual command confuses[9] the subordinate, undermines[10] order and discipline, and creates havoc[11] within the formal hierarchy of authority.	[8] *adj.* 例外的，异常的 [9] *vt.* 搞乱，使糊涂 [10] *v.* 破坏 [11] *n.* 大破坏，浩劫

4. Line of authority

The line of authority is the chain of command[12] extending from the top to the bottom of an organization. The greater the number of levels in the hierarchy, the longer communication between managers at the top and bottom takes and the slower the pace of planning and organizing.

When organizations are split into different departments, each with its own hierarchy, it is important to allow middle and first-line mangers in each department to interact with managers at similar levels in other departments. This interaction helps to speed decision-making, because managers know each other and know whom to go to when problems arise.

5. Centralization

Centralization[13] is the concentration of authority at the top of the managerial hierarchy. Fayol believed that authority should not be concentrated at the top of the chain of command. One of the most significant issues that top managers face is how much authority to centralize at the top of the organization and what authority to decentralize[14] to mangers and workers at lower hierarchical levels.

6. Unity of direction

Just as there is a need for unity of command, there is also a need for unity of direction, the singleness of purpose[15] that makes possible the creation of one plan of action to guide managers and workers as they use organizational resources. An organization without a single guiding plan becomes inefficient and ineffective; its activities become unfocused, and individuals and groups work at cross-purposes.

7. Equity

Equity is the justice, impartiality[16] and fairness to which all organizational members are entitled. As Fayol wrote: "For personnel to be encouraged to carry out their duties with all the devotion and loyalty of which they are capable, they must be treated with respect for their own sense of integrity, and equity results from the combination of respect and justice."

8. Order

Order meant the methodical[17] arrangement of positions to provide the organization with the greatest benefit and to provide employees with career opportunities to satisfy their needs. Thus, the use of organizational charts to show the position and duties of each employee and to indicate which positions an employee might move to or be promoted into in the future.

---

[12] 指挥系统，行政管理系统

[13] n. 集中，中央集权化

[14] n. 分散

[15] 目的专一，一心一意

[16] n. 不偏不倚，公正，公平

[17] adj. 有方法的，有系统的

9. Initiative

Although order and equity are important means to fostering[18] commitment and loyalty among employees, managers must also encourage employees to exercise initiative, the ability to act on their own, without direction from a superior. Used properly, initiative can be a major source of strength for an organization because it leads to creativity[19] and innovation[20]. Managers need skill and tact[21] to achieve the difficult balance between the organization's need for order and employees' desire for initiative.

10. Discipline

Discipline is obedience[22], energy, application, and other outward marks of respect for a superior's authority. Discipline results in respectful relations between organizational members and reflects the quality of an organization's leadership and a manger's ability to act fairly and equitably.

11. Remuneration[23] of personnel

Reward systems, including bonuses and profit-sharing plans, are increasingly utilized to motivate employees. An organization's payment system has important implication[24] for organizational success. Effective reward system should be equitable for both employees and the organization, encourage productivity by rewarding well-directed effort, not be subject to abuse[25], and be uniformly applied to employees.

12. Stability of tenure of personnel

Fayol also recognized the importance of long-term employment. When employees stay with an organization for extended[26] periods of time, they develop skills that improve the organization's ability to utilize its resources.

13. Subordination of individual interests to the common interest

The interests of the organization as a whole must take precedence[27] over the interests of any one individual or group if the organization is to survive. Equitable[28] agreements must be established between the organization and its members to ensure that employees are treated fairly and rewarded for their performance and to maintain the disciplined organizational relationships so vital to an efficient system of administration.

14. Esprit de corps[29]

Esprit de corps is a French expression that refers to shared feelings of comradeship[30], enthusiasm, or devotion to a common cause among members of a group. Esprit de corps is a key element in a successful organization. Esprit de corps can result when managers encourage personal, verbal contact between managers and workers and by encouraging communication to solve problems and implement solutions.

---

[18] *vt.* 促进，培养

[19] *n.* 创造力
[20] *n.* 创新
[21] *n.* 机智，策略

[22] *n.* 服众，顺从

[23] *n.* 报酬

[24] *n.* 含义，暗示

[25] *v.* 滥用

[26] *adj.* 伸出的，延长的

[27] *n.* 优先，居先
[28] *adj.* 公平的，公正的

[29] *n.* 团队精神，集体荣誉感
[30] 同志之友谊

参考译文

管 理

　　在企业和组织中，管理的功能就是协调人的努力，有效地利用现有资源来实现目标和目的。

　　管理包括确定使命、目标、过程、规则以及控制企业人力资本，以帮助企业获得成功。这意味着需要有效的沟通、人的动机，以及某种成功的进度或系统的结果。因此，管理不是处理机制（机械或自动化程序），也不是放牧动物，合法的企业和环境或非法的企业或环境中都可以有管理。没有必要只从企业角度来审视管理，因为管理的本质是提高人的生活水平以及人际关系的能力。因此，管理无处不在，其应用更广泛。在此基础上，管理必须包含人、沟通和企业的积极努力。计划、度量、动机的心理工具、目标和经济措施（利润等），这些都可以是或不是管理的必要组成部分。起初，人们从功能的角度认为管理就是检测数量、调整计划、制定目标。这甚至适用于没有计划的情况下。从这个角度来看，亨利·法约尔（1841—1925）认为管理包括六大功能：预测、计划、组织、指挥、协调和控制。

　　然而，当今管理的概念出现在广泛领域中，其边界已经大大扩展。除了营利组织，甚至非营利组织（如 NGO）也应用了管理的概念。其概念和用途不受限制。总的来说，管理是计划、组织、安排员工、领导和控制的过程。

1. 管理角色

　　除了宽泛的管理功能之外，层次结构中不同级别的管理者担当了不同的管理角色。研究员亨利·明茨伯格把这些角色分为三大类：决策、人际交往和信息化。

1.1 决策角色

　　决策角色需要管理者做出战略规划并利用资源。决策有四个具体的角色。企业家要求管理者分配资源，以开发创新性的商品和服务或者拓展业务。虽然授权的中层管理人员也能做出这样的决定，但这些角色大多数由高层管理人员担任。干扰处理者纠正来自内部或外部环境的组织无法预料的问题。各级管理人员都可以担任该角色。例如，初级经理可能解决导致组装线停顿的问题，中层经理可能解决一个店被抢劫的善后问题，高层管理者更多的是应对重大危机，如对缺陷产品的召回。第三个决策的作用是资源分配者，包括确定哪些工作单位将获得哪些资源。高层管理者有可能做大的、总的预算决策，而中层管理人员可以做出更具体的分配。在一些组织中，主管经理负责给员工涨工资。最后，谈判代表负责与其他人（如供应商、经销商或工会）协商，以达成产品和服务协议。主管管理者可以与员工进行加薪或加班问题商谈，也可与其他主管商谈共享所需要的资源。中层管理人员也与其他管理人员进行谈判并合作，以从供应商和分销商获得理想的价格。高层管理者商谈更大的问题，如劳动合同，甚至是与其他公司的兼并和收购谈判。

1.2 人际角色

　　人际角色要求管理人员指导和监督员工和组织。一般中层管理人员的上级通常是象征性的领导。该经理人可通过公司会议与员工就组织的未来目标或道德准则进行沟通。领导者为其他员工作一个榜样、给下属命令和指示并做决定，也要动员员工。组织的各级领导都是管理者，通常基层管理者向高层管理人员学习，以他们为榜样。管理者还肩负联络的角色，协调不同工作单位人员的工作，建立相互联盟并分享资源。这个角色对中层管理者尤为关键，他必须经常与其他管理者争夺重要资源，但也要与他们保持长期的成功合作关系。

1.3 信息化角色

信息化角色是那些获取和传递信息的管理者。随着技术进步，这些角色发生了巨大变化。监管者评估他人的业绩，并采取纠正措施以改善其业绩。他要察看环境变化，也要留意公司内部会影响个人和组织绩效的变化。虽然组织的高层管理者比中层和初级管理者更容易监测环境的外部威胁，但各级管理人员都要进行监管。传播者的角色要求管理者告知员工对他们以及组织有影响的变化。他们还传达公司的愿景和目标。

每个级别的管理者都给其下级发布信息，这种信息的本质是自上向下流动。最后，发言人与外部环境沟通，从发布公司商品和服务到告知社会该组织的发展方向。发布重大公告（如战略方向的改变）的发言人很可能是高级经理。但是，其他更常规的信息可以由公司中任何级别的管理者提供。例如，一个中层经理可能给当地报纸提供新闻稿，或者主管经理可能会在社区会议上做演讲。

2. 管理层次

大多数组织都有三个管理层次：初级层次、中层和高层管理人员。这些管理人员按权威等级分类并执行不同的任务。在许多组织中，管理者在每个级别的数量类似于金字塔。每个级别的职责和可能的职务头衔的规范如下。

2.1 高层

高层包括董事会（包括非执行董事和执行董事）、总裁、副总裁、首席执行官和其他C级管理人员。他们负责控制和监督整个组织。他们在顶部定调，并制定战略计划、公司政策并就业务方向做出决定。此外，高层管理人员的主要作用是调动外部资源，并向股东和公众负责。

董事会通常主要由受股东信托的非执行董事组成，并不密切参与该组织的日常活动，尽管这会因公司类型（例如，公有与私有）、规模和组织文化的不同而不同。理论上，这些董事对违反义务负责，并通常投董事及高级职员责任保险。董事会制定企业战略，对重大收购等重要事项做决策，并雇用、评估和解聘高层经理（首席执行官或总裁），而CEO通常聘任其他岗位人员。然而，董事会也更多地参与到其他职位（如首席财务官（CFO））的招聘中来。在2013年，对超过160家的公有与私人公司的CEO和董事的调查发现，CEO们最主要的弱点是"监管技能"和"董事会参与"不足，而10%的企业从来没有评估过CEO。董事会还可能有一些向他们报告的员工（例如，内部审计人员），或直接聘请独立承包商。例如，董事会通常（通过审计委员会）选择审计师。

对高层管理人员有用的技能因组织类型而异，但通常包括广泛了解竞争、世界经济与政治。此外，CEO负责执行和确定（董事会的框架内）组织的广泛政策。执行日常细节管理包括：准备部门预算、程序、时间安排的说明，任命中层管理人员（如部门经理），协调各部门之间关系，协调媒体和政府的关系，以及与股东沟通。

2.2 中层

中层包括普通经理、分公司经理和部门经理。他们向高级管理人员负责，完成本部门的工作。他们投入更多时间到组织和把握方向中。他们的角色可以被强调为执行符合公司政策的组织计划和实现高层管理人员制定的目标，他们定义并讨论从高层管理到较低层管理的信息和政策，最重要的是他们鼓舞和指导较低级别管理人员，使之业绩更好。

中层管理是一个分类组织的中间管理，仅次于高层管理人员，但高于其他所有的运营成员。一个运营经理可能由中层管理人员深思熟虑选出，也可以归类为非经营管理，负责制定特定的组织政策。在任何组织里中层的效率至关重要，因为他们是高层与低层人员之间的桥梁。

其作用包括：
- 设计和实施有效的分组，协调组与组之间的工作和信息系统。
- 定义和监控组级的任务执行。
- 诊断并解决工作组之间的问题。
- 设计和实施支持合作行为的奖励制度。他们还做决策并与高层管理者分享想法。

2.3 低层

由主管、部门领导和领班等组成，他们专注于控制和指挥。他们通常负责给员工分配任务，指导和监督员工的日常活动，确保质量和产量，向上推荐、提议并反映员工的问题。初级管理者是员工的榜样，他们实施基本监督，激励员工，制定职业生涯规划，绩效反馈。

Unit 2

Text A

Business Plan

A business plan is a formal statement of business goals, reasons they are attainable, and plans for reaching them. It may also contain background information about the organization or team attempting to reach those goals.

Business plans may target changes in perception and branding by the customer, client, taxpayer, or larger community. When the existing business is to assume a major change or when planning a new venture, a 3 to 5 year business plan is required, since investors will look for their investment return in that timeframe.

1. Audience

Business plans may be internally or externally focused. Externally focused plans target goals that are important to external stakeholders, particularly financial stakeholders. They typically have detailed information about the organization or team attempting to reach the goals. With for-profit entities, external stakeholders include investors and customers. External stakeholders of non-profits include donors and the clients of the non-profit's services.

For government agencies, external stakeholders include taxpayers, higher-level government agencies, and international lending bodies such as the International Monetary Fund, the World Bank, various economic agencies of the United Nations, and development banks.

Internally focused business plans target intermediate goals required to reach the external goals. They may cover the development of a new product, a new service, a new IT system, a restructuring of finance, the refurbishing of a factory or a restructuring of the organization. An internal business plan is often developed in conjunction with a balanced scorecard or a list of critical success factors. This allows success of the plan to be measured using non-financial measures. Business plans that identify and target internal goals, but provide only general guidance on how they will be met are called strategic plans.

Operational plans describe the goals of an internal organization, working group or department. Project plans, sometimes known as project frameworks, describe the goals of a particular project. They may also address the project's place within the organization's larger strategic goals.

2. Content

Business plans are decision-making tools. The content and format of the business plan is determined by the goals and audience. For example, a business plan for a non-profit might discuss the fit between the business plan and the organization's mission. Banks are quite concerned about defaults, so a business plan for a bank loan will build a convincing case for the organization's ability to repay the loan. Venture capitalists are primarily concerned about initial investment, feasibility, and exit valuation. A business plan for a project requiring equity financing will need to explain why current resources, upcoming growth opportunities, and sustainable competitive advantage will lead to a high exit valuation.

Preparing a business plan draws on a wide range of knowledge from many different business disciplines: finance, human resource management, intellectual property management, supply chain management, operations management, and marketing, among others. It can be helpful to view the business plan as a collection of subplans, one for each of the main business disciplines.

A good business plan can help to make a good business credible, understandable, and attractive to someone who is unfamiliar with the business. Writing a good business plan can't guarantee success, but it can go a long way toward reducing the odds of failure.

3. Presentation

The format of a business plan depends on its presentation context. It is common for businesses, especially start-ups, to have three or four formats for the same business plan.

An "elevator pitch" is a short summary of the plan's executive summary. This is often used as a teaser to awaken the interest of potential investors, customers, or strategic partners.

A pitch deck is a slide show and oral presentation that is meant to trigger discussion and interest potential investors in reading the written presentation. The content of the presentation is usually limited to the executive summary and a few key graphs showing financial trends and key decision making benchmarks. If a new product is being proposed and time permits, a demonstration of the product may be included.

A written presentation for external stakeholders is a detailed, well written, and pleasingly formatted plan targeted at external stakeholders.

An internal operational plan is a detailed plan describing planning details that are needed by management but may not be of interest to external stakeholders. Such plans have a somewhat higher degree of candor and informality than the version targeted at external stakeholders and others.

3.1 Typical Structure for a Business Plan for a Start up Venture

- cover page and table of contents.
- executive summary.
- mission statement.
- business description.
- business environment analysis.
- SWOT analysis.
- industry background.
- competitor analysis.
- market analysis.
- marketing plan.
- operations plan.
- management summary.
- financial plan.
- attachments and milestones.

3.2 Typical Questions Addressed by a Business Plan for a Start up Venture

- What problem does the company's product or service solve? What niche will it fill?
- What is the company's solution to the problem?
- Who are the company's customers, and how will the company market and sell its products to them?
- What is the size of the market for this solution?
- What is the business model for the business (how will it make money)?
- Who are the competitors and how will the company maintain a competitive advantage?
- How does the company plan to manage its operations as it grows?
- Who will run the company and what makes them qualified to do so?
- What are the risks and threats confronting the business, and what can be done to mitigate them?
- What are the company's capital and resource requirements?
- What are the company's historical and projected financial statements?

4. Open Business Plans

Traditionally business plans have been highly confidential and quite limited in audience. The business plan itself is generally regarded as secret. However, the emergence of free software and open source has opened the model and made the notion of an open business plan possible.

An open business plan is a business plan with unlimited audience. The business plan is typically web published and made available to all.

In the free software and open source business model, trade secrets, copyright and patents can no longer be used as effective locking mechanisms to provide sustainable advantages to a particular business and therefore a secret business plan is less relevant in those models.

New Words

formal ['fɔ:məl] adj. 正式的，形式的
attainable [ə'teinəbl] adj. 可到达的，可得到的
background ['bækgraund] n. 背景，后台
target ['tɑ:git] n. 目标，对象
branding [brænd] n. 品牌定位，品牌化
customer ['kʌstəmə] n. 消费者
taxpayer ['tæks,peiə] n. 纳税人
investor [in'vestə] n. 投资者
investment [in'vestmənt] n. 投资
stakeholder ['steikhəuldə] n. 股东
non-profit [nɔn-'prɔfit] adj. 非盈利的
development [di'veləpmənt] n. 开发；发展
restructure [ri'strʌktʃə] vt. 重构，调整，改组
refurbish [ri:'fə:biʃ] vt. 翻新，刷新
factor ['fæktə] n. 因素，要素
framework ['freimwə:k] n. 构架，框架，结构
format ['fɔ:mæt] n. 形式，格式 vt. 安排……的格局（或规格）
default [di'fɔ:lt] n. 食言，不履行责任
loan [ləun] n.（借出的）贷款，借出 v. 借给
repay [ri(:)'pei] v. 偿还，报答
capitalist ['kæpitəlist] n. 资本家
feasibility [,fi:zə'biləti] n. 可行性，可能性
valuation [vælju'eiʃən] n. 估价，评价，计算
sustainable [sə'steinəbl] adj. 足可支撑的，可持续的

subplan ['sʌb,plæn] n. 子计划，辅助方案
credible ['kredəbl] adj. 可信的，可靠的
understandable [ʌndə'stændəbl] adj. 可以理解的，可懂的
unfamiliar ['ʌnfə'miljə] adj. 新奇的，不熟悉的，没有经验的
guarantee [,gærən'ti:] n. 保证，保证书，担保，抵押品 vt. 保证，担保
odds [ɔdz] n. 机会，可能性
awaken [ə'weikən] v. 唤醒，醒来，唤起
slide [slaid] n. 幻灯片
trigger ['trigə] vt. 引发，引起，触发
graph [grɑ:f] n. 图表，曲线图
benchmark ['bentʃmɑ:k] n. 衡量标准，基准
demonstration [,deməns'treiʃən] n. 示范，实证
candor ['kændə] n. 直截了当，坦白，直率
informality [,infɔ:'mæliti] n. 非正式
attachment [ə'tætʃmənt] n. 附件
milestone ['mailstəun] n. 里程碑，重要事件，转折点
qualify ['kwɔlifai] vt. 限制，限定
mitigate ['mitigeit] v. 减轻
confidential [kɔnfi'denʃəl] adj. 秘密的，机密的
emergence [i'mə:dʒəns] n. 浮现，露出，出现
unlimited [ʌn'limitid] adj. 无限的，无约束的
patent ['peitənt] n. 专利权，执照

Unit 2

Phrases and Expressions

business plan 商业计划
business goal 商业目标
investment return 投资回报
International Monetary Fund 国际货币基金组织
World Bank 世界银行
in conjunction with 与……联合，与……协力
balanced scorecard 平衡记分卡
a list of... ……的清单
strategic plan 战略计划
operational plan 运营计划
project plan 项目计划
decision-making tool 决策工具
equity financing 资本筹措，股本融资，发行股票筹资

sustainable competitive advantage 可持续发展的竞争优势
draw on 利用，凭借
intellectual property 知识产权
supply chain management 供应链管理
a collection of 很多，一批，一组
elevator pitch 电梯推销，电梯游说
strategic partner 战略伙伴
pitch deck 融资演讲稿
oral presentation 口头陈述
start up 启动，新兴公司
business model 商业模式
open source 开源，开放资源

Abbreviations

SWOT (Strengths Weaknesses Opportunities Threats) 竞争优势、竞争劣势、机会和威胁
IT (Information Technology) 信息技术

Notes

1 When the existing business is to assume a major change or when planning a new venture, a 3 to 5 year business plan is required, since investors will look for their investment return in that timeframe.

本句中，When the existing business is to assume a major change or when planning a new venture 作条件状语，修饰和限定谓语 is required。since investors will look for their investment return in that timeframe 也作状语，说明 a 3 to 5 year business plan is required 的原因。

❷ Business plans that identify and target internal goals, but provide only general guidance on how they will be met are called strategic plans.

本句中，that identify and target internal goals, but provide only general guidance on how they will be met 是一个定语从句，修饰和限定主语 Business plans。在该定语从句中，how they will be met 是一个宾语从句，作介词 on 的宾语。

❸ A business plan for a project requiring equity financing will need to explain why current resources, upcoming growth opportunities, and sustainable competitive advantage will lead to a high exit valuation.

本句中，for a project requiring equity financing 是一个介词短语，作定语，修饰和限定主语 A business plan。在该短语中，requiring equity financing 是一个现在分词短语，作定语，修饰和限定 a project。why current resources, upcoming growth opportunities, and sustainable competitive advantage will lead to a high exit valuation 是一个宾语从句，作 explain 的宾语。

❹ An internal operational plan is a detailed plan describing planning details that are needed by management but may not be of interest to external stakeholders.

本句中，describing planning details that are needed by management but may not be of interest to external stakeholders 是一个现在分词短语，作定语，修饰和限定 a detailed plan。在该短语中，that are needed by management but may not be of interest to external stakeholders 是一个定语从句，修饰和限定 planning details。

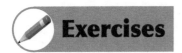

EX. 1 根据课文内容，回答以下问题。

1. What is a business plan?
2. What do external stakeholders include with for-profit and non-profits entities respectively?
3. What do internally focused business plans cover?
4. How is the content and format of the business plan determined?
5. What does one need when preparing a business plan?
6. What can a good business plan do?
7. What is an "elevator pitch"?
8. What is a pitch deck?
9. What is an internal operational plan?
10. What is an open business plan?

EX. 2 把下列中文单词和词组译成英文，英文单词和词组译成中文。

1.（借出的）贷款，借出_____

Unit 2

2. 偿还，报答_____
3. 里程碑，重要事件，转折点_____
4. 专利权，执照_____
5. 衡量标准，基准_____
6. 保证，保证书，担保，抵押品_____
7. 估价，评价，计算_____
8. 投资_____
9. 因素，要素_____
10. 股东_____
11. investment return_____
12. decision-making tool_____
13. equity financing_____
14. elevator pitch_____
15. strategic partner_____

EX. 3 把下列句子翻译为中文。

1. With a low-cost strategy, managers try to drive the organization's costs down below the costs of its rivals.
2. Formulating strategies is the job of managers at the corporate, business, and functional levels.
3. Although goals should be challenging, they should be realistic.
4. In the fast-changing market where customers' needs change and evolve, companies must learn to define and redefine their businesses to satisfy those needs.
5. A plan helps coordinate managers of the different functions and divisions of an organization to ensure that they all pull in the same direction.
6. Organizations that successfully pursue a differentiation strategy may be able to charge a premium price for their products.
7. Both the differentiating strategy and the low-cost strategy are aimed at serving many or most segments of a particular market.
8. Makes SWOT analysis is an integral part of the planning process.
9. Each organizational function has an important role to play in the process of lowering costs or adding value to a product.
10. If customers see more value in one organization's products than in the products of its competitors, they may be willing to pay premium prices.

EX. 4 把下面的短文翻译成中文。

In today's competitive environment, there is an increasing recognition of the need for more dynamic approaches to formulating as well as implementing strategies. Strategy is not a static, analytical process; it requires vision, intuition, and employee participation. Many organizations are abandoning central planning departments, and strategy is becoming an everyday part of the job for workers at all level.

Text B

Five Ps For Strategy

Human nature insists on a definition for every concept. But the word Strategy has long been used implicitly in different ways even if it has traditionally been defined in only one. Explicit recognition of multiple definitions can help people to maneuver through this difficult field. Accordingly, five definitions of strategy are presented here as plan, ploy, pattern, position, and perspective.

1. Strategy as Plan

To almost anyone you care to ask, strategy is a plan—some sort of consciously intended course of action, a guideline to deal with a situation. As a kid has a "strategy" to get over a fence, a corporation has one to capture a market. By this definition, strategies have two essential characteristics: they are made in advance of the actions to which they apply, and they are developed consciously and purposefully.

2. Strategy as Ploy

As plans, strategies may be general or they can be specific. There is one use of the word in the specific sense that should be identified here. As a plan, a strategy can be a ploy, too. It is really just a specific "maneuver" intended to outwit an opponent or competitor. The kid may use the fence as a ploy to draw a bully into his yard, where his Doberman pinscher awaits intruders. Likewise, a corporation may threaten to expand plant capacity to discourage a competitor from building a new plant. Here the real strategy is the threat, not the expansion itself, and as such is a ploy.

3. Strategy as Pattern

But if strategies can be intended, surely they can also be realized. In other words, defining strategy as a plan is not sufficient; we also need a definition that encompasses the resulting behavior. Thus, a third definition is proposed: strategy is a pattern—specifically, a pattern in a stream of actions. By this definition, when Picasso painted blue for a time, that was a strategy, just as was the behavior of the Ford Motor Company when Henry Ford offered his Model T only in black. In other words, by this definition, strategy is consistency in behavior, whether or not intended.

This may sound like a strange definition for a word that has been so bound up with free will. But the fact of the matter is that while hardly anyone defines strategy in this way, many people seem at one time or another to use it so. Consider this quotation from a business executive: "Gradually the successful approaches merge into a pattern of action that becomes our strategy. We certainly don't have an overall strategy on this." This comment is inconsistent only if we restrict ourselves to one definition of strategy: what this man seems to be saying is that his firm has strategy as pattern, but not as plan.

The definition of strategy as plan and pattern can be quite independent of each other: plans may go unrealized, while patterns may appear without preconception. To paraphrase Hume, strategies may result from human actions but not human beings. If we label the first definition intended strategy and the second realized strategy, then we can distinguish deliberate strategies, where intentions that existed previously were realized, from emergent strategies, where patterns developed in the absence of intentions, or despite them when went unrealized.

4. Strategy as Position

The fourth definition is that strategy is a position—specifically, a means of locating an organization in what organization theorists like to call an "environment". By this definition, strategy becomes the mediating force—or "match" between organization and environment, that is, between the internal and the external context. In ecological terms, strategy becomes a "niche"; in economic terms, a place that generates "rent"; in management terms, formally, a product-market "domain", the place in the environment where resources are concentrated.

Note that this definition of strategy can be compatible with either of the preceding ones, a position can be pre-selected and aspired to through a plan (or a ploy) and/or it can be reached, perhaps even found, through a pattern of behavior.

5. Strategy as Perspective

While the fourth definition of strategy looks out, seeking to locate the organization in the external environment, and down to concrete positions, the fifth looks inside the organization, indeed inside the heads of the collective strategies, but up to a broader view. Here, strategy is a perspective, its content consisting not just of a chosen position, but of an ingrained way of perceiving the world. There are organizations that favor marketing and build a whole ideology around that; HP has developed the "H-P way," based on its engineering culture, while McDonald's has become famous for its emphasis on quality, service, and cleanliness.

This fifth definition suggests above all that strategy is a concept. This has one important implication, namely, that all strategies are abstractions which exist only in the minds of interested parties. It is important to remember that no one has ever seen a strategy or touched one; every strategy is an invention, a figment of someone's imagination, whether conceived of as intentions to regulate behavior before it takes place or inferred as patterns to describe behavior that has already occurred.

What is of key importance about this fifth definition, however, is that the perspective is shared. As implied in the words Weltanschauung, culture, and ideology, but not the word personality, strategy is a perspective shared by the members of an organization, through their intentions and/or by their actions. In effect, when we are talking of strategy in this context, we are entering the realm of the collective mind—individuals united by common thinking and/or behavior.

New Words

concept ['kɔnsept] n. 观念，概念
implicitly [im'plisitli] adv. 含蓄地，暗中地
explicit [iks'plisit] adj. 外在的，清楚的
recognition [rekəg'niʃ(ə)n] n. 承认；认可
maneuver [mə'nu:və] n. 运用，操作
ploy [plɔi] n. 策略，计谋
pattern ['pætən] n. 模式
perspective [pə'spektiv] n. 设想，洞察力
consciously ['kɔnʃəsli] adv. 有意识地，自觉地
purposefully ['pə:pəsfuli] adj. 有目的的，自觉的
outwit [aut'wit] vt. 以智取胜；瞒骗
opponent [ə'pəunənt] n. 对手，反对者
bully ['buli] n. 欺凌弱小者；恶棍 vt. 威吓，威逼
await [ə'weit] vt. 等候，准备
intruder [in'tru:də] n. 入侵者
threaten ['θretn] vt. 恐吓，威胁
discourage [dis'kʌridʒ] vt. 使气馁，阻碍
propose [prə'pəuz] vt. 计划，建议
Picasso ['pika:sou] n. 毕加索
consistency [kən'sistənsi] n. 一致性，连贯性
quotation [kwəu'teiʃən] n. 引用语，价格，报价单，行情表
merge [mə:dʒ] v. 合并，并入
inconsistent [,inkən'sistənt] adj. 不一致的，不协调的，矛盾的

preconception [pri:kən'sepʃən] n. 成见，偏见；先入为主的概念
paraphrase ['pærəfreiz] vt. 解释，释义；意译
deliberate [di'libərət] adj. 周密计划的；深思熟虑的
despite [dis'pait] prep. 不管，不论；尽管
mediate ['mi:diit] v. 仲裁，调停，作为引起……的媒介
context ['kɔntekst] n. 背景，上下文
ecological [,ekə'lɔdʒikəl] adj. 生态学的，社会生态学的
niche [nitʃ] n. 小生境，合适的环境
economic [,i:kə'nɔmik] adj. 经济（上）的
rent [rent] n. 租金
domain [dəu'mein] n. 范围，领域
preceding [pre'si:diŋ] adj. 在前的，前述的
aspire [əs'paiə] vi. 热望，立志
ingrained [in'greind] adj. 彻底的，根深蒂固的
ideology [aidi'ɔlədʒi] n. 意识形态
cleanliness ['klenlinis] n. 干净，清洁
figment ['figmənt] n. 臆造的事物，虚构的事
infer [in'fə:] v. 推断
Weltanschauung ['velt'ɑ:nʃauəŋ] n. 世界观，人生观
personality [,pə:sə'næliti] n. 个性，人格，人物
realm [relm] n. 领域

Unit 2

Phrases and Expressions

insist on 坚持，坚决要求，强调
course of action 做法，行动过程
get over 爬过，克服
capture market 争取市场
in advance of 在……前面，超过
Doberman pinscher 一种德国种的短毛猎犬
plant capacity 工厂设备(生产)能力

as such 同样地，同量地
be bound up with 与……有密切关系
in the absence of 没有
free will 自愿，自由意志
be compatible with 适合，一致
aspire to 渴望，追求
interested party 有关的当事人
conceive of 想象

Exercises

EX. 5 根据文章所提供的信息判断正误。

1. Human nature insists on a definition for not all the concepts.
2. The author uses the example of a kid has a "strategy" to get over a fence to support his idea strategy is a plan.
3. Strategies may be general or they can be specific.
4. Unlike a plan, a strategy can be a ploy.
5. Regarding the definition that strategy is a pattern, we mean that strategy is consistency in behavior, whether or not intended.
6. The definition of strategy as plan and pattern is quite dependent of each other.
7. The fourth definition is that strategy is a position.
8. The definition that strategy is a position can be compatible with either of the preceding ones.
9. This fifth definition implies that all strategies are abstractions which exist only in the minds of interested parties.
10. The key importance about the definition of strategy as perspective is that perspective cannot be shared.

SWOT Analysis and Five Competitive Forces

Strategy formulation[1] involves managers analyzing an organization's current situation and then developing strategies to accomplish[2] its mission and achieve its goals. Strategy formulation begins with managers analyzing the factors within an organization and outside, in the task and general environments that affect or may affect the organization's ability to meet its goals now and in the future. SWOT analysis and the Five Forces Model are two useful techniques[3] managers use to analyze these factors.

1. SWOT analysis

SWOT analysis is a planning exercise in which managers identify organizational strength[4] (S), and weakness[5] (W), and environmental opportunities (O), and threats (T). Based on a SWOT analysis, managers at different levels of the organization select the corporate-, business-, and functional-level strategies to best position the organization to achieve its mission[6] and goals.

• Internal strengths and weaknesses.

Strengths are positive internal characteristics that the organization can exploit[7] to achieve its strategic performance goals. Weaknesses are internal characteristics that may inhibit[8] or restrict[9] the organization's performance. The information sought typically pertains[10] to specific functions such as marketing, finance, production, and R&D. Internal analysis also examines overall organization structure, management competence[11], and quality, and human resource characteristics. Based on their understanding of these areas, managers can determine their strength or weakness vis-a-vis[12] other companies. For example, Marriott Corporation has been able to grow rapidly because of its financial strength. It has strong financial base[13], enjoys an excellent reputation with creditors[14], and has always been able to acquire financing needed to support its strategy of constructing hotels in new locations.

• External opportunities and threats.

Threats are characteristics of the external environment that may prevent the organization from achieving its strategic goals. Opportunities are characteristics of the external environment that

Notes

[1] *n.* 用公式表示，明确地表达，作简洁陈述

[2] *vt.* 完成，达到，实现

[3] *n.* 技术，技巧，方法

[4] *n.* 长处，优点
[5] *n.* 弱点，缺点

[6] *n.* 使命，任务

[7] *vt.* 开拓，开发，
[8] *v.* 抑制，约束
[9] *vt.* 限制，约束，限定
[10] *v.* 适合，属于

[11] *n.* 能力，特长

[12] *prep.* 和……面对面，同……相比，关于

[13] *n.* 底部，基础
[14] *n.* 债权人

have the potential to help the organization achieve or exceed[15] its strategic goals. Executives evaluate the external environment with information about nine sectors. The task environment sectors are the most relevant[16] to strategic behavior and include the behavior of competitors, customers, suppliers, and the labor supply. The general environment contains[17] those sectors that have an indirect influence[18] on the organization but nevertheless must be understood and incorporated[19] into strategic behavior. The general environment includes technological developments, the economy, legal-political and international events, and sociocultural[20] changes. Additional areas that might reveal[1] opportunities or threats include pressure groups[21], interest groups, creditors, natural resources, and potentially[22] competitive industries.

2. Porter's five competitive forces

A well-known model that helps managers isolate[23] particular forces in the external environment that are potential threats is Michael Porter's five forces model. Porter identified five factors that are major threats because they affect how much profit organizations competing within the same industry can expect to make.

• Potential new entrants[24].

Capital requirements and economies of scale[25] are examples of two potential barriers to entry that can keep out new competitors. It is far more costly to enter the automobile industry, for example, than to start a specialized mail-order[26] business.

• Bargaining[27] power of buyer.

Informed customers become empowered customers. As advertising and buyer information educate customers about the full range of price and product options[28] available in the marketplace, their influence over a company increases. This is especially true when a company relies on one or two large, powerful customers for the majority of its sales.

• Bargaining power of suppliers.

The concentration of suppliers and the availability[29] of substitute[30] suppliers are significant factors in determining supplier power. The sole[31] supplier of engines to a manufacturer of small airplanes will have great power. Other factors include whether a supplier can survive without a particular purchaser, or whether the purchaser can threaten[32] to self-manufacture the needed supplies.

[15] *vt.* 超越,胜过

[16] *adj.* 有关的,相应的

[17] *vt.* 包含,容纳,容忍
[18] *n.* 影响,感化,势力
[19] *vt.*(使)合并,并入,合编

[20] *adj.* 社会文化的

[21] *n.* 压力集团
[22] *adv.* 潜在地

[23] *vt.* 使隔离,使孤立

[24] *n.* 进入者,新到者
[25] *n.* 规模经济

[26] *n.* 邮购
[27] *n.* 议价,讨价,商讨

[28] *n.* 选项,选择权

[29] *n.* 可用性,有效性
[30] *n.* 代用品,代替者,替代品
[31] *adj.* 单独的,唯一的
[32] *vt.* 恐吓,威胁,预示(危险)

• Threat of substitute products.

The power of alternatives[33] and substitutes for a company's product may be affected by cost changes or trends such as increased health consciousness[34] that will deflect[35] buyer loyalty to companies. Companies in the sugar industry suffered from the growth of sugar substitutes; manufacturers of aerosol[36] spray cans[37] lost business as environmentally conscious consumers chose other products.

• Rivalry[38] among competitors.

The scrambling[39] and jockeying[40] for position is often exemplified[41] by what Porter called the "advertising slugfest[42]." The rivalries are influenced by the preceding[43] four forces as well as by cost and product differentiation[44]. A famous example of competitive rivalry is the battle between Pepsi and Coke. Rivalry between Federal Express and United Parcel Service is becoming almost as fierce[45] as the two companies grapple[46] for dominance[47] of the express delivery business. UPS has rolled out a new 8:00 A.M. delivery, two hours earlier than Federal Express. When Federal Express introduced FedEx Ship, offering a free PC-based system that lets even the smallest customers order pickups, print shipping labels, and track delivery without ever using a telephone, UPS fired back[48] by unveiling[49] a new alliance[50] to enable customers to book orders through Prodigy online services.

[33]	*n.* 二中择一，可供选择的办法、事物
[34]	*n.* 意识，知觉
[35]	*v.*（使）偏斜，（使）偏转
[36]	*n.* 浮质
[37]	*n.* 喷壶，喷雾器
[38]	*n.* 竞争，竞赛，敌对
[39]	*n.* 爬行，攀缘
[40]	*n.* 谋取
[41]	*vt.* 例证，例示
[42]	*n.* 激烈的殴斗
[43]	*adj.* 在前的，前述的
[44]	产品差别化
[45]	*adj.* 凶猛的，猛烈的，热烈的
[46]	*v.* 格斗
[47]	*n.* 优势，统治
[48]	回火
[49]	*vt.* 揭开，揭幕
[50]	*n.* 联盟，联合

商业计划

　　商业计划是阐述企业目标、可以实现的理由以及如何实现的计划。它也可能包含试图实现这些目标的组织或团队的背景信息。

　　商业计划的目标是客户、顾客、纳税人或更大的团体对品牌认知的变化。当现有的业务发生重大变化或规划新的合资公司时，一个3至5年的商业计划是必需的，因为投资者将寻找在那段时间内他们的投资回报率。

1. 受众

　　商业计划可以着眼于内部或外部。着眼于外部的计划针对的是外部利益相关者，特别是金融的利益相关者。他们通常有试图达到目标的组织或团队的详细信息。对以营利为目的的实体而言，外部利益相关者包括投资者和客户；对于非营利组织而言，外部利益相关者包括捐助者和非营利性服务的客户。

　　对于政府机构而言，外部利益相关者包括纳税人、上级政府机构和国际贷款机构（如国际货币基金组织、世界银行、联合国各经济机构和开发银行）。

着眼于内部的商业计划是外部目标所需的中期目标。它们可能会涵盖开发新产品、新服务、新的 IT 系统、财务重组、工厂的翻新或组织的转型。内部商业计划往往与平衡计分卡或一些关键的成功因素相关联。这允许使用非财务指标来衡量这一计划的成功。标明和确定内部目标但对如何实现只提供一般性指导的商业计划被称为战略计划。

运营计划描述了一个内部组织、工作组或部门的目标。项目计划（有时也被称为项目框架）描述一个特定项目的目标。它们还可以说明该项目在企业更大的战略目标中的位置。

2. 内容

商业计划是决策工具。商业计划的内容与格式由目标和受众来决定。例如，一个非营利性的商业计划可能会讨论业务计划和组织使命之间是否匹配。银行颇为关注拖欠问题，所以一个银行贷款的商业计划应给出该组织具有令人信服的偿还贷款能力的理由。风险投资主要关注初始投资和可行性以及退出估值。需要股权融资的项目的商业计划需要说明现有资源、未来的增长机会以及持续竞争优势将导致高退出估值的原因。

要从许多不同的商业领域汲取广泛知识来准备商业计划，这些领域包括财务、人力资源管理、知识产权管理、供应链管理、运营管理和营销等。把商业计划看作每个主要商业领域子计划的集合是有益的。

一个好的商业计划有助于建立良好商业信誉，并且能让不熟悉业务的人理解并对他们产生吸引力。写一个好的商业计划并不能保证成功，但它可以有效降低失败的概率。

3. 介绍

商业计划的格式取决于应用环境。在企业（尤其是初创企业）中经常见到同一商业计划有三或四种格式。

"电梯推销"是对计划执行要点的简短总结。它经常用作预热广告，以召唤潜在的投资者、客户或战略合作伙伴。

融资演讲稿是一个幻灯片演示，以引发讨论并引起读到这个计划的潜在投资者的兴趣为目的。演讲稿的展示内容通常仅限于执行摘要和显示财政发展趋势的一些关键图表以及关键决策基准。如果要推出新产品并且时间允许，也可包括该产品的演示。

对于外部股东的书面陈述应当是详细的、写得很好、并且是令人愉快和格式化的。

内部运营计划是一个详细计划，它可以满足管理需要，但未必会引起外部股东的兴趣。这类计划更直截了当一些，也没有提供给外部股东和其他人的版本那么正式。

3.1 用于初始投资的商业计划的典型结构

- 封面及目录
- 执行摘要
- 使命宣言
- 业务描述
- 商业环境分析
- SWOT 分析

- 行业背景
- 竞争对手分析
- 市场分析
- 营销计划
- 运营计划
- 管理总结
- 财务计划
- 附件和里程碑

3.2 用于初始投资的商业计划的典型问题

- 该公司的产品或服务解决什么问题？它将填补什么样的市场空白？
- 该公司如何解决这些问题？
- 谁是公司的客户？该公司如何营销，以及如何销售产品？
- 这一解决方案所面对的市场有多大？
- 该公司的商业模式是什么（它将如何赚钱）？
- 谁是竞争对手？公司将如何保持竞争优势？
- 随着业务增长，公司计划如何管理？
- 谁来管理这家公司？他们应该具有什么资格？
- 面临的业务风险和威胁是什么？怎样降低风险？
- 公司的资金和资源需求是什么？
- 公司的历史和预测的财务报表是什么？

4. 开放商业计划

传统的商业计划一直高度保密，能够看到的受众相当有限。商业计划本身通常被视为机密。然而，自由软件和开源的出现已经突破了这一模式，使开放业务计划概念成为可能。

一个开放商业计划是不限受众的商业计划。商业计划书通常在网站公布，并提供给所有人。

在自由软件和开源商业模式中，商业秘密、版权和专利不再被作为在特定业务中有可持续的、优势的、有效的锁定机制。因此在这种模式中秘密商业计划并不那么重要。

Unit 3

Text A

Human Resource Management

Undoubtedly, any organization's success depends on how it manages its resources. A firm's resources propel it toward its goals, just as an engine propels an automobile toward its destination. Many of an organization's resources are nonhuman, such as land, capital, and equipment. Although the management of these resources is very important, a business cannot succeed without also managing its human resources (i.e., its people) properly. Just as automobiles will not operate efficiently if they are not driven by capable people, organizations will not operate successfully unless they too are "driven" by capable people. People determine the organization's objectives, and people run the operations that allow the organization to reach its objectives.

Human resource management, focusing on the people aspect of management, consists of practices that help the organization deal effectively with its people during the various phases of the employment cycle: pre-selection, selection, and post-selection.

The HRM pre-selection practices, which are human resource planning and job analysis, lay the foundation for the other HRM practices. The organization must decide what type of job openings will exist in the upcoming period and determine what qualifications are necessary to perform these jobs. In other words, firms must analyze and plan for their treatment of workers before they can carry out the remaining HRM practices.

Human resource planning helps managers anticipate and meet changing needs relating to the acquisition, deployment and utilization of its employees. The organization first maps out an overall plan (called a strategic plan). Then, through a process called demand and supply forecasting, it estimates the number and types of employees needed to carry out successfully its overall plan. Such information enables a firm to plan its recruitment, selection, and training strategies. For example, let's say that a firm's HR plan estimates that 15 additional engineers will be needed during the next year. The firm typically hires recent engineering graduates to fill such positions. Because these majors are in high demand, the firm decides to begin its campus recruiting early in the academic year, before other companies can "snatch away" the best candidates.

Job analysis is a systematic procedure of gathering, analyzing, and documenting information about particular jobs. The analysis specifies what each worker does, the work conditions, and the worker qualifications necessary to perform the job successfully. Job analysis information is used to plan and coordinate nearly all HRM practices, such as these: determining job qualifications for recruitment purposes, choosing the most appropriate selection techniques, developing training programs, helping to determine pay rates. For example, an organization may decide to use a mechanical aptitude test to screen applicants because a job analysis indicated that the nature of the work had recently changed and was now more demanding.

HRM selection practices are policies and procedures used by organizations to staff their positions, which include recruiting applicants, assessing their qualifications, and ultimately selecting those who are deemed to be the most qualified. Organizations use recruitment to locate and attract job applicants for particular positions. Organizations may recruit candidates internally or externally. The aim of recruitment practices is to identify a suitable pool of applicants quickly, cost efficiently, and legally. Selection involves assessing and choosing among job candidates. To be effective, selection processes must be technically sound (i.e. accurate) and legal.

In the post-selection phase, the organization develops HRM practices for effectively managing people once they have "come through the door". These practices are designed to maximize the performance and satisfaction levels of a firm's employees by providing them with the necessary knowledge and skills to perform their job and by creating conditions that will energize, direct, and facilitate the employees' efforts toward meeting the organization's objectives.

Training and development are planned learning experiences that teach workers how to perform their current or future jobs effectively. Training focuses on present jobs, whereas development prepares employees for possible future jobs. Training and development practices are designed to improve organizational performance by enhancing the knowledge and skill levels of employees. Training and development is an ongoing process, changes in technology and the environment, as well as in an organization's goals and strategies often require organizational members to learn new techniques and ways of working.

Through the performance appraisal process, organizations measure the adequacy of their employees' job performances and communicate these evaluations to them. One aim of appraisal systems is to motivate employees to continue appropriate behaviors and correct inappropriate ones. Management may also use performance appraisals as tools for making HRM-related decisions, such as promotion, demotions, discharges and pay raises.

On the basis of performance appraisals, managers distribute pay to employees. By rewarding high-performing organizational members with pay raises, bonuses, and the like, managers increase the likelihood that an organization's most valued human resources are motivated to continue their high levels of contribution to the organization. Moreover, by linking pay to performance, high-performing employees are more likely to stay with the organization, and managers are more likely to fill positions that become open with highly talented individuals. Benefits, such as health insurance or employee discounts, are important outcomes that employees receive by virtue of their membership in an organization.

Last, but not least, labor relations encompass the steps that managers take to develop and maintain good working relationship with the labor unions that may represent their employees' interests.

Managers must ensure that all these practices fit together and complement their company's structure and control system. For example, if managers decide to decentralize authority and empower employees, they need to invest in training and development to ensure that lower level employees have the knowledge and expertise they need to make the decisions that top managers would make in a more centralized structure.

New Words

undoubtedly [ʌnˈdaʊtidli] *adv.* 毋庸置疑地，的确地
propel [prəˈpel] *vt.* 推进，驱使
destination [ˌdestiˈneɪʃ(ə)n] *n.* 目的地，终点
nonhuman [ˈnɒnˈhjuːmən] *adj.* 非人类的
equipment [iˈkwɪpmənt] *n.* 装备，设备，器材，装置
properly [ˈprɒpəli] *adv.* 适当地，完全地
capable [ˈkeɪpəbl] *adj.* 有能力的，能干的
aspect [ˈæspekt] *n.* （问题等的）方面

phase [feɪz] *n.* 阶段，状态
firm [fəːm] *n.* 公司，商行，（合伙）商号
employment [imˈplɔimənt] *n.* 雇用，使用，利用
analysis [əˈnælisis] *n.* 分析；分解
analyze [ˈænəlaiz] *vt.* 分析；分解
opening [ˈəʊpnɪŋ] *n.* 空缺，机会
upcoming [ˈʌpˌkʌmɪŋ] *adj.* 即将来临的，预定将要
qualification [ˌkwɒlifiˈkeɪʃən] *n.* 资格，条件
treatment [ˈtriːtmənt] *n.* 待遇；处置，处理

anticipate [æn'tisipeit] vt. 预期，期望；占先，抢先
acquisition [,ækwi'ziʃən] n. 获得，获得物
deployment [di'plɔimənt] n. 展开，部署，调度
utilization [,ju:tilai'zeiʃən] n. 利用，使用，应用
overall [əuvər'ɔ:l] adj. 全部的，总的
strategic [strə'ti:dʒik] adj. 战略的，战略上的
forecasting ['fɔ:kɑ:stiŋ] n. 预测，预报
recruitment [ri'kru:tmənt] n. 补充，征募新兵
selection [si'lekʃən] n. 选拔，挑选
document ['dɔkjumənt] vt. 用文件证明；为……提供文件
specify ['spesifai] vt. 指定，详细说明
purpose ['pə:pəs] n. 目的，意图，用途，效果，决心，意志 vt. 打算，企图，决心
additional [ə'diʃənl] adj. 另外的，附加的，额外的
aptitude ['æptitju:d] n. 天资，才能，聪颖
screen [skri:n] v. 初选，遴选，选拔，筛选
applicant ['æplikənt] n. 申请者，请求者
locate [ləu'keit] vt. 确定，找出，找到
systematic [,sisti'mætik] adj. 系统的，体系的
policy ['pɔlisi] n. 政策，方针；手段；计谋；策略
staff [stɑ:f] vt. 供给人员，充当职员

ultimately ['ʌltimətli] adv. 最后，终于
deem [di:m] v. 认为，相信
qualified ['kwɔlifaid] adj. 有资格的
legally ['li:gəli] adv. 法律上，合法地
maximize ['mæksmaiz] vt. 使……最大化，使……达到最大（程度）
facilitate [fə'siliteit] vt. 使容易，使便利，推动
whereas [wɛər'æz] conj. 然而，反之
enhance [in'hɑ:ns] vt. 提高，增强
adequacy ['ædikwəsi] n. 适当，足够
appraisal [ə'preizəl] n. 评定；鉴定；评价，估价
inappropriate [,inə'prəupriit] adj. 不适当的，不相称的
demotion [,di:'məuʃən] n. 降级
discharge [dis'tʃɑ:dʒ] n. 解雇，遣走 vt. 免……的职；解雇
reward [ri'wɔ:d] n. 报酬，奖金 vt. 酬劳，奖赏
bonus ['bəunəs] n. 奖金，红利
likelihood ['laiklihud] n. 可能，可能性
talented ['tæləntid] adj. 有才能的；能干的
discount ['diskaunt] n. 折扣；贴现
represent [,ri:pri'zent] vt. 代表；表现
interest ['intrist] n. 利益，利害；兴趣，关心；利息
ensure [in'ʃuə] vt. 确保，确保，保证
complement ['kɔmplimənt] vt. 补助，补足
decentralize [di:'sentrəlaiz] n. 分散
empower [im'pauə] v. 授权与，使能够

Unit 3

Phrases and Expressions

just as 正像……，如同
consist of 包括，由……组成
deal with 对付，应付；对待
lay the foundation for 给……打下基础，为……奠定基础
map out 制订
human resource planning 人力资源规划
job analysis 工作分析
demand and supply 供与求，供求
in high demand 需要量很大
campus recruiting 校园招聘

academic year 学年
snatch away 迅速拿走
aptitude test 能力倾向测验
come through 经历，成功
performance appraisal 绩效考核
be likely to do sth. 可能做某事
by virtue of 依靠，由于
health insurance 健康保险
labor relation 劳资关系
labor union 工会

Abbreviations

HRM (Human Resource Management) 人力资源管理

Notes

1 Although the management of these resources is very important, a business cannot succeed without also managing its human resources (i.e., its people) properly.

本句中，Although the management of these resources is very important 是一个让步状语从句，Although 的意思是"尽管"、"虽然"。

注意：在英语中，从句中有 although 时，主句中不能再用连接词 but, 但可用副词 yet, nevertheless 等。请看下例：
Although it was so cold, he went out without an overcoat.
天气虽然很冷，他没有穿大衣就出去了。

2 Just as automobiles will not operate efficiently if they are not driven by capable people, organizations will not operate successfully unless they too are "driven" by capable people.

本句中，Just as automobiles will not operate efficiently if they are not driven by capable people 是一个比较状语从句，在该从句中，if they are not driven by capable people 是一个条件状语从句，修饰 will not operate efficiently。unless they too are "driven" by capable people 也是一个条件状语从句，修饰 will not operate successfully。unless 的意思是"如

41

果不，除非"，等于 if not。请看下例：

I shall go there tomorrow unless I'm too busy.

如果我不太忙，明天将到那儿去。

Unless he studies hard, he will never pass the examination.

他如果不努力学习，就永远不能考及格。

3 HRM selection practices are policies and procedures used by organizations to staff their positions, which include recruiting applicants, assessing their qualifications, and ultimately selecting those who are deemed to be the most qualified.

本句中，used by organizations to staff their positions 是一个动词不定式短语，作定语，修饰和限定 policies and procedures，该短语也可以扩展为一个定语从句：which are used by organizations to staff their positions。which include recruiting applicants, assessing their qualifications, and ultimately selecting those who are deemed to be the most qualified 是一个非限定性定语从句，对 policies and procedures 作进一步补充说明。在该非限定性定语从句中，who are deemed to be the most qualified 是一个定语从句，修饰和限定 those。

4 These practices are designed to maximize the performance and satisfaction levels of a firm's employees by providing them with the necessary knowledge and skills to perform their job and by creating conditions that will energize, direct, and facilitate the employees' efforts toward meeting the organization's objectives.

本句中，to maximize the performance and satisfaction levels of a firm's employees 是一个动词不定式短语，作目的状语，修饰谓语 are designed。by providing them with the necessary knowledge and skills to perform their job and by creating conditions that will energize, direct, and facilitate the employees' efforts toward meeting the organization's objectives 是方式状语，也修饰谓语。在该方式状语中，to perform their job 是一个动词不定式短语，作定语，修饰和限定 knowledge and skills，that will energize, direct, and facilitate the employees' efforts toward meeting the organization's objectives 是一个定语从句，修饰和限定 conditions。

5 By rewarding high-performing organizational members with pay raises, bonuses, and the like, managers increase the likelihood that an organization's most valued human resources are motivated to continue their high levels of contribution to the organization.

本句中，By rewarding high-performing organizational members with pay raises, bonuses, and the like 是方式状语，修饰谓语 increase，that an organization's most valued human resources are motivated to continue their high levels of contribution to the organization 是一个同位语从句，作 the likelihood 的同位语，对其进行说明。to continue their high levels of contribution to the organization 是一个动词不定式短语，作目的状语，修饰谓语 are motivated。

6 Last, but not least, labor relations encompass the steps that managers take to develop and maintain good working relationship with the labor unions that may represent their employees' interests.

Unit 3

本句中，that managers take 是一个定语从句，修饰和限定 the steps，to develop and maintain good working relationship with the labor unions 是一个动词不定式短语，作定语，也修饰和限定 the steps。that may represent their employees' interests 是一个定语从句，修饰和限定 the labor unions。

7 For example, if managers decide to decentralize authority and empower employees, they need to invest in training and development to ensure that lower level employees have the knowledge and expertise they need to make the decisions that top managers would make in a more centralized structure.

本句中，if managers decide to decentralize authority and empower employees 是一个条件状语从句，to ensure that lower level employees have the knowledge and expertise they need to make the decisions that top managers would make in a more centralized structure 是一个动词不定式短语，作目的状语，修饰谓语 need to invest。在该短语中，they need 是一个定语从句，修饰和限定 the knowledge and expertise，to make the decisions 是一个动词不定式短语，作定语，也修饰和限定 the knowledge and expertise。that top managers would make in a more centralized structure 是一个定语从句，修饰和限定 the decisions。

EX. 1 根据课文内容，回答以下问题。

1. What does any organization's success depend on?
2. What does Human resource management, focusing on the people aspect of management, consists of?
3. What is job analysis? What does it specify?
4. What is job analysis information used to do?
5. What are HRM selection practices? What do they include?
6. What is the difference between training and development? What are these practices designed to do?
7. What do organizations do through the performance appraisal process? What may management use performance appraisals as?
8. How do managers increase the likelihood that an organization's most valued human resources are motivated to continue their high levels of contribution to the organization?
9. What do labor relations encompass?
10. If managers decide to decentralize authority and empower employees, what do they need to do?

EX. 2 根据下面的英文释义，写出相应的英文词汇（使用本单元所学的单词、词组或缩略语）。

英文释义	词 汇
having capacity or ability; efficient and able	
to separate into parts or basic principles so as to determine the nature of the whole	
a quality, an ability, or an accomplishment that makes a person suitable for a particular position or task	
of, characterized by, based on, or constituting a system	
to state explicitly or in detail	
to increase or make as great as possible	
a sum of money or the equivalent given to an employee in addition to the employee's usual compensation	
to serve as the official and authorized delegate or agent for, stand for	
to distribute the administrative functions or powers of (a central authority) among several local authorities	
to invest with power, especially legal power or official authority	

EX. 3 把下列句子翻译为中文。

1. On the basis of performance appraisals, managers distribute pay to employees.
2. Managers are responsible for acquiring, developing, protecting, and utilizing the resources.
3. Recruitment is what managers do to develop a pool of qualified candidates for open positions.
4. Trainees should be encouraged and expected to use their new-found expertise on the job.
5. Before recruiting and selecting employees, managers must engage in human resource planning and job analysis.
6. Training focuses on teaching organizational members how to perform effectively in their current jobs.
7. Organizations are legally required to provide certain benefits to their employees, such as social security and unemployment insurance.
8. In determining pay levels, managers should take into account their organization's strategy.
9. Formal performance appraisals supply both managers and subordinates with valuable information.
10. Managers often dislike providing performance feedback, especially when the feedback is negative, but doing so is an important managerial activity.

EX. 4 把下面的短文翻译成中文。

Managers are responsible for acquiring, developing, protecting, and utilizing the resources that an organization needs to be efficient and effective. One of the most important resources in all organizations is human resources—the people involved in the production and distribution of goods and services. Effective managers realize how valuable human resources are and take active steps to make sure that their organizations build and fully utilize their human resources to gain a competitive advantage.

Text B

The Nature of Motivation

Even with the best strategy in place and an appropriate organizational architecture, an organization will be effective only if its members are motivated to perform at a high level. One reason why leading is such an important managerial activity is that it entails ensuring that each member of an organization is motivated to perform highly and help the organization achieve its goals. When managers are effective, the outcome of the leading process is a highly motivated workforce. A key challenge for managers of organizations both large and small is to encourage employees to perform at a high level. Thus, it is important for us to understand what motivation is, where it comes from, and why managers need to promote high levels of it for an organization to be effective and achieve its goals.

Motivation may be defined as psychological forces that determine the direction of a person's behavior in an organization, a person's level of effort, and a person's level of persistence in the face of obstacles. The direction of a person's behavior refers to the many possible behaviors that a person could engage in. For example, employees at The Container Store know that they should do whatever is required to meet a customer's container needs and don't have to ask permission to do something out of the ordinary. Effort refers to how hard people work. Employees at The Container Store exert high levels of effort to provide superior customer service. Persistence refers to whether, when faced with roadblocks and obstacles, people keep trying or give up. For example, when Hayden Tidwell, a salesperson at The Container Store in Dallas couldn't find a box in the store that would hold a customer's painting, rather than giving up and telling the customer he was sorry, he persisted and made a custom-size box with cardboard and tape.

Motivation is so central to management because it explains why people behave the way they do in organizations—why employees at The Container Store provide such excellent customer service and enjoy doing so. Motivation also explains why a waiter is polite or rude, and why a kindergarten teacher really tries to get children to enjoy learning or just goes through the motions.

It explains why some managers themselves truly put their organizations' best interests first whereas others are more concerned with maximizing their salaries, and why some workers put forth twice as much effort as others.

Motivation can come from intrinsic sources. Intrinsically motivated behavior is behavior that is performed for its own sake; the source of motivation is actually performing the behavior, and motivation comes from doing the work itself. Many managers are intrinsically motivated; they derive a sense of accomplishment and achievement from helping their organization to achieve their goals and gain competitive advantages. Jobs that are interesting and challenging are more likely to lead intrinsic motivation than are jobs that are boring or do not make use of a person's skills and abilities. An elementary school teacher who really enjoys teaching children, a computer programmer who loves solving programming problems, and a commercial photographer who relishes taking creative photographs are all intrinsically motivated. For these individuals, motivation comes from performing their jobs whether it be teaching children, finding bugs in computer programs, or taking pictures.

Extrinsically motivated behavior is behavior that is performed to acquire material or social rewards or to avoid punishment; the source of motivation is the consequences of the behavior, not the behavior itself. A car salesperson who is motivated by the high salary and status that go along with the job, and a factory worker who is motivated by the opportunity to earn a secure income are all extrinsically motivated. Their motivation comes from the consequences they receive as a result of their work behaviors.

People can be intrinsically motivated, extrinsically motivated, or both intrinsically and extrinsically motivated. A top manager who derives a sense of accomplishment and achievement from managing a large corporation and strives to reach year-end targets to obtain a hefty bonus is both intrinsically and extrinsically motivated. Similarly, a nurse who enjoys helping and taking care of patients and is motivated by having a secure job with good benefits is both intrinsically and extrinsically motivated.

Regardless of whether people are intrinsically or extrinsically motivated, they join and are motivated to work in organizations to obtain certain outcomes. An outcome is anything a person gets from a job or organization. Some outcomes, such as autonomy, responsibility, a feeling of accomplishment, and the pleasure of doing interesting or enjoyable work, result in intrinsically motivated behavior. Other outcomes, such as pay, job security, benefits, and vacation time, result in extrinsically motivated behavior.

Organizations hire people to obtain important inputs. An input is anything a person contributes to the job or organization, such as time, effort, education, experience, skills, knowledge, and actual work behaviors. Inputs such as these are necessary for an organization to achieve its goals. Managers strive to motivate members of an organization to contribute inputs that help the organization achieve its goals. How do manages do this? They ensure that members of an organization obtain the outcomes they desire when they make valuable contributions to the organization. Managers use outcomes to motivate people to contribute their inputs to the organization. Giving people outcomes when they contribute inputs and perform well aligns the interests of employees with the goals of the organization as a whole because when employees do what is good for the organization, they personally benefit. Managers seek to ensure that people are motivated to contribute important inputs to the organization, that these inputs are put to good use or focused in the direction of high performance, and that high performance results in workers obtaining the outcomes they desire.

New Words

motivation [ˌməutiˈveiʃən] n. 动机
architecture [ˈɑːkitektʃə] n. 建筑，体系机构
managerial [mænəˈdʒiəriəl] adj. 经理的，管理的
motivated [ˈməutiveitid] adj. 有动机的，由……推动的
challenge [ˈtʃælindʒ] n. 挑战 vt. 向……挑战
encourage [inˈkʌridʒ] vt. 鼓励，怂恿
psychological [ˌsaikəˈlɔdʒikəl] adj. 心理(上)的
persistence [pəˈsistəns] n. 坚持，持续
permission [pəˈmiʃən] n. 许可，允许
obstacle [ˈɔbstəkl] n. 障碍(物)；妨碍，阻碍，干扰
salesperson [seilˈpəːsn] n. 售货员
persist [pəˈsist] vi. 坚持，持续
cardboard [ˈkɑːdbɔːd] n. 纸板
tape [teip] n. 带子，带；胶带
central [senˈtrɑːl] adj. 中心的，中央的，重要的
excellent [ˈeksələnt] adj. 卓越的，极好的
polite [pəˈlait] adj. 有礼貌的，客气的，有教养的，文雅的

rude [ruːd] adj. 粗鲁的，无礼的；猛烈的，残暴的
kindergarten [ˈkindəˌgɑːtn] n. 幼儿园 adj. 幼儿园的，初级的，启蒙阶段的
behave [biˈheiv] v. 行为表现
motion [ˈməuʃən] n. 运动，动作
intrinsic [inˈtrinsik] adj. (指性质)固有的，内在的
sake [seik] n. 缘故，理由
derive [diˈraiv] vt. 得到；得自，起源
accomplishment [əˈkɔmpliʃmənt] n. 成就，完成，技艺
programming [ˈprəugræmiŋ] n. 规划，设计
commercial [kəˈməːʃəl] adj. 商业的，贸易的
photographer [fəˈtɔgrəfə] n. 摄影师，摄影家
relish [ˈreliʃ] vt. 喜欢，爱好
bug [bʌg] n. 缺陷，瑕疵；小虫，臭虫
extrinsically [eksˈtrinsikəli] adj. 非固有的，非本质的
consequence [ˈkɔnsikwəns] n. 结果，因果关系
target [ˈtɑːgit] n. 目标；标的；靶子

secure [si'kjuə] *adj.* 安全的，可靠的，放心的	autonomy [ɔː'tɔnəmi] *n.* 自治，自主
hefty ['hefti] *adj.* 重的，强壮的，有力的	enjoyable [in'dʒɔiəbəl] *adj.* 令人愉快的，可享受的
benefit ['benifit] *n.* 利益，好处，津贴	align [ə'lain] *vt.* 使结盟，使成一行

Phrases and Expressions

in the face of 面对，面向，面临	be concerned with 关心，注重
ask permission 得到允许	take pictures 照相
out of the ordinary 不平常的，非凡的	put forth 放出，提出，发表
customer service 客户服务	elementary school 小学
give up 放弃(念头、希望等)，停止	go along with 一起去，赞同
enjoy doing sth. 喜爱，喜欢；享受……的乐趣	regardless of 不管，不顾
go through 经历，经受，仔细检查，参加，履行	make contributions to… 为……做贡献
	in the direction of 朝……方向

Exercises

EX. 5 根据文章所提供的信息回答问题。

1. Why is leading such an important managerial activity?
2. What is motivation defined as?
3. What does the direction of a person's behavior refer to? What about effort?
4. Why is motivation so central to management?
5. What is intrinsically motivated behavior?
6. What is extrinsically motivated behavior?
7. Can people be both intrinsically and extrinsically motivated? Please give examples.
8. What is an outcome?
9. What is an input?
10. Why does giving people outcome when they contribute inputs and perform well align the interests of employees with the goals of the organization as a whole?

Unit 3

Text	Notes
Who Appraises Performance?	
We have been assuming[1] that managers or the supervisors[2] of employees evaluate performance. This is a pretty fair assumption, for supervisors are the most common appraisers of performance; indeed each year, 70 million U.S. citizens have their job performance appraised by their managers or supervisors. Performance appraisal[3] is an important part of most managers' job duties. Managers are responsible for not only motivating their subordinates to perform at a high level but also making many decisions hinging[4] on performance appraisals, such as pay raises or promotions. • Self, Peers, Subordinates, and Clients. When self-appraisals are used, managers supplement[5] their evaluations with an employee's assessment[6] of his or her own performance. Peer appraisals are provided by an employee's coworkers. Especially when subordinates work in groups or teams, feedback from peer appraisals can motivate team members while providing managers with important information for decision making. A growing number of companies are having subordinates appraise their manager's performance and leadership as well. And sometimes customers or clients provide assessments of employee performance in terms of responsiveness[7] to customers and quality of service. Although appraisals from each of these sources can be useful, managers need to be aware of potential issues that may arise when they are used. Subordinates sometimes may be inclined[8] to inflate[9] self-appraisals, especially if organizations are downsizing[10] and they are worried about their job security[11]. Managers who are appraised by their subordinates may fail to take needed but unpopular[12] actions out of fear that their subordinates will appraise them negatively[13]. • 360-degree performance appraisals.[14] To improve motivation and performance, some organizations include 360-degree appraisals and feedback in their performance appraisal systems, especially for managers. In a 360-degree appraisal, a manager's performance is appraised by a variety of people, beginning with the manager's self-appraisal and including peers or co-workers, subordinates, superiors and sometimes even customers or clients. The manager receives feedback based on evaluations from these multiple sources.	[1] *vt.* 假定，设想 [2] *n.* 监督人，管理人 [3] *n.* 绩效评估 [4] *v.* 使依靠，使基于 [5] *v.* 补遗，补充 [6] *n.* 评估，评价 [7] *n.* 响应，反应 [8] *adj.* 倾向……的 [9] *vi.* 充气，膨胀 [10] *v.* 减少规模，缩小化 [11] *n.* 安全 [12] *adj.* 不流行的，不受欢迎的 [13] *adv.* 否定地，消极地 [14] 360度绩效评估

The growing number of companies begins to use 360-degree appraisals and feedback. A 360-degree appraisal and feedback is not always as clear-cut[15] as it might seem. On the other hand, some subordinates try to get back at[16] their bosses by giving managers negative evaluations, especially when evaluations are anonymous [17] (to encourage honesty and openness). A top manger at CITIC indicated that he received a highly negative appraisal from a subordinate who tried to smear[18] him personally. The manager was pretty sure that the evaluation came from a very poor performer. On the other hand, some managers coach[19] subordinates to give, or even threaten sanctions[20] if they fail to give, positive evaluations.

Peers often are very knowledgeable[21] about performance, but may be reluctant to provide an accurate[22] and negative appraisal of someone they like or a positive appraisal of someone they dislike. At Baxter International, when peer appraisals were used in the information technology unit, workers tended to provide each other with uniformly[23] positive evaluations because they knew the evaluations were going to be used for pay raise decisions and they were not able to provide negative feedback anonymously. Managers at Baxter continued conducting the peer appraisals but decided to use them primarily for self-development activities and not for pay decisions.

In addition, whenever peers, subordinates, or anyone else evaluates a worker's performance, managers must be sure that the evaluators are actually knowledgeable about the performance dimensions[24] being assessed. For example, subordinates should not evaluate their supervisor's decision making if they have little opportunity to observe this dimension of performance.

These potential problems with 360-degree appraisals and feedback do not mean that they are not useful. Rather they suggest that for 360-degree appraisals and feedback to be effective, there has to be trust throughout an organization. More generally, trust is a critical ingredient[25] in any performance appraisal and feedback procedure. In addition, research suggests that 360-degree appraisals should focus on behaviors rather than traits[26] or results, and that managers need to carefully select appropriate raters. Moreover, appraisals tend to be more honest when made anonymously and when raters have been trained in how to use 360-degree appraisal forms. Additionally, managers need to think carefully about the extent to which 360-degree appraisals are appropriate for certain jobs and be willing to modify any system they implement when they become aware of unintended[27] problems the appraisal system is responsible for.

[15] adj. 轮廓鲜明的，清晰的
[16] [俚] 实行报复
[17] adj. 匿名的
[18] v. 涂上，涂污，诽谤
[19] v. 训练，指导
[20] n. 批准，同意，支持
[21] adj. 知识渊博的，有见识的
[22] adj. 正确的，精确的
[23] adv. 一律地，均一地
[24] n. 尺度，维数
[25] n. 成分，因素
[26] n. 显著的特点，特性
[27] adj. 非故意的，无意识的

Unit 3

Even when 360-degree appraisals are used, it is sometimes difficult to design an effective process by which subordinates' feedback can be communicated to their managers. Advances in information technology provide organizations with a potential solution to this problem. For example, ImproveNow.com has on-line questionnaires[28] that subordinates can fill out to evaluate the performance of their managers and provide the managers with feedback. Each subordinate of a particular manager completes the questionnaire on-line independently[29], all responses are tabulated[30], and the manager is given specific feedback on behaviors in a variety of areas such as rewarding good performance, looking out for the subordinates' best interest and being supportive, and having a vision for the future.

For example, Sonia Russomanno, a manager at Alliance Funding, a New Jersey mortgage[31] lending organization, received feedback from her nine subordinates on-line from ImproveNow. She received an overall grade of B and specific feedback on a variety of dimensions. This experience drove home to Russomanno the importance of getting honest feedback from her subordinates and listening to it to improve her performance as a manager. She has changed how she rewards her subordinates as a result and plans on using this service in the future to see how she is doing.

[28] *n.* 调查表，问卷

[29] *adv.* 独立地，自立地

[30] *vt.* 把……制成表格

[31] *n.* 抵押

人力资源管理

毫无疑问，组织的成功取决于它如何管理资源。一个企业的资源驱动它去实现目标，有如发动机发动汽车到达目的地。组织的大多数资源都是非人化的，如土地、资本和设备。尽管这些对资源的管理非常重要，但是企业必须通过恰当地管理其人力资源才能取得成功。正如汽车不可能有效地运转，除非有能力的人来驱动它；组织也不可能成功地运转，除非有能力的人来驾驭它。是人决定了组织的目标，也是通过人的有效运作，组织才能够实现其目标。

人力资源管理关注管理中人的因素，包括那些帮助组织在雇佣周期中有效地处理人力资源方面的实践，如挑选前实践、挑选实践和挑选后的实践。

人力资源管理挑选前的实践由人力资源规划和工作分析构成，它们为其他的人力资源管理实践奠定了基础。组织必须决定在近期将有何种类型的工作空缺，并决定胜任该工作需要何种素质。换言之，在企业实施余下的人力资源管理实践前，必须首先分析和规划如何对待其员工。

人力资源规划帮助管理者预见并满足不断变化的、与其员工的获取、配置和使用相关的需求。首先，组织会制订一个整体计划（战略计划），然后，通过人力资源供求预测过程来估计为完成该整体计划所需要的员工数量和类型。这样的信息使企业能够规划其招聘、挑选和培训战略。例如，假设一个企业的人力资源计划在下一年度新增15个工程师，企业通常会雇佣工程专业的大学毕业生来填补空缺。因为这些专业在市场上的需求较高。在其他公司"迅速抢走"最好的候选人之前，企业会决定在学年的年初就启动校园招聘。

　　工作分析是收集、分析、记录特定工作信息的一个系统程序。分析结果详细说明每位员工的工作内容、工作条件和成功完成该工作所必需的工作资格。工作分析信息被用于计划和协调几乎所有的人力资源管理实践，如决定招聘时的工作资格，选择最恰当的选拔技术，开发培训项目，帮助决定工资水平。例如，一个组织可能决定使用能力倾向测试来筛选应征者，因为工作分析显示该工作的性质最近已发生改变，对人员的要求更加严格。

　　人力资源管理挑选实施是组织用于安置员工的政策和程序，它包括招募申请人，评价其资格，以及最后挑选出组织认为最胜任的申请人。组织使用招募来搜寻和吸引申请特定职位的应征者。组织既可在组织内部也可在组织外部吸引候选人。招募实践的目的是为了快速地、低成本地、合法地识别出合适的应征者群体。挑选实践包括对工作候选人的评价和选择。为了能够有效地进行，挑选过程必须在技术上精确且符合法律要求。

　　在挑选后阶段，组织将开发人力资源管理实践以有效地管理那些顺利进入企业的员工。设计这些实践的目的是：通过向员工提供完成工作所必需的知识和技能，以及通过创造激发、指导、促进员工努力实现组织目标的条件，使得企业员工的绩效水平和满意度水平最大化。

　　培训和开发是有计划的学习体验，它教会员工如何有效地执行当前和未来的工作。培训关注于当前工作，而开发则是让员工为未来工作做好准备。组织设计培训与开发实践是为了通过提高员工的知识和技能水平来改进组织的绩效。培训与开发是一个持续不断的过程，技术和环境的变化，或组织目标和战略的变化常常会要求组织成员学习新的工作技术和方法。

　　通过绩效评估过程，组织测评员工的工作绩效，并将评价结果告诉员工。工作评价系统的一个目的是为了激励员工保持正确的行为并纠正不恰当的行为。管理层也可能使用绩效评估工具来做出与人力资源管理相关的决策，如晋升、降级、解雇和增加工资。

　　在绩效评估的基础上，管理者向员工发放工资。通过增加工资、奖金等相似的方式奖励高绩效的组织成员，管理者促使组织中最具价值的人力资源以高激励水平继续其对组织的贡献。而且，通过将奖励与绩效挂钩，高绩效员工更可能留在组织中，管理者也更可能对空缺职位填补上高素质的人才。福利，如健康保险或员工折扣，都是员工作为组织成员所得到的重要回报。

　　最后，但同样重要的是劳动关系管理，它包括管理者与代表员工利益的工会发展和保持良好工作关系所采取的一系列措施。

　　管理者必须确保上述所有实践相互结合并辅助公司的结构与控制系统。例如，如果管理者决定分散权力，对员工授权，那么他们必须投资于员工的培训与开发，以确保较低级别的员工拥有必要的知识和专业技术做出决策，而这些决策在更加集权的结构下通常是由高层管理者负责的。

Unit 4

Text A

Marketing Management

What makes a company excellent? This question exploded across America in the early 1980. Several of America's blue-chip companies were slipping badly in sales and profits. There were the normal problems—changing customer tastes, rising material costs, falling prices. There were also some newer factors—foreign competition, particularly the invasion of high-quality products coming from Japan, Singapore, Korea and so on. Markets were undergoing dizzying rates of change, and yet many companies failed to acknowledge or respond to these change.

A handful of other American companies continued to rack up high and continuously improving sales and profits. By interviewing forty-three high-performing companies, Tom Peters and Bob Waterman found that all of these companies shared a set of basic operating principles, among them a keen sense of customer, a keen sense of the market, and a high ability to motivate their employees to produce high quality and high value for the customers. Half of what they found relates to what marketers call the "marketing concept".

It is recognized today that companies cannot survive today by simply doing a good job. They must do an excellent job if they are to succeed in markets characterized by slow growth and fierce competition at home and abroad. Consumer and business buyers face an abundance of choices in seeking to satisfy their needs and therefore look for excellence in quality or value or cost when they choose their suppliers. Recent studies have demonstrated that knowing and satisfying the customers with competitively superior offers is the key to profitable performance. And marketing is the company function charged with defining customer targets and the best way to satisfy their needs and wants competitively and profitably.

Marketing has its origins in the fact that humans are creatures of needs and wants. Needs and wants create a state of discomfort in people, which is resolved through acquiring products to satisfy these needs and wants. Since many products can satisfy a given need, product choice is guided by the concepts of utility, value, and satisfaction. These products are obtainable in several ways: self-production, coercion, begging, and exchange. Most modern societies work on the principle of exchange, which means that people specialize in producing particular products and trade them for the other things they need. They engage in transactions and relationship building. A market is a group of people who share a similar need. Marketing encompasses those activities that represent working with markets, that is, trying to actualize potential exchanges.

Marketing management takes place when at least one party to a potential exchange gives thought to objectives and means of achieving desired responses from other parties. Marketing management is the process of planning and executing the conception, pricing, promotion, and distribution of ideas, goods, and services to create exchanges that satisfy individual and organizational objectives.

Marketing management can occur in an organization in connection with any of its markets. Consider an automobile manufacturer. The vice-president of personnel deals in the labor market; the vice-president of purchasing, the raw-materials market; and the vice-president of finance, the money market. They must set objectives and develop strategies for achieving satisfactory results in these markets. Traditionally, however, these executives have not been called marketers, nor have they been trained in marketing. Instead marketing management is historically identified with tasks and personnel dealing with the customer market.

Marketing work in the customer market is formally carried out by sales managers, sales people, advertising and promotion managers, marketing managers, customer-service mangers, product managers, market managers, and the marketing vice-president. Each job carries well-defined tasks and responsibilities. Many of these jobs involve managing particular marketing resources such as advertising, sales people, or marketing research. On the other hand, product managers, market managers, and the marketing vice-president manage programs. Their job is to analyze, plan, and implement programs that will produce a desired level and mix of transactions with target market.

The popular image of the marketing manger is someone whose task is primarily to stimulate demand for the company's products. However, this is too limited a view of the diversity of marketing tasks performed by marketing mangers. Marketing management has the task of influencing the level, timing, and composition of demand in a way that will help the organization achieve its objectives. Marketing management is essentially demand management.

The organization presumably forms an idea of a desired level of transactions with a target market. At times, the actual demand level may be below, equal to, or above the desired demand level. That is, there may be no demand, weak demand, adequate demand, excessive demand, and so on, and marketing management has to cope with these different states. Marketing managers cope with these different states by carrying out marketing research, planning, implementation, and control. Within marketing planning, marketers must make decisions on target markets, market positioning, product development, pricing, channel of distribution, physical distribution, communication, and promotion. Marketing managers must acquire several skills to be effective in the marketplace.

Five alternative philosophies can guide organizations in carrying out their marketing work. The production concept holds that consumers will favor products that are affordable and available, and therefore management's major task is to improve production and distribution efficiency and bring down prices. The product concept holds that consumers favor quality products that are reasonably priced, and therefore little promotional effort is required. The selling concept holds that consumers will not buy enough of the company's product unless they are stimulated through a substantial selling and promotion effort. The marketing concept holds that the main task of the company is to determine the needs, wants, and preferences of a target group of customers and to deliver the desired satisfaction. Its four principles are market focus, customer orientation, coordinated marketing, and profitability. The societal marketing concept holds that the main task of the company is to generate customer satisfaction and view long-run consumer and societal well-being as the key to satisfying organizational goals and responsibilities.

Interest in marketing is intensifying as more organizations in the business sector, the nonprofit sector, and the international sector recognize how marketing contributes to improved performance in the marketplace.

New Words

explode [iks'pləud] *vi.* 爆炸, 爆发, 破除, 激发

blue-chip [blu:-tʃip] *adj.* 独特的; 值钱的

slip [slip] *vi.* 滑动; 滑倒 *n.* 滑倒, 事故, 片, 纸片

sale [seil] *n.* 销路, 销售额; 出售, 卖出; 廉价出售

taste [teist] *n.* 喜爱, 爱好; 味道, 味觉 *v.* 品尝, 辨味; 领略; 体验, 感到

invasion [in'veiʒən] *n.* 入侵

undergo [ʌndə'gəu] *vt.* 经历, 遭受, 忍受

dizzying ['diziiŋ] *adj.* 令人昏乱的, 灿烂的

acknowledge [ək'nɔlidʒ] *vt.* 承认, 公认

interview ['intəvju:] *vt.* 访问, 采访; 接见; 会见

share [ʃɛə] *v.* 共享, 共用; 分摊; 共有 *n.* 共享, 参与

principle ['prinsəpl] *n.* 法则, 原则, 原理

keen [ki:n] *adj.* 敏锐的, 敏捷的, 热心的

marketer ['mɑ:kitə] *n.* 市场商人

survive [sə'vaiv] *v.* 幸免于, 幸存, 生还

characterize ['kæriktəraiz] *vt.* 表示……特点, 具有……特征; 描绘, 刻画, 形容(人或物)

fierce [fiəs] *adj.* 凶猛的, 猛烈的, 热烈的

excellence ['eksələns] *n.* 优秀, 卓越

abundance [ə'bʌndəns] *n.* 丰富, 充裕, 丰富充裕

demonstrate ['demənstreit] vt. 示范，证明，论证
offer ['ɔfə] n. 出价，提议
profitable [,prɔfitə'bl] adj. 有利可图的
origin ['ɔridʒin] n. 起源，由来，起因
discomfort [dis'kʌmfət] n. 不便之处，不适
resolve [ri'zɔlv] vt. 解决
guide [gaid] vt. 指导，支配，管理 n. 领路人，导游者，向导；引导者；指南
utility [ju:'tiliti] n. 效用，有用
satisfaction [,sætis'fækʃən] n. 满意，满足
obtainable [əb'teinəbl] adj. 能得到的，可到手的
coercion [kəu'ə:ʃən] n. 强迫，威压
transaction [træn'zækʃən] n. 交易，业务，事务，交易办理
actualize ['æktjuəlaiz] vt. 实现，实施
potential [pə'tenʃ(ə)l] adj. 可能的，潜在的
objective [əb'dʒektiv] n. 目标，目的 adj. 客观的，公正的，无偏见的
mean [mi:n] vt. 意为，想要 adj. 低劣的，卑鄙的；吝啬的；普通的，简陋的
means [mi:nz] n. 手段，方法
pricing ['praisiŋ] n. 定价
promotion [prə'məuʃən] n. 促销；促进
distribution [,distri'bju:ʃən] n. 分销
occur [ə'kə:] vi. 发生，出现
executive [ig'zekjutiv] n. 执行者，经理主管人员，决策人，董事会；行政官 adj. 决策和执行的，实行的，执行的，行政的

alternative [ɔ:l'tə:nətiv] adj. 选择性的，二中择一的
popular ['pɔpjulə] adj. 通俗的，流行的，受欢迎的
image ['imidʒ] n. 形象；肖像；图像
stimulate ['stimjuleit] vt. 刺激，激励；增强；增加活力
presumably [pri'zju:məbəli] adv. 可能，大概，推测起来
diversity [dai'və:siti] n. 多样，不同，千变万化，差异
excessive [ik'sesiv] adj. 过多的，过分的，额外
philosophy [fi'lɔsəfi] n. 基本原理，观点，哲学，哲学体系
favor ['feivə] vt. 喜欢，支持，赞成 n. 喜爱，好感，宠爱
affordable [ə'fɔ:dəbl] vt. 提供，给予，供应得起
available [ə'veiləbəl] adj. 可得到的；可利用的
reasonable ['ri:znəbl] adj. 合理的，有道理的
substantial [səb'stænʃəl] adj. 坚固的，实质的
orientation [,ɔrien'teiʃən] n. 方向，方位，定位
preference ['prefərəns] n. 偏爱，优先选择
societal [sə'saiətəl] adj. 社会的
well-being [wel-'bi:iŋ] adj. 康乐，安宁，福利
intensify [in'tensifai] vt. 加强

Unit 4

Phrases and Expressions

a handful of 少数；一把
rack up 获胜，击倒
operating principle 运作原则
succeed in 在……方面成功
on the principle of 根据……的原则
home and abroad 国内外
satisfy sb.'s needs 满足某人的需要
an abundance of 丰富，许多
specialize in 擅长于，专攻
engage in 使从事于，参加
at least 至少
give thought to 留意，注意；考虑，深思

in connection with 与……有关，连同
automobile manufacturer 汽车制造厂
money market 金融市场，货币市场，短期资金市场
be identified with 视……为一体，认同
target market 目标市场
demand management 需求的监督和调节
cope with 处理，对付，应付；克服
market positioning 市场定位
product development 产品开发
channel of distribution 分销渠道
physical distribution 物理分销

Notes

1 They must do an excellent job if they are to succeed in markets characterized by slow growth and fierce competition at home and abroad.

本句中，characterized by slow growth and fierce competition at home and abroad 是一个过去分词短语，作定语，修饰和限定 markets。该短语可以扩展为一个定语从句：which is characterized by slow growth and fierce competition at home and abroad。be characterized by 的意思是"具有……的特点"，at home and abroad 的意思是"在国内外"。

2 Most modern societies work on the principle of exchange, which means that people specialize in producing particular products and trade them for the other things they need.

本句中，which means that people specialize in producing particular products and trade them for the other things they need 是一个非限定性定语从句，对其前面的整句话进行补充说明。

英语中，which 引导的非限定性定语从句可以修饰一个词，也可以修饰整个句子。请看下例：

The river, which flows through London, is called the Thames.
这条流经伦敦的河叫泰晤士河。
He changed his mind, which made me very angry.
他改变了主意，这使我很生气。

3. Marketing management has the task of influencing the level, timing, and composition of demand in a way that will help the organization achieve its objectives.

本句中，that will help the organization achieve its objectives 是一个定语从句，修饰和限定 a way。in a way 作程度状语，意思是"在某种程度上"。

4. The societal marketing concept holds that the main task of the company is to generate customer satisfaction and view long-run consumer and societal well-being as the key to satisfying organizational goals and responsibilities.

本句中，that the main task of the company is to generate customer satisfaction and view long-run consumer and societal well-being as the key to satisfying organizational goals and responsibilities 是一个宾语从句，作 holds 的宾语。在该从句中，the main task of the company 是主语，is 和它后面的动词不定式短语作谓语。view... as 的意思是"把……看作是，认为"。请看下例：

She doesn't view herself as a success.

她不认为她自己成功了。

The United States is viewed as a melting pot.

美国被认为是一个大熔炉。

EX. 1 根据课文内容，回答以下问题。

1. What were the causes that several of America's blue-chip companies were slipping badly in sales and profits in the early 1980?
2. By interviewing forty-three high-performing companies, what did Tom Peters and Bob Waterman find?
3. What have recent studies demonstrated?
4. What is marketing management?
5. Who carries out marketing work in the customer market formally?
6. What does the production concept hold?
7. What does the product concept hold?
8. What does the selling concept hold?
9. What does the marketing concept hold?
10. What does the societal marketing concept hold?

Unit 4

EX. 2 根据下面的英文释义，写出相应的英文词汇（使用本单元所学的单词、词组或缩略语）。

英文释义	词　汇
the exchange of goods or services for an amount of money or its equivalent; the act of selling	
a personal preference or liking	
to admit the existence, reality, or truth of	
to be a distinctive trait or mark of; distinguish	
to realize in action or make real	
accepted by or prevalent among the people in general	
to be partial to; indulge a liking for	
variety or multiformity; The fact or quality of being diverse; difference	
to make intense or more intense	
a great or plentiful amount	

EX. 3 把下列句子翻译为中文。

1. Marketing is a social and managerial process by which individuals and groups obtain what they need and want.
2. People satisfy their needs and wants with products and services.
3. Manufacturers get into a lot of trouble by paying more attention to their products than to the services produced by these products.
4. Exchange must be seen as a process than as an event.
5. To make successful exchange, the marketer analyzes what each party expects to give and get.
6. Economists use the term market to refer to a collection of buyers and sellers who transact over a particular product or product class.
7. Marketing must be well coordinated with the other departments in the company.
8. Marketing department only works when all employees appreciate how they impact on customer satisfaction.
9. Marketing emerges when people decide to satisfy needs and wants through exchange.
10. A satisfied customer tells three people about a good product experience, while a dissatisfied customer gripes to eleven people.

EX. 4 把下面的短文翻译成中文。

In the past, marketers faced a number of tough decisions. They had to determine product features and quality, establish accompanying services, set the price, determine the distribution channels, decide how mush to spend on marketing. Today's marketers, of course, face the same tough decisions. But today's marketplace is enormously more complex. Domestic markets, at one time safe from foreign invaders, are now the happy hunting grounds of giant global corporations. Major strides in technology have considerably shortened time and distance: New products are launched at an astonishing pace and are available worldwide in a short time. Communication media are proliferating. New distribution channels and formats keep appearing. Competitors are everywhere and hungry.

Text B

Marketing Management Philosophies

We describe marketing management as carrying out tasks to achieve desired exchanges with target markets. What philosophy should guide these marketing efforts? What weight should be given to the interests of the organization, customers and society? Very often these interests conflict.

There are five alternative concepts under which organizations conduct their marketing activities: the production, product, selling, marketing, and societal marketing concepts.

1. The Production Concept

The production concept holds that consumers will favor products that are available and highly affordable. Therefore, management should focus on improving production and distribution efficiency. This concept is one of the oldest philosophies that guide sellers.

The production concept is still a useful philosophy in two situations. The first occurs when the demand for a product exceeds the supply. Here, management should look for ways to increase production. The second situation occurs when the product's cost is too high and improved productivity is needed to bring it down. For example, Henry Ford's whole philosophy was to perfect the production of the Model T so that its cost could be reduced and more people could afford it. He joked about offering people a car of any color as long as it was black.

For many years, Texas Instruments followed a philosophy of increased production and lower costs in order to bring down prices. It won a major share of the North American handheld calculator market using this approach. However, companies operating under a production philosophy run a major risk of focusing too narrowly on their own operations.

2. The Product Concept

Another major concept guiding sellers, the product concept, holds that consumers will favor products that offer the most quality, performance, and innovative features. Thus, an organization should devote energy to making continuous product improvements. Some manufacturers believe that if they can build a better mousetrap, the world will beat a path to their door. But they are often rudely shocked. Buyers may well be looking for a better solution to a mouse problem, but not necessarily for a better mousetrap. The solution might be a chemical spray, an exterminating service, or something that works better than a mousetrap. Furthermore, a better mousetrap will not sell unless the manufacturer designs, packages, and prices it attractively; places it in convenient distribution channels; brings it to the attention of people who need it; and convinces buyers that it is a better product.

3. The Selling Concept

Many organizations follow the selling concept, which holds that consumers will not buy enough of the organization's products unless it undertakes a large-scale selling and promotion effort. The concept is typically practiced with unsought goods—those that buyers do not normally think of buying, such as encyclopedias or insurance. These industries must be good at tracking down prospects and selling them on product benefits. The selling concept also is practiced in the non-profit area. A political party, for example, will vigorously sell its candidate to voters as a fantastic person for the job.

Most firms practice the selling concept when they have overcapacity. Their aim is to sell what they make rather than make what the market wants. Thus, marketing based on hard selling carries high risks. It focuses on creating sales transactions rather than on building long-term, profitable relationships with customers. It assumes that customers who are coaxed into buying the product will like it. Or, if they don't like it, they will possibly forget their disappointment and buy it again later. These are usually poor assumptions to make about buyers. Most studies show that dissatisfied customers do not buy again. Worse yet, while the average satisfied customer tells three others about good experiences, the average dissatisfied customer tells 10 others his or her bad experiences.

4. The Marketing Concept

The marketing concept holds that achieving organizational goals depends on determining the needs and wants of target markets and delivering the desired satisfactions more effectively and efficiently than competitors do. The marketing concept has been stated in colorful ways such as "We make it happen for you"; "Reliability is our service"; and "We are not satisfied until you are".

The selling concept and the marketing concept are sometimes confused. The selling concept takes an inside-out perspective. It starts with the factory, focuses on the company's existing products, and calls for heavy selling and promotion to obtain profitable sales. It focuses heavily on customer conquest—getting short-term sales with little concern about who buys or why. In contrast, the marketing concept takes an outside-in perspective. It starts with a well-defined market, focuses on customer needs, coordinates all the marketing activities affecting customers, and makes profits by creating long-term customer relationships based on customer value and satisfaction. Under the marketing concept, companies produce what consumers want, thereby satisfying consumers and making profits.

5. The Societal Marketing Concept

The societal marketing concept holds that the organization should determine the needs, wants, and interests of target markets. It should then deliver superior value to consumers in a way that maintains or improves the consumer's and the society's well-being. The societal marketing concept is the newest of the five marketing management philosophies.

The societal marketing concept questions whether the pure marketing concept is adequate in an age of environmental problems, resource shortages, rapid population growth, worldwide economic problems, and neglected social services. It asks if the firm that senses, serves, and satisfies individual wants is always doing what's best for consumers and society in the long run. According to the societal marketing concept, the pure marketing concept overlooks possible conflicts between consumer short-run wants and consumer long-run welfare.

conflict [ˈkɔnflikt] n. 冲突，斗争
conduct [ˈkɔndʌkt] v. 实施，处理；经营；引导
perfect [pəˈfikt] vt. 使完美无瑕 adj. 完美的，全然的，理想的
reduce [riˈdjuːs] vt. 减少；缩减；降低
calculator [ˈkælkjuleitə] n. 计算器
devote [diˈvəut] vt. 投入于，献身
manufacturer [ˌmænjuˈfæktʃərə] n. 制造业者，厂商
mousetrap [ˈmausətræp] n. 捕鼠器
exterminate [iksˈtəːmineit] v. 消除
convince [kənˈvins] vt. 使确信，使信服；说服
unsought [ˈʌnˈsɔːt] adj. 未追求的，未寻求的
encyclopedia [enˌsaikləuˈpiːdiə] n. 百科全书
insurance [inˈʃuərəns] n. 保险，保险单

vigorously [ˈvigərəsli] adv. 精神旺盛地
voter [ˈvəutə] n. 投票者，有投票权者
fantastic [fænˈtæstik] adj. 极好的，极妙的；幻想的，奇异的
overcapacity [ˌəuvəkəˈpæsiti] n. 生产能力过剩
coax [kəuks] v. 哄，用好话相劝；诱出
disappointment [disəˈpɔintmənt] n. 失望
assumption [əˈsʌmpʃən] n. 假定，设想
reliability [riˌlaiəˈbiliti] n. 可靠性，安全性；可信赖性
confused [kənˈfjuːzd] adj. 混乱的；困惑的
inside-out [ˈinˈsaid-aut] adv. 彻底地，里面翻到外面
conquest [ˈkɔŋkwest] n. 征服
outside-in [ˈautˈsaid-in] adv. 里面翻到外面，彻底地
neglected [niˈglektid] adj. 被忽视的

Unit 4

rapid ['ræpid] *adj.* 迅速的，快的
population [ˌpɔpju'leiʃən] *n.* 人口
worldwide ['wɜːldwaid] *adj.* 遍及全世界的，世界范围的；世界性的

sense [sens] *vt.* 感到，理解，认识
overlook [ˌəuvə'luk] *vt.* 忽略；没注意；俯瞰，俯视
welfare ['welfɛə] *n.* 福利，安宁，幸福

Phrases and Expressions

give weight to 重视；加强
bring down 降低
run a risk 冒险
devote energy to 把精力投到
chemical spray 化学喷雾（器）
brings sth. to the attention of sb. 使某人注意到某物/某事

start with 以……开始
call for 要求，提倡
track down 追捕到
hard sell 硬卖，强行推销
environmental problem 环境问题
resource shortage 资源短缺
in the long run 最后

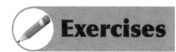

EX. 5 根据文章所提供的信息填空。

1. There are _____ alternative concepts under which organizations conduct their marketing activities: _____, _____, _____, _____ and _____.
2. The production concept is still a useful philosophy in two situations. The first occurs ____ _____. The second situation occurs _____ and _____ is needed to bring it down.
3. Another major concept guiding sellers is the product concept, which holds that consumers will favor products _____.
4. Most firms practice the selling concept when _____. Their aim is _____. rather than _____.
5. The marketing concept has been stated in colorful ways such as _____; _____. and _____.
6. _____. is the newest of the five marketing management philosophies. It holds that the organization should determine, _____, wants, and _____ of _____. It should then deliver _____ to consumers in a way that _____ the consumer's and the society's well-being.

Text	Notes
Target Consumers	
To succeed in today's competitive marketplace, companies must be customer-centered—winning customers from competitors by delivering greater value. But before it can satisfy consumers, a company must first understand their needs and wants. Thus, sound marketing requires a careful analysis of consumers[1].	[1] *n.* 消费者
Being able to successfully devise[2] a strategy or revise an existing strategy often depends on the strategist's[3] ability to understand the benefits a customer desires, the criteria used when making choices, and the behaviors followed when seeking information and selecting alternatives.	[2] *vt.* 设计，发明，图谋 [3] *n.* 战略家
Companies know that they cannot satisfy all consumers in a given market—at least not all consumers in the same way. There are too many different kinds of consumers with too many different kinds of needs. And some companies are in a better position to serve certain segments[4] of the market. Thus, each company must divide up the total market, choose the best segment, and design strategies for profitable serving chosen segments better than its competitors do. This process involves four steps: demand measurement and forecasting[5], market segmentation, market targeting, and market positioning[6].	[4] *n.* 段，节，片断 [5] *n.* 预测；预报 [6] *n.* 定位
• Demand Measurement and Forecasting.	
Suppose a company is looking at possible markets for a potential new product. First, the company needs to make a careful estimate of the current and future of the market and its various segments. To estimate current market size, the company would identify all competing products, estimate the current sales of these products, and determine whether the market is large enough to profitable support another product.	
Equally important is future market growth. Companies want to enter markets that show strong growth prospects. Growth potential may depend on the growth rate of certain age, income, and nationality groups that use the product. Growth also may be related to larger developments in the environment, such as economic conditions, the crime rate, and lifestyle[7] changes. For example, the future market for quality children's toys and clothing is strongly related to current birth rates, trends in consumer affluence[8], and projected family lifestyle.	[7] *n.* 生活方式 [8] *n.* 富裕，富足

• Market Segmentation.

Suppose the demand forecast looks good. The company must now decide how to enter the market. The market consists of many types of customers, products and needs, and the marketer has to determine which segments offer the best opportunity for achieving company objectives. Consumers can be grouped in various ways based on geographic factors; demographic[9] factors; psychographic[10] factor; and behavioral factors. The process of dividing a market into distinct groups of buyers with different needs, characteristics, or behavior who might require separate products or marketing mixes is called market segmentation[11].

Every market has market segments, but not all ways of segmenting a market are equally useful.

A market segment consists of consumers who respond in a similar way to a given[12] set of marketing efforts. In the car market, for example, consumers who choose the biggest, most comfortable car regardless of price make up one market segment. Another market segment would be customers who care mainly about price and operating economy. It would be difficult to make one model of car that was the first choice of every consumer. Companies are wise to focus their efforts on meeting the distinct[13] needs of one or more market segments.

• Market Targeting.

After a company has defined market segments, it can enter one or many segments of a given market. Market targeting involves evaluating each market segment's attractiveness[14] and selecting one or more segments to enter. A company should target segments in which it can generate the greatest customer value and sustain it over time. A company with limited resources might decide to serve[15] only one or a few special segments. This strategy limits sales but can be very profitable. Or a company might choose to serve several related segments—perhaps those with different kinds of customers but with the same basic wants. Or a large company might decide to offer a complete range of products to serve all market segments.

Most companies enter a new market by serving a single segment, and if this proves successful, they add segments. Large companies eventually seek full market coverage. They want to be the "General Motors[16]" of their industry. GM says that it makes a car for every "person, purse, and personality[17]." The leading[18] company normally has different products designed to meet the special needs of each segment.

[9] *adj.* 人口统计学的
[10] *adj.* 心理的
[11] *n.* 市场细分
[12] *adj.* 给定的
[13] *adj.* 清楚的，明显的
[14] *adj.* 吸引人的
[15] *v.* 服务，服役
[16] *n.* 通用汽车
[17] *n.* 个性，人格，人物
[18] *adj.* 领导的，第一位的，最主要的

- Market Positioning.

After a company has decided which market segments to enter, it must decide what "position" it wants to occupy in those segments. A product's position is the place the product occupies relative to competitors in consumers' minds. If a product is perceived[19] to be exactly like another product on the market, consumers would have no reason to buy it.

Market positioning[20] is arranging for a product to occupy a clear, distinctive, and desirable place in the minds of target consumers relative to competing products. Thus, marketers plan positions that distinguish their products from competing brands and give them the greatest strategic advantage in their target markets.

In positioning its product, the company first identifies possible competitive advantages on which to build the position. To gain competitive advantage, the company must offer greater value to chosen target segments, either by charging lower prices than its competitors or by offering more benefits to justify higher prices.

But if a company positions the product as offering greater value, it must then deliver that greater value. Thus, effective positioning begins with actually differentiating[21] the company's marketing offer so that it gives consumers more value than the competition offers. Once the company has chosen a desired position, it must take strong steps to deliver and communicate that position to target consumers. The company's entire marketing program should support the chosen positioning strategy.

[19] v. 感知，感到，认识到

[20] n. 定位

[21] v. 差异化

市场营销管理

什么使一家企业卓越？这个问题在20世纪80年代早期在美国爆炸式地铺开。美国一些很有价值的企业的销售额与盈利额急剧下滑。这里既有常规的问题，如变化的顾客口味、上升的物料成本、下降的价格；同时也有其他新的因素，如来自国外的竞争，尤其是来自日本、新加坡和韩国等高质量产品的进入。市场经历了令人眩晕的变化，而许多企业未能够认识到这些变化并做出反应。

部分美国的其他公司却持续获胜，并不断地提升销售额和盈利额。通过调查43家高绩效企业汤姆·彼得和鲍伯·沃特曼发现，所有这些企业都拥有一系列基本的运作原则，其中有敏锐地感知关注顾客、敏锐地感知市场，以及具备激励其雇员为顾客生产出高质量、高价值产品的能力。过半数原则与市场商人所谓的"营销概念"相关。

今天，人们意识到公司仅仅将事情做好是不能生存的。要在缓慢增长且竞争激烈的国

Unit 4

内外市场中获胜，公司必须表现卓越。顾客和企业购买者在寻求能满足他们的需求时面对丰富充裕的选择，因此他们趋向于寻找那些在质量、价值或成本方面卓越的供应商。最近的研究证明，用完全优质的产品和服务来了解和满足顾客是获得盈利绩效的关键。市场营销承担具有竞争性和盈利性地定义顾客目标和满足顾客需求和需要的途径的职能。

市场营销起源于人类是有需求和动机的动物。需求和动机造就了人们一种不适的状态，只有通过获得产品满足才能化解这种状态。既然许多产品能够满足给定的需求，产品的选择就受到效用、价值和满意等概念的引导。产品的获取有几种方式：自制、强迫获得、乞求获得、交换。现代社会大多数是基于交换的原则运作的，这意味着人们专注于生产特定产品并将其产品与其他产品交换以满足需求。为此人们从事交易与关系的建立。一个市场就是一群人的集合，他们分享着相似的需求。市场营销包括那些与市场打交道的活动，即，尽力将潜在的交易付诸实现。

当至少一方对潜在的交换提出使另一方做出反应的目标和手段的想法时，营销管理就发生了。营销管理是规划和实施想法、商品和服务的定义以及定价、促销和分销的过程，它创造了满足个体和组织目标的交换。

营销管理也发生在当企业与市场发生关联时。例如，一个汽车制造商中的人事副总处理劳动力市场，采购副总处理原材料市场，财务副总则面对资金市场。他们必须设定目标和开发战略从而在这些市场中得到满意的结果。然而，传统来说，这些执行副总并不被称为市场营销者，他们也没有接受市场营销方面的专门训练。而从历史的观点来看，是运用与顾客市场打交道的任务和人员来识别市场营销管理的。

顾客市场上开展的营销工作在形式上是由销售经理、销售人员、广告和促销经理、营销经理、顾客服务经理、产品经理、市场经理以及市场营销副总来执行的。每项工作要承担良好的任务和责任。这些工作涉及管理特定的市场营销资源，如广告、销售人员或市场营销研究。另一方面，产品经理、市场经理、市场营销副总管理项目。他们的工作是分析、规划、实施项目，这些项目将为目标市场生产期望的交易水平和交易组合。

市场营销经理的普遍形象就是其任务主要是刺激对公司产品的需要。然而，这是一种对市场营销经理执行的多样性营销任务的一个非常局限的认知。营销管理以一种帮助企业实现目标的方式执行具有影响需求的水平、时间和构成的任务。营销管理本质上是需求管理。

组织预先构想了对目标市场的期望交易水平。随着时间变化，实际的需求水平可能低于、等于或者高于期望的需求水平。换言之，可能市场上没有需求、需求弱、需求充分、过量需求等，而营销管理必须应对这些不同的市场状态。营销经理通过开发市场研究、规划、实施和控制来解决这些不同的情形。在市场营销规划中，营销者必须就目标市场、市场定位、产品开发、产品定价、分销渠道、物理分销、沟通和促销做出决策。营销经理必须具备许多的技术才能在市场中表现出色。

五种营销哲学能指导组织开展市场营销工作。生产观点认为消费者偏好能够负担得起且买得到的产品，因此管理的主要任务是改进生产和分销的效率，降低成本。产品观念认为，消费者喜欢高质量且价格合理的产品，因此不需要太多的促销活动。销售观念认为消费者不会购买足量的产品，除非对他们进行实实在在的销售和促销刺激。营销观念认为，公司的主要任务是决定顾客目标群体的需求、动机和偏好，并为顾客带来期望的需求满足。

这四种原则都是在关注市场、以顾客为导向并且旨在营利。社会营销观点认为，公司的主要任务是使顾客满意，而长期的消费者与社会福利是实现组织目标和责任的关键。

　　随着商业部门、非营利部门以及国际部门的更多组织认识到市场营销是如何有助于改进企业市场绩效的，对市场营销的兴趣与关注将继续加强。

Unit 5

Text A

Operations Management

Organizations, ranging from sports teams, schools, and churches to hospitals, legal institutions, military bases, and large and small businesses, are found in any industrial society. These formal groups enable people to produce a vast range of products and services that would be beyond the capabilities of the individual. Operations management is crucial to each type of organization because only through successful management of people, capital, information, and materials can an organization meet its goals.

At one time, the term "operations management" referred primarily to manufacturing production. The growing economic importance of a wide range of non-manufacturing business activities, however, broadened the scope of the operations management function. Today, the term operations management refers to the direction and control of the processes that transform inputs into finished goods and services. This function is essential to systems producing goods and services in both profit and nonprofit organizations.

Operations management, as is the case with every functional area within an organization, can be defined from several perspectives: one is with respect to its overall role and contribution within an organization and the other focuses more on the day-to-day activities that fall within its area of responsibility. From an organizational perspective, operations management may be defined as the management of the direct resources that are required to produce and deliver an organization's goods and services.

The marketplace—the firm's customers for its goods and services—determines the corporate strategy of the firm. This strategy is based on the corporate mission, and in essence reflects how the firm plans to use all of its resources and functions to gain an advantage over its competition. The operations strategy specifies how the firm will employ its production capabilities to support its corporate strategy.

Within the operations function, management decisions can be divided into three broad areas: strategic (long-range) decisions, tactical (medium-range) decisions, operational planning and control (short-range) decisions. These three areas can be viewed as a top-down approach to operations management, with the decisions made at the higher levels acting as constraints on the lower levels. The strategic issues are usually very broad in nature, addressing such questions as: how well we make the product? Where do we locate the facility or facilities? How much capacity do we need? When should we add more capacity? Consequently, by necessity, the time frame for strategic decisions is typically very long, usually several years or more, depending on the specific industry.

Operations management decisions at the strategic level impact the long-range effectiveness of the company in terms of how well it can address the needs of its customers. Thus, for the firm to succeed, these decisions must be closely aligned with the corporate strategy. Decisions made at the strategic level then define the fixed conditions or constraints under which the firm must operate in both the intermediate and short term. For example, a decision made at the strategic level to increase capacity by building a new plant becomes a capacity constraint with respect to tactical and operational decisions.

Looking at the next level in the decision-making process, tactical planning primarily addresses the issue of how to efficiently schedule material and labor over a specific time horizon and within the constraints of the strategic decisions that were previously made. Thus, some of the OM issues at this level are: how many workers do we need? When do we need them? Should we work overtime or put on a second shift? When should we have material delivered? Should we have a finished goods inventory? These tactical decisions, in turn, define the operating constraints under which the operational planning and control decisions are made.

The management decisions with respect to operational planning and control are very narrow and short term, by comparison. For example, issues at this include: what jobs do we work on today or this week? To whom do we assign what tasks? What jobs have priority?

From an operational perspective, the day-to-day activities within the operations management function focus on adding value for the organization through its transformation process, which is sometimes referred to as the technical core, especially in manufacturing organizations. Some examples of the different types of transformations are: physical as in manufacturing; locational as in transportation, exchange as in retailing, storage as in warehousing, physiological as in health care, informational as in telecommunications.

The inputs are customers and/or materials which undergo the transformation. Also part of the transformation process are a variety of components supplied by the organization, such as labor, equipment, and facilities, which convert the inputs into outputs. Every transformation process is affected by external factors, which are outside the control of management. External factors include random, unexpected events such as natural disasters, economic cycles, changes in government policies and laws, as well as changes in consumer preferences and tastes.

Unit 5

These external factors can also include anticipated changes, such as seasonality, over which management has little or no control.

Another important role of the operations management function is the measurement and control of the transformation process. This consists of monitoring the outputs in various ways, including quality and quantity, and then using this information as feedback to make the necessary adjustments that will improve the process.

New Words

range [reindʒ] vi. (在一定范围内)变化，变动 n. 范围
team [ti:m] n. 队，组
church [tʃə:tʃ] n. 教堂，礼拜堂
institution [ˌinsti'tju:ʃən] n. 公共机构，协会，制度
society [sə'saiəti] n. 群体，团体
capability [ˌkeipə'biliti] n.(实际)能力，性能，容量
enable [i'neibl] vt. 使能够，使成为可能，使实现
crucial ['kru:ʃəl] adj. 极重要的；有决定性的
broaden ['brɔ:dn] vt. 加宽，使扩大，加阔
scope [skəup] n. 范围，范畴，领域
employ [im'plɔi] v. 使用，运用
tactical ['tæktikəl] adj. 战术的
approach [ə'prəutʃ] n. 方法，步骤，途径，通路
constraint [kən'streint] n. 约束，强制，局促
intermediate [ˌintə'mi:djət] adj. 中间的
schedule ['ʃedju:l; 'skedʒjul] vt. 预定，安排 n. 时间表，进度表
overtime ['əuvətaim] adv. 超时；加班 n. 超时；加班；加班费

shift [ʃift] n. 轮班，轮班职工；轮班工作时间
inventory ['invəntri] n. 商品目录；清单；存货，库存量
assign [ə'sain] vt. 分配，指派
priority [prai'ɔriti] n. 优先，优先权
transformation [ˌtrænsfə'meiʃən] n. 变化，转化，改造
manufacturing [ˌmænju'fæktʃəriŋ] n. 制造业 adj. 制造业的
locational [ləu'keiʃənəl] adj. 位置上的
affect [ə'fekt] vt. 影响
facility [fə'siliti] n. 设施，设备
retailing ['ri:teiliŋ] n. 零售业
storage ['stɔridʒ] n. 贮藏(量)，贮藏库，存储
warehousing ['wɛəhauziŋ] n. 仓库费；入仓库；仓库贮存
physiological [ˌfiziə'lɔdʒikəl] adj. 生理学的，生理学上的
informational [ˌinfə'meiʃənəl] adj. 报告的，情报的
telecommunication ['telikəmju:ni'keiʃən] n. 电信，长途通信，无线电通信
convert [kən'və:t] vt. 使转变,转换,使……改变信仰

工商管理 英语

random ['rændəm] *adj.* 任意的，随便的，胡乱的
unexpected [ˌʌniks'pektid] *adj.* 想不到的，意外的，未预料到

disaster [di'zɑːstə] *n.* 灾难，天灾，灾祸
cycle ['saikl] *n.* 周期，循环
seasonality ['siːzənliti] *n.* 季节的，季节性
adjustment [ə'dʒʌstmənt] *n.* 调整，调节

 Phrases and Expressions

operations management 运营管理
military base 军事基地
industrial society 工业社会
in essence 本质上；大体上；其实
in nature 实际上，本质上
time frame 期限，时帧
with respect to 关于
work overtime （超出时间的工作）加班
in turn 反过来；轮流地；挨个，依次

corporate strategy 公司战略
top-down approach 由上至下的方法
act as 担当
time horizon 时间范围
by comparison 比较起来
health care 卫生保健
external factor 外部因素
natural disaster 自然灾害

 Abbreviations

OM (Operations Management) 运营管理

Notes

1 These formal groups enable people to produce a vast range of products and services that would be beyond the capabilities of the individual.

本句中，that would be beyond the capabilities of the individual 是一个定语从句，修饰和限定 products and services。beyond 是一个介词，意思是"为……所不能及；多于；超出"。enable sb. to do sth. 的意思是"使某人能够做某事，赋予某人做某事的权力"。请看下例：

Understanding this article is beyond my capacity.
我看不懂这篇文章。

It's quite beyond me why she married such a heavy smoker.
我实在无法理解为什么她会嫁给这样一个烟鬼。
This dictionary enable you to understand English words.
这本词典使你能理解英语词汇。
The rights protection law for the consumers enables any impaired consumers to claim money from the company.
消费者权益保护法使任何受损害的消费者有向公司索赔的权利。

2 Operations management is crucial to each type of organization because only through successful management of people, capital, information, and materials can an organization meet its goals.

本句中，because only through successful management of people, capital, information, and materials can an organization meet its goals 是一个原因状语从句，在该从句中，only through successful management of people, capital, information, and materials 作条件状语，can an organization meet its goals 是一个倒装句，是原因状语从句的主句。

英语中，only 和它所修饰的状语放在句首时，必须使用倒装语序。请看下例：
Only in this way can you improve your English.
Only then did he realize the importance of English.
但是，若 only 和它所修饰的状语不在句首时，则不倒装。若放在句首的 only 修饰的是句子的主语时，也不倒装。请看下例：
You can understand it only when you grow up.
只有当你长大成人后才能明白这件事情。
It was reported only five people were injured in the accident.
据报道只有五个人在这起事故中受伤。
You seem to be getting fatter — the only answer is to do more exercise.
你好像越来越胖了。唯一的解决办法是多活动些。

3 Operations management, as is the case with every functional area within an organization, can be defined from several perspectives: one being with respect to its overall role and contribution within an organization; the other focusing more on the day-to-day activities that fall within its area of responsibility.

本句中，as is the case with every functional area within an organization 是一个非限定性定语从句，对 Operations management 进行说明，as 在从句中作主语。请看下例：
He opposed the idea, as could be expected.
正如可以预料到的，他反对这个意见。

one being with respect to its overall role and contribution within an organization 和 the other focusing more on the day-to-day activities that fall within its area of responsibility 是独立主格结构，对 several perspectives 进行解释。that fall within its area of responsibility 是一个定语从句，修饰和限定 the day-to-day activities。请看下例：
The class is divided into four groups, each working on one subject.

班级被分成四个小组，每组完成一个主题。
Everywhere you see people in their holiday dresses, their faces shining with smiles.
到处都可以看到人们穿着节日服装满面笑容。

4. Decisions made at the strategic level then define the fixed conditions or constraints under which the firm must operate in both the intermediate and short term.

本句中，made at the strategic level 是一个过去分词短语，作定语，修饰和限定主语 decisions，它可以扩展为一个定语从句：which are made at the strategic level。under which the firm must operate in both the intermediate and short term 是一个介词前置的定语从句，修饰和限定宾语 the fixed conditions or constraints。

英语中，如果关系代词在从句中作介词的宾语时，通常用 whom、which 或 that。此时，介词放在句子的后面，关系代词可以省略。但是在正式书面语中，介词放在关系代词之前，此时，只能使用关系代词 whom 或 which，并且不能省略关系代词。请看下例：

Have you met the person about whom he was speaking?
你见过他说的那个人吗？
The only thing about which he is not sure is how to use this tool.
他唯一没有把握的是如何使用这个工具。

5. Looking at the next level in the decision-making process, tactical planning primarily addresses the issue of how to efficiently schedule material and labor over a specific time horizon and within the constraints of the strategic decisions that were previously made.

本句中，Looking at the next level in the decision-making process 是一个现在分词短语，作状语。how to efficiently schedule material and labor over a specific time horizon and within the constraints of the strategic decisions that were previously made 是副词 how + 动词不定式短语作介词 of 的宾语。that were previously made 是一个定语从句，修饰和限定 the strategic decisions。

6. From an operational perspective, the day-to-day activities within the operations management function focus on adding value for the organization through its transformation process, which is sometimes referred to as the technical core, especially in manufacturing organizations.

本句中，From an operational perspective 是一个介词短语，作状语。within the operations management function 是一个介词短语，作定语，修饰和限定主语 the day-to-day activities。adding value for the organization 是一个动名词短语，作谓语 focus on 的宾语。through its transformation process 作方式状语，修饰 adding。which is sometimes referred to as the technical core, especially in manufacturing organizations 是一个非限定性定语从句，对 transformation process 作进一步补充说明。

7. Also part of the transformation process are a variety of components supplied by the organization, such as labor, equipment, and facilities, which convert the inputs into outputs.

本句是一个表语提前的倒装句，正常的语序应该是：A variety of components supplied by the organization, such as labor, equipment, and facilities, which convert the inputs into outputs, are also part of the transformation process。使用倒装句主要是为了保

持句子平衡，避免头重脚轻。

本句中，supplied by the organization 是一个过去分词短语，作定语，修饰和限定 a variety of components。such as 的意思是"例如"，用于举例说明。labor, equipment, and facilities 解释 a variety of components 时举的例子。which convert the inputs into outputs 是一个非限定性定语从句，对 a variety of components 进行补充说明。

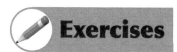

EX. 1 根据课文内容，回答以下问题。

1. Why is operations management crucial to each type of organization?
2. What did the term "operations management" refer primarily to at one time?
3. What does the term "operations management" refer to today?
4. What may operations management be defined as from an organizational perspective?
5. What is the difference between the corporate strategy and the operations strategy?
6. Within the operations function, how many broad areas can management decisions be divided into? What are they?
7. What are the strategic issues usually in nature? Can you list some of the questions they address?
8. What do decisions made at the strategic level define?
9. Looking at the next level in the decision-making process, what does tactical planning primarily address?
10. What is another important role of the operations management function? What does it consist of?

EX. 2 根据下面的英文释义，写出相应的英文词汇（使用本单元所学的单词、词组或缩略语）。

英文释义	词汇
to vary within specified limits	
to make or become broad or broader	
of, relating to, or using tactics	
to direct the efforts or attention of (oneself); To deal with	
an established right to precedence	
the functions and activities involved in the selling of commodities directly to consumers	

the electronic systems used in transmitting messages, as by telegraph, cable, telephone, radio, or television	
an occurrence causing widespread destruction and distress; a catastrophe	
the act or an instance of transforming	
having no specific pattern, purpose, or objective	

EX. 3 把下列句子翻译为中文。

1. Operations management deals with the production of goods and services that people buy and use every day.
2. Operations managers are responsible for ensuring that an organization has sufficient supplies of high-quality, low-cost input.
3. Because satisfying customers is so important, managers try to design production systems that can produce the outputs that have the attributes customers desire.
4. Customers usually prefer a higher-quality product to a lower-quality product.
5. Achieving high product quality lowers operating costs because of the effect of quality on employee productivity.
6. One way that businesses attempt to become more productive is to examine critically whether the operations performed by their workers add value.
7. The way in which machines and workers are organized or grouped together into workstations affects the efficiency of the production system.
8. One of the central tasks of operations management is to develop new and improved production systems that enhance the ability of the organization.
9. The ability of an organization to satisfy the demands of its customers for lower prices, acceptable quality, better features, and so on, depends critically on the nature of the organization's production system.
10. The company that customizes every product to the unique demands of individual customers is likely to see its cost structure become very high.

EX. 4 把下面的短文翻译成中文。

The importance of operations management, both for organizations and society, should be fairly obvious: the consumption of goods and services is an integral part of our society. Operations management is responsible for creating those goods and services. Organizations exist primarily to provide services or create goods. Hence, operations management is the core function of an organization. Without this core, there would be no need for any of the other functions.

Unit 5

Text B

The Ever Changing World of Operations Management

Operations management is continuously changing to meet the new and exciting challenges of today's business world. This ever-changing world is characterized by increasing global competition and advances in technology. Emphasis is also shifting within the operations function to link it more closely with both customers and suppliers.

1. Increased Global Competition

The world is rapidly transforming itself into a single global economy, which is also referred to as a global village or global landscape. Markets once dominated by local or national companies are now vulnerable to competition from literally all corners of the world. Consequently, as companies expand their businesses to include foreign markets, so too must the operations management function take a broader, more global perspective in order for companies to remain competitive. To survive and prosper in such a global marketplace companies must excel in more than one competitive dimension, which previously was the norm. With the rise of the global economy, companies are no longer limited as to where they can make or buy their products and components.

2. Advances in Technology

Advances in technology in recent years also have had a significant impact on the operations management function. Information technology now allows us to collect detailed customer data so that we can "mass customize" products to meet the needs of individual customers. The increased use of automation and robotics also has permitted us to improve the quality of the goods that are being manufactured. Automated teller machines (ATM), which can provide customers with 24-hours service, are a good example of technology being applied in service operations, particularly in those countries with high labor costs.

The explosive growth of the Internet in recent years also has had an impact on operations. Electronic marketplace, a major factor in the emergence of B2B transactions, quickly identifies the lowest-priced suppliers. The wide use of e-mail now allows companies to communicate rapidly with suppliers, customers, and other operations within their respective organizations. Customer contact centers, be they for making hotel or airline reservations, receiving customer orders, or handling customer complaints, can now be located anywhere in the world.

However, advances in technology place new requirement on the workforce and even on customers, especially in service operations. Consequently, skilled workers are replacing unskilled workers in all types of operations.

3. Linking Operations Management to Customers and Suppliers

In the past, most manufacturing organizations viewed operations strictly as an internal function that had to be buffered from the external environment by other organizational functions. Orders were generated by the marketing function; suppliers and raw materials were obtained through the purchasing function; capital for equipment purchases came from the finance function; the labor force was obtained through the human resources function; and the product was delivered by the distribution function.

Buffering the transformation process from the external environment was traditionally desirable for several reasons:

- Interaction with environmental elements could have a disturbing influence on the transformation process.
- The transformation process was often more efficient than the processes required for obtaining inputs and distributing finished goods.
- With certain processes, maximum productivity was achieved only by operating at a continuous rate that assumed the market could absorb all of the products being manufactured. This meant that the production process had to shift at least some of the input and output activities to other parts of the firm.
- The managerial skills required for the successful operation of the transformation process were often different from those required for the successful operation of boundary functions such as marketing and human resources, for example.

However, there were some inherent disadvantages when the transformation process was totally isolated. One was that information lagged between the process and the boundary function, which inevitably led to inflexibility. Another was that for high-tech products in particular, communications between the shop floor and the customer could be extremely valuable in solving technical problems during production.

More and more firms recognize the competitive advantage achieved when the transformation process is not isolated, as when customers are invited to view their operating facilities firsthand. For example, Green Giant believes that the tours of their production facilities that they provided to Japanese distributors were a major factor in their ability to penetrate that market with their Green Giant food products.

In a like manner, companies are working more closely with suppliers. Firms like Toyota, for example, have suppliers deliver product directly to the factory floor, eliminating any need for a stockroom. Texas Instruments encourages many of its vendors to automatically replenish items on the factory floor without individual purchase orders or incoming reports every time a delivery is made.

This trend toward having the transformation process work more closely with both suppliers and customers alike is often referred to as a product's value chain. We can define a value chain as consisting of all those steps that actually add value to the product without distinguishing where they are added. This concept attempts to eliminate all non-value added steps, and consequently results in a higher degree of dependence among the value-added functions within the chain.

The integration of both suppliers and customers into the transformation process begins to blur the boundaries between what were previously totally independent organizations. What appears to be emerging now is a concept known as the virtual enterprise, which is fully integrated and interlocked network of interdependent organizations. With this new approach, it is often difficult to determine where one organization leaves off and the next one begins. As one example, FedEx has several employees who work full time at the L.L. Bean Mail Order Distribution Center in Freeport, Maine.

continuously [kən'tinjuəsli] *adv.* 不断地；连续地

advance [əd'vɑːns] *n.* 前进；提升

emphasis ['emfəsis] *n.* 强调；重点

transform [træns'fɔːm] *vt.* 转换；改变；改造

landscape ['lændskeip] *n.* 风景；景观；庭园；山水

dominate ['dɔmineit] *v.* 支配；控制；占优势

vulnerable ['vʌlnərəbəl] *adj.* 易受攻击的；易受……的攻击

literally ['litərəli] *adv.* 照字面意义；逐字地

consequently ['kɔnsikwəntli] *adv.* 从而；所以；因此

excel [ik'sel] *vt.& vi.* 优于；胜过

dimension [di'menʃən] *n.* 范围；尺寸；尺度；维；规模

norm [nɔːm] *n.* 标准；规范

customize [kʌstəmaiz] *v.* 定制；用户化

automation [ɔːtə'meiʃən] *n.* 自动化操作；自动控制；自动操作

robotics [rəu'bɔtiks] *n.* 机器人技术；机器人学

permit [pə(ː)'mit] *v.* 许可；允许；准许 *n.* 通行证；许可证；执照

apply [ə'plai] *vt.* 应用；实施；运用；使用

explosive [iks'pləusiv] *adj.* 爆炸(性)的；爆发(性)的

emergence [i'məːdʒəns] *n.* 显露；出现；发生

respective [ri'spektiv] *adj.* 各自的；各个的

reservation [ˌrezə'veiʃən] *n.* 预定；预约

order ['ɔːdə] *n.* 定单；定购

complaint [kəm'pleint] *n.* 诉苦；抱怨；牢骚

requirement [ri'kwaiəmənt] *n.* 需求；要求；必要条件

workforce ['wəːkfɔːs] *n.* 劳动力

replace [ri(ː)'pleis] *vt.* 取代；替换；代替

strictly ['striktli] *adv.* 严格地；严厉地；精确地

buffer ['bʌfə] *vt.* 减轻；缓冲；保护

disturbing [di'stəːbiŋ] *adj.* 烦扰的

工商管理 英语

absorb [əb'sɔ:b] vt. 吸收
boundary ['baundəri] n. 边缘；界线；边界；境界
inherent [in'hiərənt] adj. 固有的；内在的
isolate ['aisəleit] vt. 使隔离；使孤立
lag [læg] vi. 落后；滞后；跟不上；落伍 n. 落后
inevitably [in'evitəbli] adv. 不可避免地；必然地
inflexibility [in'fleksəbliti] n. 不屈性；顽固；不变性
invite [in'vait] vt. 邀请
firsthand [fə:st'hænd] adv. 第一手地；直接地 adj. 直接的；直接得来的；直接采购的
tour [tuə] n. 巡回展；旅行；游历；旅游 v. 旅行；游历；巡回

distributor [dis'tribjutə] n. 发行人；销售者；批发商
penetrate ['penitreit] vt. 穿透；渗透；看穿
stockroom ['stɔkrum] n. 商品储藏室；仓库
vendor ['vendɔ:] n. 卖方；卖主
Texas ['teksəs] n. 得克萨斯州 (美国州名)
automatically [ɔ:tə'mætikli] adv. 自动地；机械地
replenish [ri'pleniʃ] v. 补充
trend [trend] n. 倾向；趋势
dependence [di'pendəns] n. 依靠；依赖；信任
integration [,inti'greiʃən] n. 整合；综合
blur [blə:] vt. 使模糊；使看不清
interlock [intə'lɔk] vt.&vi. 连锁；连串

Phrases and Expressions

global village 地球村
all corners of the world 世界各地；世界每个角落
no longer 不再
have a significant impact on... 对……有重大影响

finished goods 成品
Texas Instruments 得州仪器公司
value chain 价值链
virtual enterprise 虚拟企业
leave off 停止

Abbreviations

ATM (Automated Teller Machine) 自动取款机
B2B (Business to Business) 企业对企业的电子商务

Unit 5

EX. 5 根据课文内容，回答以下问题。

1. Why is operations management continuously changing?
2. What is this ever-changing world characterized by?
3. What is the world rapidly transforming itself into? What is it also referred to?
4. Have advances in technology in recent years had a significant impact on the operations management function? What does information technology now allow us to do?
5. What are a good example of technology being applied in service operations, particularly in those countries with high labor costs?
6. What does the wide use of e-mail now allow companies to do?
7. What is the result of advances in technology on the workforce?
8. In the past, what did most manufacturing organizations view operations strictly as?
9. How were orders generated? How were suppliers and raw materials obtained? Where did capital for equipment purchases come from? How was the labor force obtained? And how was the product delivered?
10. How many inherent disadvantages when the transformation process was totally isolated mentioned? What are they?

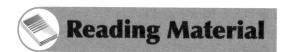

Text	Notes
Manufacturing and Services: Differences and Similarities In the early history of operations management and until the middle of the twentieth century, the focus was on manufacturing organizations, and the field was thus called industrial management or production management[1]. Service organizations, because they performed almost at handicraft[2] levels, were largely ignored. Today's managers apply concepts of process analysis, quality, job design[3], capacity, facility location, layout, inventory, and scheduling[4] to both manufacturing and the provision of services. The benefits of these applications are improved quality, reduced costs, and increased value to the customers, all of which give a firm a competitive edge. **1. Differences Between Manufacturing and Services.** The differences between manufacturing and service operations fall into the eight categories.	[1] *n.* 生产管理 [2] *n.* 手工艺，手工艺品，手艺 [3] *n.* 工作设计 [4] *n.* 行程安排

The first distinction arises from the physical nature[5] of the product. Manufactured goods are physical, durable[6] products. Services are intangible[7], perishable[8] products—often being ideas, concepts, or information.

The second distinction also relates to the physical nature of the product. Manufactured goods are outputs that can be produced, stored, and transported in anticipation[9] of future demand. Creating inventories allows managers to cope with fluctuations[10] in demand by smoothing output levels. By contrast, services can't be pre-produced. Service operations don't have the luxury[11] of using finished goods inventories as a cushion[12] against erratic[13] customer demand.

A third distinction is customer contact. Most customers for manufactured products have little or no contact with the production system. Primary customer contact is left to distributors and retailers. However, in many service organizations the customers themselves are inputs and active participants in the process. For example, at a college the student studies, attends lectures, takes exams, and finally receives a diploma[14]. Hospitals, jails[15], and entertainment centers are other places where the customer is present during the provision of most of the services. Some service operations have low customer contact at one level of the organization and high customer contact at other levels. For example, the branch offices of parcel delivery, banking, and insurance organizations deal with customers daily, but their central offices have little direct customer contact. Similarly, the back-room operations of a jewelry store require little customer contact, whereas sales counter operations involve a high degree of contact.

A related distinction is response time[16] to customer demand. Manufacturers generally have days or weeks to meet customer demand, but many services must be offered within minutes of customer arrival. The purchaser of a forklift[17] truck may be willing to wait 16 weeks for delivery. By contrast, a grocery store customer may grow impatient[18] after waiting five minutes in a checkout line. Because customers for services usually arrive at times of their choosing, service operations may have difficulty matching capacity with demand. Furthermore, arrival patterns may fluctuate daily or even hourly, creating even more short-term demand uncertainty.

Two other distinctions concern the location and size of an operation. Manufacturing facilities often serve regional[19], national, or even international markets and therefore generally require larger facilities, more automation, and greater capital investment than for service facilities. In general, services can't be shipped to distant locations. For example, a hairstylist[20] in Manhattan[21] can't give a haircut to someone in Topeka[22]. Thus service organizations requiring direct customer contact must locate relatively near their customers.

[5] *n.* 物理性质
[6] *adj.* 持久的，耐用的
[7] *adj.* 无形的
[8] *adj.* 容易腐烂的
[9] *n.* 预期，预料
[10] *n.* 波动，起伏
[11] *n.* 奢侈，华贵
[12] *n.* 垫子，软垫
[13] *adj.* 无确定路线，不稳定的，奇怪的
[14] *n.* 文凭，毕业证书
[15] *n.* 监狱
[16] *n.* 响应时间
[17] *n.* [美][机]铲车，叉式升降机
[18] *adj.* 不耐烦的，急躁的
[19] *adj.* 地区性的；地域性的
[20] *n.* 发式专家，发式师
[21] *n.* 曼哈顿岛（美国纽约一区）
[22] 托皮卡[美国堪萨斯州首府]

A final distinction is the measurement of quality. As manufacturing systems tend to have tangible products and less customer contact, quality is relatively easy to measure. The quality of service systems, which generally produce intangibles, is harder to measure. Moreover, individual preferences[23] affect assessments of service quality, making objective measurement difficult. For example, one customer might value a friendly chat with the salesclerk during a purchase, whereas another might assess quality by the speed and efficiency of a transaction.

2. Similarities Between Manufacturing and Services.

Despite these distinctions, the similarities between manufacturing and service operations are compelling[24]. Every organization has processes that must be designed and managed effectively. Some type of technology, be it manual or computerized[25], must be used in each process. Every organization is concerned about quality, productivity, and the timely response to customers. A service provider, like a manufacturer, must make choices about the capacity, location, and layout of its facilities. Every organization deals with suppliers of outside services and material, as well as scheduling problems. Matching staffing levels and capacities with forecasted demands is a universal[26] problem. Finally, the distinctions between manufacturing and service operations can get cloudy.

Manufacturers do not just offer products, and service organizations do not just offer services. Both types of organizations normally provide a package of goods and services. Customers expect both good service and good food at a restaurant and both good service and quality goods from a retailer. Manufacturing firms offer many customer services, and a decreasing proportion of the value added by them directly involves the transformation of materials.

Despite the fact that service providers can't inventory[27] their outputs, they must inventory the inputs for their products. These inputs must undergo further[28] transformations during provision of the service. Hospitals, for example, must maintain an adequate supply of medications. As a result, wholesale and retail firms hold 48 percent of the U.S. economy's inventory. In addition, manufacturing firms that make customized[29] products or limited-shelf-life[30] products can't inventory their outputs.

As for customer contact, many service operations have little outside customer contact, such as the back-room[31] operations of a bank or the baggage handling area at an airport. However, everyone in an organization has some customers—outside customers or inside customers—whether in services or in manufacturing.

[23] *n.* 优先考虑

[24] *adj.* 引人注目的

[25] *vt.* 用计算机处理，使计算机化

[26] *adj.* 普遍的，全体的，通用的

[27] *vt.* 编制详细目录，开清单，清点存货

[28] *adj.* 进一步的

[29] *adj.* 定制的，用户化的

[30] *n.* 有限保存期限

[31] *n.* 后台

运营管理

在工业化社会中，从体育团队、学校、教会，到医院、法律机构、军事基地，以及大中小型企业，都能发现组织的存在。这些正式的团体帮助人们生产大量的产品和服务，而这超越了个人能力范围。对每一种类型的组织而言，运营管理都是极为关键的，因为唯有对人、财、信息、物料进行成功地管理，组织才能实现其目标。

曾经有一段时间，"运营管理"这个术语主要指制造业的生产。然而，随着大量非制造业商业活动在经济中的地位被提升，运营管理的功能得到了扩展。今天，运营管理是对将投入转变为商品和服务过程的指导与控制，这项管理功能对于营利或非营利组织的商品和服务生产系统至关重要。

正如组织中的每一个职能领域，我们可以从几个角度对运营管理进行定义：一种是考虑它在组织中扮演的角色以及做出的贡献；另一种则是更多关注属于其职责范围内的日常活动。从组织角度，运营管理可以被定义为：对用于生产和传递组织产品和服务的直接资源进行管理。

市场——对企业商品和服务有需求的顾客——决定了企业的公司战略。这种战略建立在公司使命的基础上，本质上反映了企业如何计划运用其所有的资源和功能以获得竞争优势。运营战略则详细指明了企业如何使用其生产能力来支持公司战略的实现。

在运营职能中，管理决策可以划分为三大类型：战略（长期）决策、战术（中期）决策、运营规划和控制（短期）决策。这三类决策可以视为一个从上至下的运营管理方法，上层的决策限定了下层决策的方向。战略问题通常是非常宽泛的，如：如何生产产品？在何处放置设备或工具？需要多大的产能？什么时候应该增加生产容量？因此，从必要性而言，典型的战略决策期限是非常长的，通常几年甚至更久，这取决于特定的产业。

在战略层面的运营管理决策影响着企业在多大程度上满足其顾客需求的长期效力。因此，企业为了成功，所做出的运营管理决策必须紧密地与公司战略相一致。在战略层面做出的决策定义了企业在中期和短期运作中的固定条件或限制。例如，在战略层面做出通过建设一个新厂房以增加产能的决策，成为限定战术和运营决策的产能约束。

关注决策过程的下一层次，战术规划主要涉及在一个特定的时间范围内，以及之前确定的战略决策约束条件下，如何有效地安排物料和人力进程。因此，运营管理的问题通常有：需要多少工人？什么时候需要他们？应该加班还是推迟到下一轮？什么时候传送物料？是否需要准备商品库存？反过来，这些战术决策将定义运营规划与控制决策的约束条件。

比较而言，运营规划和控制方面的管理决策是较为狭窄和短期性的。例如，决策问题包括：本周或本日我们的主要工作有哪些？我们应将什么任务分配给谁？什么任务具有优先权？

从运营角度，运营管理职能下的日常活动主要关注如何通过其运作过程为组织增加价值，这通常被视为技术核心，尤其是对于制造业组织。不同类型运作转换的例子有制造业中的物质、运输业中的定位、零售业中的交换、仓库业中的存贮、健康保健中的生理、电信中的信息。

经历运作转换的投入包括顾客和/或物质。当然，该运作过程的一部分是由组织提供的，例如劳动力、设备和工具，它们将投入转变为产出。每一次转换过程都受到外部因素的影响，这不在组织的控制范围之内。外部因素包括随意的、不可预计的事件，例如自然灾害、经济周期、政府政策和法律的变动，以及顾客偏好与口味的变化。这些外部因素也包括那些可预期的变化，例如季节性，对此管理层的控制力较小，甚至不能控制。

运营管理的另外一个重要角色就是对转换过程的衡量和控制。这包括用多种方式监测产出，包括质量和数量，然后使用这些信息作为反馈进行必要调整，进而改进转换过程。

Unit 6

Text A

Logistic Management

During the past three decades, logistics has emerged as a major concern of business managers. The objective of logistical operations is to deliver finished inventory and material assortments, in correct quantities, when required, at the location desired, and in usable condition at the lowest total dollar cost. It is through the logistic process that raw materials flow into the vast manufacturing complex of an industrial nation and finished products are distributed for consumption.

Logistical performance provides time and place utility in the business system. Thus value is added to either raw materials or finished products as the result of the logistical process. The value associated with time and place utility is costly to achieve.

There are various managerial activities involved in logistical operations of an individual enterprise. To achieve an orderly flow of products to the marketplace, managerial attention must be directed to the design and administration of a logistical system. The purpose of the logistical system is to control the flow of raw material and finished products. The goal of logistics is to achieve efficiently a predetermined level of manufacturing marketing support at the lowest possible total cost expenditure. The logistical manager has the fundamental responsibility to design an operating system capable of realizing this goal. Once designed, his responsibility extends to the administration of the system.

From the perspective of the individual firm, the over-all field of logistics is subdivided into three main areas of managerial concern: physical distribution management, material management, and logistical coordination.

The process of physical distribution management is concerned with the movement of finished inventory to customers. The availability of inventory is a vital part of the marketing efforts of a firm. Unless the product is delivered at the appropriate time and in an economic manner, a great deal of the promotional efforts of a firm may be diluted. It is through the physical distribution process that time and space are introduced into marketing. Thus physical distribution links a firm with its customers. To support the wide variety of marketing systems that exist in a highly commercialized nation, many physical distribution systems are utilized. In total, such systems link together manufacturers, wholesalers, and retailers into a channel network for providing inventory availability in support of marketing.

The process of material management, sometimes referred to as physical supply, is concerned with the procurement and movement of raw materials and parts from geographical points of purchases to manufacturing and assembly plants. Similar to physical distribution, material management is concerned with making available the correct assortment of materials, at the desired location, when needed, and in an economical manner. Whereas physical distribution is concerned with satisfying customer requirements, material management is concerned with the support of manufacturing and assembly operations.

Logistical coordination is concerned with the identification of internal requirements and the establishment of specifications that tie together a particular firm's physical distribution and material management. Coordination is required to establish operational continuity. Between physical distribution and material management substantially different operational requirements exist. The function of logistical coordination is to reconcile these differentials to the maximum benefit of the enterprise.

Logistical coordination constitutes a combination of planning and operational matters. The establishment of objectives to guide operations requires that estimates be compiled concerning future expectations and requirements. Forecasting is therefore an integral part of logistical coordination. Finally, to operationalize what a firm plans to accomplish during a specific time period, forecasts must be synthesized into specific plans. Such plans encompass material planning, production scheduling, and internal product replenishment. Forecasting, material planning, and production scheduling constitute the planning aspects of logistical coordination. Product replenishment represents the operational aspect of logistical coordination.

Product replenishment operations maintain control over semi-finished goods between stages of manufacturing and finished inventory to and between warehouses utilized by the enterprise. Product replenishment has one major difference in contrast to either physical distribution or material management operations. Product replenishment operations are limited to movements within and under the complete control of the enterprise. Therefore, the uncertainties introduced by random order entry and erratic performances are removed from operational planning, thereby permitting more optional allocation.

From a vantage point of the total enterprises, the three subdivisions of logistics have

Unit 6

substantial overlap. They combine to provide management of all material and finished inventory moving among locations, supply sources, and customers in the total enterprise. In this sense logistics is concerned with the integrated management for maximum benefit and economy of all material and finished inventory movement.

New Words

logistic [ləuˈdʒistik] *adj.* 后勤学的，后勤的，物流的

logistics [ləˈdʒistiks] *n.* 物流；后勤学，后勤

assortment [əˈsɔːtmənt] *n.* 分类

quantity [ˈkwɔntiti] *n.* 量，数量

location [ləuˈkeiʃən] *n.* 位置，场所，特定区域

usable [ˈjuːzəbl] *adj.* 可用的，合用的，便于使用的

vast [vɑːst] *adj.* 巨大的，辽阔的，大量的

consumption [kənˈsʌmpʃən] *n.* 消费，消费量

logistical [ləuˈdʒistikəl] *adj.* 后勤学的，后勤的，物流的

orderly [ˈɔːdəli] *adv.* 依次地，顺序地

administration [ədminisˈtreiʃən] *n.* 管理，经营

predetermine [ˈpriːdiˈtəːmin] *v.* 预定，预先确定

expenditure [iksˈpenditʃə] *n.* 支出，花费

subdivide [ˈsʌbdiˈvaid] *v.* 再分，细分

extend [iksˈtend] *vi.* 延伸，延续，继续扩张

availability [əˌveiləˈbiliti] *n.* 可用性，有效性，实用性

promotional [prəuˈməuʃənəl] *adj.* 促进的；促销的；奖励的

diluted [daiˈljuːtid] *adj.* 无力的；冲淡的

commercialize [kəˈməːʃəlaiz] *v.* 使商业化，使商品化

wholesaler [ˈhəulseilə] *n.* 批发商

retailer [riːˈteilə] *n.* 零售商人

channel [ˈtʃænl] *n.* 渠道；途径

procurement [prəˈkjuəmənt] *n.* 采购，获得，取得

geographical [ˌdʒiəˈgræfikəl] *adj.* 地理学的，地理的

assembly [əˈsembli] *n.* 组装，装配；集合

economical [ˌiːkəˈnɔmikəl] *adj.* 节约的，经济的

identification [aiˌdentifiˈkeiʃən] *n.* 辨认，鉴定，证明，视为同一

establishment [isˈtæbliʃmənt] *n.* 确立，制定

establish [iˈstæbliʃ] *vt.* 成立，建立

specification [ˌspesifiˈkeiʃən] *n.* 详述，规格，说明书，规范

continuity [ˌkɔntiˈnjuiti] *n.* 连续性，连贯性

substantially [səbˈstænʃəli] *adv.* 主要地；实质上地；重大地；相当大地

reconcile [ˈrekənsail] *vt.* 使和解，使和谐，使顺从

differential [difəˈrenʃ(ə)l] *n.* 差别，差异 *adj.* 有差别的，有区别的

89

工商管理 英语

constitute [ˈkɔnstitjuːt] vt. 组成，构成，任命
compile [kəmˈpail] vt. 编译，编辑，汇编
expectation [ˌekspekˈteiʃən] n. 期望，期待，预料，指望，展望
forecast [ˈfɔːkɑːst] vt. 预想，预测，预报
integral [ˈintigrəl] adj. 主要的，必备的；完整的，整体的
operationalize [ˌɔpəˈreiʃənlaiz] vt. 使用于操作，使开始运转，实施
synthesize [ˈsinθisaiz] v. 综合，合成
replenishment [riˈpleniʃmənt] n. 补给，补充
semi-finished [ˈsemi-ˈfiniʃt] adj. 半完成的，半制的，半成品的

warehouse [ˈwɛəhaus] n. 仓库，货栈，大商店
uncertainty [ʌnˈsəːtnti] n. 无常，不确定，不可靠
introduce [ˌintrəˈdjuːs] vt. 引起；介绍，传入，引进，提出
erratic [iˈrætik] adj. 无确定路线，不稳定的
optional [ˈɔpʃənəl] adj. 可选择的，随意的
allocation [ˌæləuˈkeiʃən] n. 分配，安置
subdivision [ˈsʌbdiˌviʒən] n. 细分，一部
overlap [ˈəuvəˈlæp] v.（与……）交叠，重叠；部分相同，在特性或功能上相似，相当

 Phrases and Expressions

logistical operations　物流管理
logistical system　物流系统
physical distribution management　货物流通管理
material management　材料管理
in support of　支持，支援
assembly plant　装配厂

tie together　捆绑在一起；配合
be similar to　类似于……
production scheduling　生产调度
under the control of　受……的控制
remove from　拿走；撤走，除去
vantage point　有利位置，优越地位，优势

Notes

1 It is through the logistic process that raw materials flow into the vast manufacturing complex of an industrial nation and finished products are distributed for consumption.

　　本句中，It is... that... 是一个强调句型，through the logistic process 是强调部分，that 后面有两个并列句。

　　英语中，It is /was... that/who 强调句型着重强调句子的某个成分，如主语、宾语或状语。请看下例：

Unit 6

It was Mr. Smith that solved this problem.
是史密斯先生解决了这个问题。
It is light and heat that the sun gives us.
太阳供给我们的是光和热。
It was last year that he took over this company.
他是在去年接管了这家公司的。

  注意：It is /was… that 句型不能强调句子的谓语。如果要强调谓语，需要用助动词 do。请看下例：
Tom does look well.
汤姆看上去确实很健康。
Do come and see me when you are free.
有空一定来看我。
They did work very hard last Sunday.
他们上个星期天确实工作很努力。

2 The logistical manager has the fundamental responsibility to design an operating system capable of realizing this goal.

  本句中，to design an operating system 是一个动词不定式短语，作定语，修饰和限定 the fundamental responsibility。capable of realizing this goal 是一个形容词短语，作定语，修饰和限定 an operating system，该短语可以扩展为一个定语从句：which is capable of realizing this goal。

3 The establishment of objectives to guide operations requires that estimates be compiled concerning future expectations and requirements.

  本句中，The establishment of objectives 作主语，等于 Establishing objectives。to guide operations 是一个动词不定式短语，作定语，修饰和限定 objectives。that estimates be compiled concerning future expectations and requirements 是一个虚拟语气的句子，作谓语 requires 的宾语，在 estimates 和 be 之间省略了 should。

  英语中，在表示命令、请求或建议等动词后的宾语从句中，谓语常用"should + 动词原形"的形式，也可以省略 should，只用动词原形。请看下例：
He suggested that the work should be finished by Friday.
他建议星期五之前完成这项工作。
The boss insisted that they go there at once.
老板坚持他们马上到那儿去。

4 Therefore, the uncertainties introduced by random order entry and erratic performances are removed from operational planning, thereby permitting more optional allocation.

  本句中，introduced by random order entry and erratic performance 是一个过去分词短语，作定语，修饰和限定 the uncertainties。thereby permitting more optional allocation 是一个现在分词短语，作结果状语。

Exercises

EX. 1 根据课文内容，回答以下问题。

1. What is the objective of logistical operations?
2. What does logistical performance provide?
3. What is the purpose of the logistical system?
4. What is the goal of logistics?
5. From the perspective of the individual firm, what is the over-all field of logistics subdivided into? What are they?
6. What is the process of physical distribution management concerned with?
7. What is the process of material management concerned with?
8. What is logistical coordination concerned with?
9. What do product replenishment operations maintain control over?
10. Does product replenishment have any major difference in contrast to either physical distribution or material management operations?

EX. 2 根据下面的英文释义，写出相应的英文词汇（使用本单元所学的单词、词组或缩略语）。

英文释义	词 汇
supply, procurement, distribution, and replacement of materiel and personnel	
the act of assorting; separation into classes	
fit for use; convenient to use	
person who sells goods, especially in large quantities, to shopkeepers, for resale to the public	
prudent and thrifty in management; not wasteful or extravagant	
a detailed, exact statement of particulars, especially a statement prescribing materials, dimensions, and quality of work for something to be built, installed, or manufactured.	
to be the elements or parts of; compose	
to combine so as to form a new, complex product	
lacking consistency, regularity, or uniformity; having no fixed or regular course	
to lie or extend over and cover part of; to have an area or a range in common with.	

Unit 6

EX. 3 把下列句子翻译为中文。

1. The logistical system is primarily concerned with support of the production and marketing systems.
2. Logistical costs have a direct relationship to a firm's selected service policy.
3. Physical distribution is essential to marketing because timely and economical product delivery is necessary to accomplish profitable transactions.
4. The basic design of the material management operating system is based upon fulfillment of the material plan.
5. It is a fundamental responsibility of material management to select the sources that most consistently meet quality specifications.
6. The speed of information flow is directly related to the integration of fixed facilities, transportation capability, and inventory.
7. The goal of logistics is to support procurement, manufacturing, and market distribution operational requirements.
8. Logistics should be managed as an integrated effort to achieve customer satisfaction at the lowest total cost.
9. While many aspects of information are critical to logistics operations, the processing of order is of primary importance.
10. Forecasting and communication of customer requirements are the two areas of logistical work driven by information.

EX. 4 把下面的短文翻译成中文。

The potential for logistical services to favorably impact customers is directly related to operating system design. The many different facets of logistical performance requirements make operational design a complex task as an operating structure must offer a balance of performance, cost, and flexibility. When one considers the variety of logistical systems used throughout the world to service widely diverse markets, it is astonishing that any structural similarity exits.

Text B

Logistical Integration Objectives

To achieve logistical integration, six operational objectives must be simultaneously achieved: responsiveness, variance reduction, inventory reduction, shipment consolidation, quality, and life cycle support. The relative importance of each is directly related to a firm's logistical strategy.

1. Responsiveness

Responsiveness is concerned with a firm's ability to satisfy customer requirements in a timely manner. Information technology is facilitating response-based strategies that permit operational commitment to be postponed to the last possible time, followed by accelerated delivery. The implementation of response-based strategies serves to reduce inventories committed or deployed in anticipation of customer requirements. Responsiveness serves to shift operational emphasis from forecasting future requirements to accommodating customers on a rapid order-to-shipment basis. In a response-based system, inventory is not deployed until a customer commits. To support such commitment, a firm must have inventory availability and timely delivery once a customer order is received.

2. Variance Reduction

All operating areas of a logistical system are susceptible to variance. Variance results from failure to perform any expected facet of logistical operations. For example, delay in customer order processing, an unexpected disruption in manufacturing, goods arriving damaged at a customer's location, and/or failure to deliver at the right location on time all create unplanned variance in the order-to-delivery cycle. A common solution to safeguard against the detrimental variance is to use inventory safety stocks to buffer operations. It is also common to use premium transportation to overcome unexpected variance that delays planned delivery. Such practices, given their associated high cost, can be minimized by using information technology to maintain positive logistics control. To the extent that variance is minimized, logistical productivity will improve. Thus, variance reduction, the elimination of system disruptions, is one basic objective of integrated logistics management.

3. Inventory Reduction

To achieve the objective of inventory reduction, an integrated logistics system must control asset commitment and turn velocity. Asset commitment is the financial value of deployed inventory. Turn velocity reflects the rate at which inventory is replenished over time. High turn rates, coupled with desired inventory availability, mean assets devoted to inventory are being efficiently and effectively utilized; that is, overall assets committed to support an integrated operation are reduced.

It is important to keep in mind that inventory can and does facilitate desirable benefits. Inventories are critical to achieving economies of scale in manufacturing and procurement. The objective is to reduce and manage inventory to the lowest possible level while simultaneously achieving performance objectives.

4. Shipment Consolidation

One of the most significant logistical costs is transportation. Approximately 60 cents of each logistics dollar is expended for transportation. Transportation cost is directly related to the type of product, size of shipment, and movement distance. Many logistical systems that feature direct fulfillment depend on high-speed, small shipment transportation, which is costly. A system objective is to achieve shipment consolidation in an effort to reduce transportation cost. As a general rule, the larger a shipment and the longer the distance it is transported, the lower is the cost per unit. Consolidation requires innovative programs to combine small shipments for timely consolidated movement. Such programs require multiform coordination because they transcend the supply chain. Successful e-commerce fulfillment direct-to-consumers require innovative ways to achieve effective consolidation.

5. Quality

A fundamental operational objective is continuous quality improvement. Total Quality Management is a major initiative throughout most facets of industry. If a product becomes defective or if service promises are not kept, little can be added by the logistics process. Logistical costs, once expended, cannot be reversed or recovered. In fact, when product quality fails after customer delivery and replacement is necessary, logistical costs rapidly accumulate. In addition to the initial distribution cost, products must be returned and replaced. Such unplanned movements typically cost more than original distribution. For this reason, commitment to zero-defect order-to-delivery performance is a major goal of logistics.

Logistics itself is performed under challenging conditions. The difficulty of achieving zero-defect logistics is magnified by the fact that logistical operations typically are performed across a vast geographical area during all times of day and night without direct supervision.

6. Life Cycle Support

The final integration design objective is life cycle support. Few items are sold without some guarantee that the product will perform as advertised. In some situations the initial value-added inventory flow to customers must be reversed. Product return is common as a result of increasingly rigid quality standards, product expiration dating, and responsibility for hazardous consequences. Reverse logistics also results from the increasing number of laws encouraging recycling of beverage containers and packaging materials. The significant point concerning reverse logistics is the need to maintain maximum control when a potential health liability exists, such as a contaminated product. The operational requirements for reverse logistics often are able to reclaim value by reducing the quantity of products that might otherwise be scrapped or sold at a discount. Sound integrative strategy cannot be formulated without careful review of reverse logistical requirements.

For some products, such as copying equipment, primary profit lies in the sale of supplies and aftermarket service to maintain the product. The importance of life cycle support is significantly different in situations wherein the majority of profits are achieved in the aftermarket. For firms marketing consumer durables or industrial equipment, the commitment to life cycle support constitutes a versatile and demanding marketing opportunity as well as one of the largest costs of logistical operations. Life cycle support requires cradle-to-cradle logistics. Cradle-to-cradle logistical support goes beyond reverse logistics and recycling to include the possibility of aftermarket service, product recall, and product disposal.

New Words

simultaneously [siməl'teiniəsly] adv. 同时地

variance ['vɛəriəns] n. 不一致，变化，变异

shipment ['ʃipmənt] n. 装船，出货

consolidation [kən,sɔli'deiʃən] n. 巩固，合并；整理；调整

postpone [pəust'pəun] v. 推迟，延期，缓办

accelerated [ək'seləreitid] adj. 加速的

deploy [di'plɔi] v. 展开，配置

accommodate [ə'kɔmədeit] vt. 供应，供给，使适应

susceptible [sə'septəbl] adj. 易受影响的，易感动的

facet ['fæsit] n. (多面体的)面，层

unplanned ['ʌn'plænd] adj. 无计划的，未筹划的

detrimental [,detri'mentl] adj. 有害的

premium ['primjəm] n. 额外费用；奖金；奖赏；保险费

associated [ə'səuʃieitid] adj. 伴随的，有关的

elimination [i,limi'neiʃən] n. 排除，除去，消除

disruption [dis'rʌpʃən] n. 中断，分裂，瓦解，破坏

velocity [vi'lɔsiti] n. 速度，速率，迅速

expend [iks'pend] vt. 花费，消耗，支出

fulfillment [ful'filmənt] n. 履行，实行

innovative ['inəuveitiv] adj. 创新的，革新的

multiform ['mʌltifɔ:m] adj. 多种形式的

defective [di'fektiv] adj. 有缺陷的

reverse [ri'və:s] vt. 颠倒；反转；翻转；(使)倒退；改变 n. 相反，背面，反面，倒退 adj. 相反的，倒转的，颠倒的

advertise ['ædvətaiz] v. 做广告，登广告

accumulate [ə'kju:mjuleit] v. 积聚，堆积

magnify ['mægnifai] vt. 放大，扩大，赞美

supervision [,sju:pə'viʒən] n. 监督，管理

rigid ['ridʒid] adj. 刚硬的，刚性的，严格的

expiration [,ekspaiə'reiʃən] n. 满期，终止

hazardous ['hæzədəs] adj. 危险的，冒险的

beverage ['bevəridʒ] n. 饮料

container [kən'teinə] n. 容器，集装箱

contaminated [kən'tæmineitid] adj. 被污染的

reclaim [ri'kleim] vt. 收回，要求归还

scrap [skræp] vt. 扔弃，敲碎，拆毁

aftermarket ['ɑ:ftə,mɑ:kit] n. 配件市场

versatile ['və:sətail] adj. 通用的，万能的

recall [ri'kɔ:l] n. 收回，召回

disposal [dis'pəuzəl] n. 处理，处置，清除

Unit 6

Phrases and Expressions

life cycle 生命周期
safeguard against 保护；防卫
coupled with 加上，外加
inventory reduction 减少库存
economy of scale 规模经济
transportation cost 运输成本
Total Quality Management 全面质量管理
product return 退货

reverse logistics 逆向物流
at a discount 打折扣
consumer durable 耐用消费品
cradle-to-cradle logistics "从摇篮到摇篮"物流
supply chain 供应链
e-commerce 电子商务
zero-defect 零缺陷

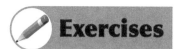

Exercises

EX. 5 根据文章所提供的信息填空。

1. To achieve logistical integration, _____ operational objectives must be simultaneously achieved: responsiveness, _____ variance reduction, _____ , _____ , quality, and _____ .

2. Responsiveness is concerned with a firm's ability to _____ in a timely manner.

3. A common solution to safeguard against _____ is to use inventory safety stocks to _____ . It is also common to use _____ to overcome unexpected variance that delays planned delivery.

4. Asset commitment is _____ of deployed inventory. Turn velocity reflects _____ _____ .

5. One of the most significant logistical costs is _____ . Approximately _____ cents of each logistics dollar is expended for transportation. Transportation cost is directly related to _____ , _____ , and _____ .

6. _____ is a major initiative throughout most facets of industry.

7. _____ is a major goal of logistics.

8. The final integration design objective is _____ . It requires _____ . Cradle-to-cradle logistical support goes beyond _____ and recycling to include the possibility of _____ , _____ , and _____ .

Reading Material

Text	Notes
Supply Chain Management A dominant logistics philosophy throughout the 1980s and into the early 1900s involved the integration of logistics with other functions in an organization in an effort to achieve the enterprise's overall success. The early to mid-1990s witnessed[1] a growing recognition[2] that there could be value in coordination the various business functions not only within organizations but across organizations as well—what can be referred to as a supply-chain management[3] philosophy. A supply chain "encompasses all activities associated with the flow and transformation[4] of goods from the raw material stage, through to the end user[5], as well as the associated information flows[6]." Supply chain management can be defined as the systemic[7], strategic coordination of the traditional business functions and the tactics[8] across these business functions within a particular company and across businesses in the supply chain, for the purpose of improving the long-term performance of the individual companies and the supply chain as a whole. Importantly, while nearly any organization can be part of a supply chain(s), SCM "requires overt[9] management efforts by the organizations within the supply chain." Successful supply-chain management requires companies to adopt an enterprise-to-enterprise point of view, which can cause organizations to accept practices and adopt behaviors that haven't traditionally been associated with buyer-seller interactions[10]. Moreover, successful supply-chain management requires companies to apply[11] the systems approach across all organizations in the supply chain. When applied to supply chains, the systems approach suggests that companies must recognize the interdependencies[12] of major functional areas within, across, and between firms. In turn, the goals and objectives of individual supply-chain participants[13] should be compatible[14] with the goals and objectives of other participants in the supply chain. For example, a company that is committed to a high level of customer service might be out of place in a supply chain comprised of companies whose primary value proposition[15] involves cost containment[16].	[1] *vt.* 目击，为……作证，证明 [2] *n.* 承认，重视，公认 [3] 供应链管理 [4] *n.* 变化，转化 [5] *n.* 最终用户 [6] *n.* 信息流 [7] *adj.* 系统的 [8] *n.* 战术，策略 [9] *adj.* 明显的，公然的 [10] *n.* 交互作用 [11] *vt.* 申请，应用 [12] *n.* 互相依赖 [13] *n.* 参与者，共享者 [14] *adj.* 谐调的，一致的，兼容的 [15] *n.* 主张，建议 [16] *n.* 围堵政策，牵制政策

One widely used model of supply-chain management, the SCOR Model, currently identifies five key processes—plan, Source, Make, Deliver, Return—associated with supply-chain management. Earlier version of the SCOR model did not include the return process; as a result, the current model explicitly[17] recognizes that returns should be considered in the design and management of supply chains.

Moreover, closer analysis of the five key processes, and their definitions, indicates the important role of logistics in supply-chain management. It can be argued[18] that logistics has some involvement in both sourcing and making. Alternatively, logistics can be heavily involved in delivering and returning; the definition of delivery specifically mentions the key logistics components[19] of order management, transportation management, and distribution management.

The food and beverage industry provides an excellent real-world example of the importance of logistics to supply-chain management. Interviews with key executives from North American and European food and beverage organizations suggested that supply-chain management is the single most important strategy for ensuring success in an industry that is experiencing tremendous[20] competitive pressures. According to these executives, the most pressing technological investments for facilitating supply-chain superiority[21] involve software associated with the logistical activity of order fulfillment.

Conventional[22] wisdom[23] suggests that company-versus-company competition will be superseded[24] in the twenty-first century by supply-chain-versus-supply-chain competition. While this may occur in a few situations, such competition may not be practical in many instances because of common or overlapping suppliers or the lack of a central control point, among other reasons.

Rather, a more realistic[25] perspective is that individual members of a supply chain will compete based on the relevant capabilities of their supply network, with a particular emphasis on immediately adjacent[26] suppliers or customers. For instance, Bose Corporation developed a supplier integration program known as JIT II. under JIT II, various suppliers have in-plant offices at Bose that allow them to personally interact with other suppliers and Bose personnel on a daily basis. The suppliers' employees stationed at Bose have the authority to place purchasing orders from Bose for their employer's goods rather than having the purchasing orders placed by Bose employees.

[17] *adv.* 明白地，明确地

[18] *vt.* 说服

[19] *n.* 部分；成分，组分

[20] *adj.* 极大的，巨大的

[21] *n.* 优越，优秀

[22] *adj.* 惯例的，常规的，习俗的

[23] *n.* 智慧，明智的行为，学识

[24] *vt.* 代替，取代，接替

[25] *adj.* 现实（主义）的

[26] *adj.* 邻近的，接近的

While much of the discussion so far has focused on domestic supply chains, one should recognize that supply chains are becoming increasingly global in nature. Reasons for the increased globalization[27] of supply chains include lower-priced[28] materials and labor, the global perspective of companies in a supply chain, and the development of global competition, among others. While supply-chain integration can be complex and difficult in a domestic setting[29], the complexity and difficulty are even greater in global supply chains due to cultural, economic, technological, political, spatial[30], and logistical differences.

[27] *n.* 全球化，全球性
[28] *adj.* （有）定价的
[29] *n.* 背景
[30] *adj.* 空间的

物流管理

在过去的三十年中，物流成为公司经理主要关注的问题。物流运作的目的是在有需要时以最低的成本将正确数量的存货与物品类别以可使用的状态传送到需要的地点。通过物流的过程，原材料流动至工业国家巨大的制造业体系中，而成品则被分销至消费者手中。

物流的成效在于为企业系统提供了时间和地点的效用，因此物流过程增加了原料或成品的价值，而与时间和地点效用相关联的价值是需要花费成本才能实现的。

在单个企业中，存在着大量涉及物流运作的管理活动。为了实现产品有序地流动至市场，管理的重心应该放在物流系统的设计和管理上。物流系统旨在控制原材料和成品的流动，物流的目标是：以最低可能的总成本支出，有效地实现预定水平的制造业市场营销支持。物流经理的基本责任是设计一个能够实现该目标的运作系统，一旦这样的系统被设计出来，其责任就延伸为对物流系统的管理。

从个体企业的角度，整个物流领域可以划分为三个主要的管理重点：货物分销管理、物料管理和物流协调。

货物分销管理的过程主要关注成品向顾客的移动。存货的可用性是企业市场营销努力的重要部分。除非产品在恰当的时间以最经济的方式被传送，否则企业大量的促销努力将被削弱。正是通过货物分销过程，时间和空间被引入到市场营销中来。因此，货物分销将企业与顾客联系起来。为支持存在于高度商业化国家的大量多样化的市场营销系统，许多货物分销系统被采用。总体上，这种系统将制造商、批发商、零售商联结并构成为一个渠道网络，为支持营销提供可用的存货。

物料管理过程，有时也被称为物料供应，它关心的是原材料从购买地点到制造和装配厂的采购和移动。与货物分销类似，物料管理考虑的是在必要时将可能的物料类别以经济的方式运送到需要的地点。当然，货物分销重点在满足顾客的需求，而物料管理重点在于支持制造与装配运作。

Unit 6

　　物流协调关注的是将特定企业的货物分销与原料管理联系在一起的内部需求识别和规格确立。为了建立运作的连续性，协调是必需的。在货物分销与原料管理之间存在着明显不同的运作需求。物流协调的功能就是调节这些差异性，实现企业利益的最大化。

　　物流协调构建了规划和运作事物的联合体。指导运作目标的建立要求在编制预算时考虑未来的期望值与需求内容。因此，预测是物流协调中的主要内容。最后，为了使企业在特定时间段内完成的计划具有可操作性，预测必须整合进特定的计划中。这样的计划包括物料计划、生产调度、内部产品补给。预测、物料计划和生产调度构成了物流协调的计划方面，产品补给则代表了物流协调的运作方面。

　　产品补充运作对半成品的控制保持在制造与完成的存货阶段和企业使用的仓库间内。产品补充与货物分销或物料运作管理存在一个主要的差异，产品补充运作受限于企业内部的移动，且完全处于企业的控制之下。因此，它远离随机订单和不确定绩效带来的不确定性，允许更多的可选择性分配。

　　从整体企业的优势角度看，上述物流的三个子部分存在显著的交叠。它们联合在一起，为整个企业提供了将全部物料和成品在地点、供应源、顾客之间移动的管理。从这个意义来讲，物流关注的是为了利益最大化以及所有物料成品最经济移动而进行的整合管理。

Unit 6

Unit 7

Text A

Total Quality Management

Total Quality Management (TQM) can be viewed as an organization-wide approach that focuses on producing high-quality goods and services. TQM, when properly used, is an integral part of an organization, not a separate, stand-alone program, and it encompasses all of the functional areas and levels within the organization, including suppliers.

There are four primary elements that are integral to every successful TQM program: leadership, employee involvement, product/ process excellence, and customer focus.

1. Leadership

The leadership provided by an organization's management is a major cornerstone in the development and implementation of a successful TQM program. When properly executed, a TQM program is companywide, transcends the traditional functional areas, and involves all of the firm's employees. It, therefore, requires vision, planning, and communication, all of which are the responsibility of top management. Studies have indicated that total commitment from management is considered to be a critical element in successfully implementing such programs.

Top management can demonstrate its commitment to a TQM program in several ways. These include incorporating TQM into the firm's overall strategy and demonstrating by actions as well as by words that quality is the number one operating priority of the organization.

2. Employee Involvement

Employee involvement is another critical element in successfully implementing a TQM program. By involving all employees in the decision-making process, management is able to receive inputs from those nearest the problems and in the best position to recommend viable solutions. Employee involvement, which appears to be prevalent in most world-class operations, also takes advantage of the skills and knowledge of all employees.

A key element in employee involvement is that each worker assumes the responsibility for inspecting the quality of his or her own work. This is referred to as quality at the source and extends beyond the worker to include the work group, all departments, and the suppliers of parts and services to the organization. This view changes the often-adversarial practice of having a QC inspector, typically from the QC department, making decisions about good or bad quality.

3. Product / Process Excellence

Product / Process Excellence involves the quality of the product's design and analysis of field failures. It also includes statistical process control (SPC) and other analytical tools.

Process control is concerned with monitoring quality while the product is being produced or the service is being performed. Typical objectives of process control plans are to provide timely information on whether currently produced items are meeting design specifications and to detect shifts in the process that signal that future products may not meet the customer's requirement. The actual control phase of process control occurs when corrective action is taken, such as when a worn part is replaced, a machine is overhauled or a new supplier is found. Process control concepts, especially statistically based control charts, are used in services as well as in manufacturing.

An underlying philosophy in achieving product/process excellence is the concept of continuous improvement. This has a general meaning as well as a specific TQM meaning. Its general meaning is an ongoing effort to improve in every part of the organization and all of its outputs. Its more specific meaning focuses on continual improvement in the processes by which work is accomplished.

In Japanese companies, the concept of continuous improvement is referred to as *kaizen*. It can be interpreted to mean a systematic approach to eliminating errors and improving the quality of the product that is delivered to the customer. One of the ways *kaizen* is achieved is through the use of foolproof in the methods that are used to make the products. In manufacturing, it often requires that a part be redesigned so that it can fit only one way.

4. Customer Focus

The customer's perception of quality must be taken into account in setting acceptable quality levels. In other words, a product isn't reliable unless the customer says it's reliable and a service isn't fast unless the customer says it's fast. Translating customer quality demand into specifications requires marketing (or product development) to accurately determine what the customer wants and product designers to develop a product (or service) that can be produced to consistently achieve that desired level of quality.

This, in turn, requires that we have an operational definition of quality, an understanding of its various dimensions, and a process for including the voice of the customer in those specifications. The quality of a product or service may be defined by the quality of its design (product quality) and the quality of its conformance to that design (process quality). Design quality refers to the inherent value of the product in the marketplace and is thus a strategic decision for the firm.

Conformance quality refers to the degree to which the product or service meets design specifications. It, too, has strategic implication, but the execution of the activities involved in achieving conformance is of a tactical day-to-day nature. It should be evident that a product or service can have high design quality but low conformance quality, and vice versa.

The operation function and the quality organization within the firm are primarily concerned with quality of conformance. Achieving all the quality specifications is typically the responsibility of manufacturing management (for products) and branch operations management (for services).

Both design quality and conformance quality should provide products that meet the customer's objectives for those products. This is often termed the product's fitness for use, and it entails identifying those dimensions of the product (or service) that the customer wants and developing a quality control program to ensure that these dimension are met.

New Words

stand-alone [stand-ə'ləun] n. 独立的
involvement [in'vɔlvmənt] n. 参与；包含
cornerstone ['kɔ:nəstəun] n. 墙角石；基础
transcend [træn'send] vt. 超越，胜过
commitment [kə'mitmənt] n. 许诺，承担义务
recommend [rekə'mend] vt. 推荐，介绍
viable ['vaiəbl] adj. 可行的
solution [sə'lju:ʃən] n. 解答，解决办法
prevalent ['prevələnt] adj. 普遍的，流行的
assume [ə'sju:m] vt. 承担
inspect [in'spekt] vt. 检查，视察
adversarial [ˌædvə'seəriəl] adj. 敌手的，对手的，对抗(性)的

detect [di'tekt] vt. 察觉，发觉，侦查
shift [ʃift] n. 移动，轮班，移位，变化
signal ['signl] n. 信号
worn [wɔ:n] adj. 用旧的；疲倦的
overhaul [ˌəuvə'hɔ:l] v. 检查
underlying [ˌʌndə'laiiŋ] adj. 在下面的，根本的，潜在的
eliminate [i'limineit] vt. 排除，消除
foolproof ['fu:lpru:f] n. 安全装置 adj. 十分简单的，十分安全的
redesign [ˌri:di'zain] v. 重新设计
perception [pə'sepʃən] n. 理解，感知，感觉
reliable [ri'laiəbl] adj. 可靠的，可信赖的
conformance [kɔn'fɔ:məns] n. 一致性，适应性

Phrases and Expressions

take… into account 考虑
control chart 控制图表
take advantage of 利用

operational definition 操作性定义
vice versa 反之亦然

Abbreviations

TQM (Total Quality Management) 全面质量管理
QC (Quality Control) 质量控制
SPC (Statistical Process Control) 统计过程控制

Notes

1. It, therefore, requires vision, planning, and communication, all of which are the responsibility of top management.

    本句中，all of which are the responsibility of top management. 是一个非限定性定语从句，which 指 vision, planning, and communication。

    英语中，定语从句可以由名词（代词或数词）+ of + which (whom) 来引导，表示部分与整体的关系。which 指物，whom 指人，注意不要误用。请看下例：

    Mary borrowed some books from the library, all of which are on computer.

    玛丽从图书馆借了一些书，全都是计算机方面的。

    He knows lots of people, few of whom are professors.

    他认识很多人，他们中间几乎没有大学教授。

    I have some friends, one of whom is a businessman.

    我有一些朋友，其中一个是商人。

2. These include incorporating TQM into the firm's overall strategy and demonstrating by actions as well as by words that quality is the number one operating priority of the organization.

    本句中，incorporating 和 demonstrating 作 include 的并列宾语；that quality is the number one operating priority of the organization 是一个宾语从句，作 demonstrating 的宾语；by actions as well as by words 作方式状语，也修饰 demonstrating。

3. This view changes the often-adversarial practice of having a QC inspector, typically from the QC department, making decisions about good or bad quality.

本句中，making decisions about good or bad quality 是一个现在分词短语，作 a QC inspector 的补足语。have sb. doing sth. 的意思是"让某人一直做某事"，have sb. do sth. 的意思是"让某人做某事"。请看下例：

"If you make trouble again, I'll have you standing outside the whole night." Mother threatened.

"如果你再惹麻烦，我就让你在门外站一夜。"妈妈威胁道。

There is something wrong with your car. I'll have Mike repair it for you tomorrow.

你的车出故障了，我明天让迈克来帮你修一下。

4. Typical objectives of process control plans are to provide timely information on whether currently produced items are meeting design specifications and to detect shifts in the process that signal that future products may not meet the customer's requirement.

本句中，to provide timely information 和 to detect shifts 由 and 连接，是两个并列的动词不定式短语作表语。whether currently produced items are meeting design specifications 是一个宾语从句，作介词 on 的宾语，与 on 一起构成介词短语，作定语，修饰和限定 information。that signal that future products may not meet the customer's requirement 是一个定语从句，修饰和限定 shifts。在该定语从句中，that future products may not meet the customer's requirement 是一个宾语从句，作 signal 的宾语。in the process 是一个介词短语，作状语，修饰 to detect。

5. Translating customer quality demand into specifications requires marketing (or product development) to accurately determine what the customer wants and product designers to develop a product (or service) that can be produced to consistently achieve that desired level of quality.

本句中，Translating customer quality demand into specifications 是一个动名词短语，作主语。requires 作谓语，marketing (or product development) 作宾语，to accurately determine what the customer wants 是一个动词不定式短语，作 marketing (or product development) 的补足语。在该不定式短语中 what the customer wants 作 determine 的宾语。and 后面省略了 requires，product designers 作 requires 宾语，to develop a product (or service) 是一个动词不定式短语，作 product designers 的补足语。that can be produced 是一个定语从句，修饰和限定 a product (or service)。to consistently achieve that desired level of quality 是一个动词不定式短语，作目的状语。

6. This is often termed the product's fitness for use, and it entails identifying those dimensions of the product (or service) that the customer wants and developing a quality control program to ensure that these dimension are met.

本句中，identifying 和 developing 由 and 连接，是两个并列的动名词短语，作 entails 的宾语。that the customer wants 是一个定语从句，修饰和限定 the product (or service)。to ensure that these dimension are met 是一个动词不定式短语，作目的状语。

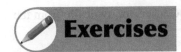

EX. 1 根据课文内容，回答以下问题。

1. What can total quality management be viewed as?
2. How many primary elements are there that are integral to every successful TQM program? What are they?
3. What have studies indicated?
4. What is a key element in employee involvement? What is it referred to?
5. What does Product / Process Excellence involve?
6. What are typical objectives of process control plans?
7. How many meanings does continuous improvement have? What are they? What is its general meaning? And what does its specific TQM meaning focus on?
8. What does design quality refer to?
9. What does conformance quality refer to?
10. What should both design quality and conformance quality provide?

EX. 2 根据下面的英文释义，写出相应的英文词汇（使用本单元所学的单词、词组或缩略语）。

英文释义	词　汇
to concentrate attention or energy	
a stone at the corner of a building uniting two intersecting walls; An indispensable and fundamental basis	
to pass beyond the limits of	
capable of success or continuing effectiveness; practicable	
relating to or characteristic of an opponent	
to examine carefully and critically, especially for flaws	
to examine or go over carefully for needed repairs	
design again	
to get rid of; remove	
insight, intuition, or knowledge gained by perceiving	

Unit 7

EX. 3 把下列句子翻译为中文。

1. For a long time, the responsibility for quality in an organization rested with its quality control department.
2. Modern quality management is now evolving toward emphasis on preventing mistakes rather than on finding and correcting them.
3. Quality is no longer the exclusive domain of the quality control department, but has become the responsibility of everybody in the organization.
4. Poor designs or defective products or services can result in loss of business.
5. Quality refers to the ability of a product or service to consistently meet or exceed customer expectation.
6. For a variety of reasons, products do not always perform as expected, and services do not always yield the desired results.
7. Quality of design refers to the intention of designers to include or exclude certain features in a product or service.
8. Poor quality can adversely affect productivity during the manufacturing process.
9. Design decisions must take into account customer wants, production or service capabilities, cost, and other similar considerations.
10. The determination of quality does not stop once the product or service has been sold or delivered.

EX. 4 把下面的短文翻译成中文。

The entire organization must be subject to the search for improved ways of performing; nothing should be regarded as sacred or untouchable. A sometimes helpful view is to consider the internal customers and strive to satisfy them; that is, every activity in an organization has one or more "customers" who receive its output. By thinking in terms of what is needed to satisfy these customers, it is often possible to improve the system and, in doing so, increase the satisfaction of the final customer.

Text B

What is Six Sigma?

In 1988, Motorola Corp. became one of the first companies to receive the Malcolm Baldrige National Quality Award. The award strives to identify those excellent firms that are worthy role models for other businesses. One of Motorola's innovations that attracted a great deal of attention was its Six Sigma program. Six Sigma stands for Six Standard Deviations. Six Sigma methodology provides the techniques and tools to improve the capability and reduce the defects in any process. Six Sigma is, basically, a process quality goal. As such, it falls into the category of a process capability technique.

The traditional quality paradigm defined a process as capable if the process's natural spread, plus and minus three sigma, was less than the engineering tolerance. Under the assumption of normality, this translates to a process yield of 99.73 percent. A later refinement considered the process location as well as its spread and tightened the minimum acceptable so that the process was at least four sigma from the nearest engineering requirement. Motorola's Six Sigma asks that processes operate such that the nearest engineering requirement is at least plus or minus six sigma from the process mean. Motorola's Six Sigma program also applies to attribute data. This is accomplished by converting the Six Sigma requirement to equivalent conformance levels.

One of Motorola's most significant contributions was to change the discussion of quality from one where quality levels were measured in percentages (parts per hundred) to a discussion of parts per million or even parts per billion. Motorola correctly pointed out that modern technology was so complex that old ideas about acceptable quality levels were no longer acceptable.

The statistical representation of Six Sigma describes quantitatively how a process is performing. To achieve Six Sigma, a process must not produce more than 3.4 defects per million opportunities. A Six Sigma defect is defined as anything outside of customer specifications. A Six Sigma opportunity is then the total quantity of chances for a defect. Process sigma can easily be calculated using a Six Sigma calculator.

The fundamental objective of the Six Sigma methodology is the implementation of a measurement-based strategy that focuses on process improvement and variation reduction through the application of Six Sigma improvement projects. This is accomplished through the use of two Six Sigma sub-methodologies: DMAIC and DMADV. The Six Sigma DMAIC process (define, measure, analyze, improve, control) is an improvement system for existing processes falling below specification and looking for incremental improvement. The Six Sigma DMADV process (define, measure, analyze, design, verify) is an improvement system used to develop new processes or products at Six Sigma quality levels. It can also be employed if a current process requires more than just incremental improvement. Both Six Sigma processes are executed by Six Sigma Green Belts and Six Sigma Black Belts, and are overseen by Six Sigma Master Black Belts.

According to the Six Sigma Academy, Black Belts save companies approximately $230,000 per project and can complete four to 6 projects per year. General Electric Co., one of the most successful companies implementing Six Sigma, has estimated benefits on the order of $10 billion during the first five years of implementation. GE first began Six Sigma in 1995 after Motorola and Allied Signal blazed the Six Sigma trail. Since then, thousands of companies around the world have discovered the far-reaching benefits of Six Sigma.

Unit 7

Even though Six Sigma was initially implemented at Motorola to improve the manufacturing process, all types of businesses can profit from implementing Six Sigma.

Businesses in various industry segments such as Services industry (Example: Call Centers, Insurance, Financial/Investment Services), E-commerce industry (Example: B2B/B2C websites), Education can definitely use Six Sigma principles to achieve higher quality. Many big businesses such as GE and Motorola have successfully implemented Six Sigma but the adaptation by smaller businesses has been very slow.

GE is a pioneer in using Six Sigma. Here are some of the reasons to explain how various GE divisions adopted and benefited from Six Sigma.

Bigger companies have resources internally who are trained in Six Sigma and also have "Train the Trainer" programs using which they churn out many more Six Sigma instructors. Also many bigger companies encourage the employees to learn Six Sigma process by providing Green Belts/Black Belts as mentors.

Effectively applying the Six Sigma techniques is difficult compared to actually learning the techniques in a class.

Big companies make Six Sigma as part of the Goals for employees and provide incentives for employees who undergo training and mentor colleagues.

Many assume that that Six Sigma works for bigger companies only as they produce in volumes and have thousands of employees. This notion is not true and Six Sigma can be effectively applied for small businesses and even companies with fewer than 10 employees.

New Words

award [ə'wɔːd] *n.* 奖，奖品 *vt.* 授予，判给
strive [straiv] *v.* 努力，奋斗
worthy ['wəːði] *adj.* 有价值的，应……的，可敬的，值得的
attention [ə'tenʃən] *n.* 注意，关心，关注，注意力
deviation [ˌdiːvi'eiʃən] *n.* 背离，偏离
methodology [ˌmeθə'dɔlədʒi] *n.* 方法学，方法论
defect [di'fekt] *n.* 过失，缺点
percentage [pə'sentədʒ] *n.* 百分率；百分比

paradigm ['pærədaim] *n.* 范例
tolerance ['tɔlərəns] *n.* 公差；宽容，忍受
normality [nɔː'mæliti] *n.* 常态
yield [jiːld] *n.* 收益；收成；回收率；生产；生产量
refinement [ri'fainmənt] *n.* 提炼，改进
tighten ['taitən] *v.* 变紧，绷紧，拉紧
equivalent [i'kwivələnt] *adj.* 相等的，相当的
quantitatively ['kwɔntitətivli] *adv.* 数量上
oversee ['əuvə'siː] *v.* 俯瞰，监视，检查
segment ['segmənt] *n.* 段，节，片断

pioneer [ˌpaiəˈniə] n. 先驱，倡导者，先遣兵	blaze [bleiz] vi. 燃烧，照耀，激发
mentor [ˈmentɔː] n. 良师益友，导师，指导者	trail [treil] n. 踪迹，痕迹，形迹
	definitely [ˈdefinitli] adv. 明确地，干脆地
incentive [inˈsentiv] n. 动机 adj. 激励的	adaptation [ˌædæpˈteiʃən] n. 适应，改编
	instructor [inˈstrʌktə] n. 教师
notion [ˈnəuʃən] n. 概念，观念，想法	internally [inˈtənəli] adv. 在内，在中心

Phrases and Expressions

Motorola Corp. 摩托罗拉公司	fall into 落入，陷于
Malcolm Baldrige National Quality Award 马尔科姆·巴里奇国家质量奖	apply to 将……应用于
	black belt 黑腰带
Six Sigma 6 西格玛	call center 呼叫中心
role model 行为榜样	churn out 艰苦地做出
stand for 代表	profit from 得益于

Abbreviations

DMAIC (Define, Measure, Analyze, Improve, Control) 定义、测量、分析、改进、控制
DMADV (Define, Measure, Analyze, Design, Verify) 定义、测量、分析、设计、校验
GE (General Electric Co.) [美] 通用电气公司

Exercises

EX. 5 根据文章所提供的信息填空。

1. _____, Motorola Corp. became one of the first companies to receive _____ _____.

2. Six Sigma stands for _____.

3. One of Motorola's most significant contributions was to _____ from one where quality levels were measured in _____ to a discussion of _____ _____ or even _____.

Unit 7

4. A Six Sigma defect is defined as _____. A Six Sigma opportunity is then _____.

5. The fundamental objective of the Six Sigma methodology is the implementation of a measurement-based strategy that _____ and _____ through the application of _____.

6. DMAIC stands for _____.

7. DMADV stands for _____.

8. The Six Sigma DMAIC process is _____ for existing processes falling below _____ and looking for _____.

9. The Six Sigma DMADV process is an improvement system used to _____ at Six Sigma quality levels. It can also be employed if a current process requires _____.

10. Six Sigma can be effectively applied for both _____ as well as _____ and even companies with fewer than 10 employees.

Reading Material

Text	Notes
International Quality Standards If each country has its own set of standards, companies selling in international markets would have difficulty complying [1] with quality documentation standards in the countries where they did business. To overcome [2] this problem, the International Organization for Standardization devised [3] a set of standards called ISO 9000 for companies doing business in the European Union. Subsequently, a new set of standards, ISO 14000, were devised for environmental management systems. **1. The ISO 9000 Standards** ISO 9000 is a set of standards governing documentation [4] of a quality program. Companies become certified [5] by proving to a qualified external examiner that they have complied with all the requirement. Once certified, companies are listed in a directory [6] so that potential customers can see which companies have been certified and to what level. Compliance with ISO 9000 standards says nothing about the actual quality of a product. Rather, it indicates to customers	[1] *vi.* 顺从，答应，遵守 [2] *vt.* 战胜，克服，胜过 [3] *vt.* 设计，发明 [4] *n.* 文件 [5] *adj.* 被鉴定的 [6] *n.* 目录

that companies can provide documentation to support whatever claims [7] they make about quality.

ISO 9000 actually consists of five documents: ISO 9000-9004. ISO 9000 is an overview document, which provides guidelines [8] for selection and use of the other standards. ISO 9001 is a standard that focuses on 20 aspects of a quality program for companies that design, produce, install, and service products. These aspects include management responsibility, quality system documentation, purchasing, product design, inspection, training, and corrective action. It is the most comprehensive and difficult standard to attain. ISO 9002 covers the same areas as ISO 9001 for companies that produce to the customer's designs or have their design and service activities at another location. ISO 9003 is the most limited in scope and addresses only the production process. ISO 9004 contains guidelines for interpreting the other standards.

2. ISO 14000—An Environmental Management System

The ISO 14000 standards require participating companies to keep track of their raw materials use and their generation [9], treatment, and disposal of hazardous [10] wastes. Although not specifying what each company is allowed to emit [11], the standards require companies to prepare a plan for ongoing improvement in their environmental performance. ISO 14000 is a series of five standards that cover a number of areas, including the following.

Environmental management system: Requires a plan to improve performance in resource use and pollutant output.

Environmental performance evaluation: Specifies guidelines for the certification of companies.

Environmental labeling: Defines terms such as recyclable, energy efficient, and safe for the ozone layer.

Life-cycle assessment: Evaluates the lifetime environmental impact from the manufacture, use, and disposal of a product.

To maintain their certification, companies must be inspected by outside, private auditors on a regular basis.

3. Benefits of ISO Certification

Completing the certification process can take as long as 18 months and involve many hours of management and employee time. For example, ABB Process Automation, Inc., a manufacturer of control system for pulp, paper, and chemical producers, spent 25,000 labor hours over nine months and $1.2 million, including a $200,000 audit

[7] n. (根据权利提出) 要求，要求权
[8] n. 指导方针
[9] n. 产生，发生
[10] adj. 危险的，冒险的
[11] vt. 发出，放射，吐露

fee, to achieve ISO 9001 certification. As much as one-third of the time necessary to establish an ISO 9000-based system is devoted to developing and creating the required documentation, which includes flow charts, computer programs, videotapes [12], and pages of written information. Like ISO 9000, ISO 14000 certification isn't cheap. A manufacturing firm of 3000 employees might expend $200,000 just in employee time. Consequently, most of the companies considering ISO 14000 certification are large global manufacturers, such as Hewlett Packard, and IBM.

Despite the expense and commitment involved in ISO certification, it bestows significant external and internal benefits. The external benefits come from the potential sales advantage that companies in compliance have. Companies looking for a supplier will more likely select a company that has demonstrated compliance [13] with ISO standards, all other factors being equal. Registered companies report an average of 48 percent increased profitability and 76 percent improvement in marketing. Consequently, more and more firms are seeking certification to gain a competitive advantage.

Internal benefits relate directly to the firm's TQM program. The British Standards Institute, a leading third-party auditor, estimates that most ISO 9000-registered companies experience a 10 percent reduction in the cost of producing a product because of the quality improvements they make. Certification in ISO 9000 requires a company to analyze and document its procedures, which is necessary in any event for implementing continuous improvement, employee involvement, and similar programs. The internal benefits can be significant. DuPont, which has 160 ISO 9000 registrations worldwide, realized significant benefits, including:

- a $ million reduction in costs at an electronics site,
- an increase in on-time delivery from 70 percent to 90 percent,
- a decrease in outgoing non conformance to specifications from 500 parts per-million to 150 ppm,
- a reduction in the number of test methods from 3200 to 1100,
- a drop in the product cycle time from 15days to 1.5 days,
- a lowering of operational costs by $750 million at one site by eliminating unnecessary tasks, overtime reduction, and job clarifications, and
- an increase in first-pass yields from 72 percent to 92 percent.

As demonstrated by the DuPont experience, the guidelines and requirements of the ISO standards provide companies with a jump [14] start in pursuing TQM programs.

[12] *n.* 录像带

[13] *n.* 依从, 顺从

[14] *n.* 跳跃, 上涨

全面质量管理

全面质量管理可以被视为组织范围内关注产品和服务高质量的方法。当被恰当应用时,全面质量管理会成为组织不可或缺的一部分,而非一个单独的孤立项目。它包括了组织中所有的职能部门和层级,也包括供应商。

为成功地实施全面质量管理项目,有四个基本要素是不可分离的,即领导、员工参与、产品/过程的卓越、顾客焦点。

1. 领导

由组织管理层提供的领导是全面质量管理项目成功开发与实施的主要基石。当恰当执行时,一个全面质量管理项目涉及全公司,并超越传统的职能领域,涵盖企业所有员工。因此,它需要远景、规划和沟通,这些都是企业高层管理团队的职责。研究表明,管理层对全面质量管理的整体承诺是成功实施该项目的关键要素。

高层管理者可以通过不同的方法证明其对全面质量管理的支持。这包括将全面质量管理整合进企业整体战略之中,通过行动和语言表明质量是企业运作最优先考虑的要素。

2. 员工参与

员工参与是成功实施全面质量管理的另一个关键因素。通过将所有员工纳入到决策过程,管理者能够从那些最接近问题和最适合提出可行方案建议的员工那里获得决策所需要的信息。在大多数世界一流的企业运作中,员工参与都是非常盛行的,它充分利用了所有员工的技能和知识。

员工参与的一个关键要素是每个员工承担了检查其工作的职责。这被理解为质量发生在来源处,同时又延伸到工作小组、所有部门以及组织部件和服务的供应商处。这种观点改变了通常对抗性的质量控制检查员的实践,主要从质量控制部门做出质量好或坏的决策。

3. 产品/过程卓越

产品/过程的卓越包括产品设计的质量和实地失效的分析。它还包括统计过程控制和其他分析工具。

过程控制关注的是当产品正在被生产或服务正在被执行的过程中对质量的监测。过程控制计划的典型目标是对当前的生产项目是否达到设计规格提供及时信息,并观察那些预示未来产品可能无法满足顾客要求的信号。过程控制的实际控制阶段发生在采取纠正性行为时,例如一个旧的零件被替换、对机器进行检查,或发现了一个新的供应商时。过程控制概念,特别是基于统计的控制图表,应用于服务业以及制造业。

实现产品/过程卓越的根本哲学是持续改进概念。它有一个普适的含义以及一个特定的全面质量管理含义。其普适的含义是为改进组织任何部分及其所有产出进行的不断努力。其特定的含义是关注工作被完成过程的持续改善。

在日本公司,持续改进的概念被理解为 *kaizen*。它可以被解释为一种消除错误和改进传递给顾客的产品质量的系统方法。实现 *kaizen* 的一种途径是通过使用用于生产产品的最简单方法。在制造业，它通常要求对部件进行重新设计使其只适合一种方式。

4. 顾客焦点

在设定可接受的质量水平时，顾客对质量的认知必须被纳入考虑。换言之，除非顾客说产品是可靠的，否则产品就是不可靠的，除非顾客说服务是快捷的，否则不能说服务是快捷的。将顾客的质量需求转换成产品规格需要进行市场营销（或产品开发），进而明确顾客想要什么，产品设计者要开发一种能持续达到顾客期望质量水平的产品或服务。这就要求我们必须对质量有一个操作性定义，从多维度进行理解，并且将顾客的声音纳入产品规格的确定过程。一项产品或服务的质量可以用其设计的质量（产品质量）和其达到该设计的质量（过程质量）表示。设计质量指的是产品在市场中的内在价值，因此是企业的一项战略决策。

质量一致性指的是产品或服务达到设计规格的程度。它也有重要的战略意义，而实现一致性的活动开展是战术性的日常工作。显然，产品或服务具有高设计质量和低一致性质量，反之亦然。

企业中的运作职能和质量组织主要关心质量的一致性。实现所有的质量规格是制造业管理（产品）和部门运作管理（服务）的典型责任。

设计质量和一致性质量应该提供那些满足顾客目标的产品。这通常被称为产品使用的匹配性，它包括识别顾客所需要的关于产品或服务的维度，并开发一个质量控制项目来确保这些维度的实现。

Unit 8

Text A

Project Management

Projects such as the 1998 Winter Olympics are unique operations with a finite life span. Generally, many interrelated activities must be scheduled and monitored within strict time, cost, and performance guidelines. A project is an interrelated set of activities that has a definite starting and ending point and that results in a unique product or service. Projects often cut across organizational lines because they need the varied skills of multiple professions and organizations. Furthermore, each project is unique, even if it is routine. Uncertainties, such as the advent of new technologies or the timing of certain events, can change the character of projects. Finally, projects are temporary activities as personnel, materials, and facilities are assembled to accomplish a goal within a specified time frame and then disbanded.

Projects are common in everyday life. Planning weddings, remodeling bathrooms, writing term papers, and organizing surprise birthday parties are examples of small projects. Projects are also pervasive in business. Conducting company audits, planning corporate relocations, creating advertising campaigns, purchasing companies, developing new products, producing motion pictures, and providing disaster relief are examples of large projects. Whether large or small, projects affect everyone.

Successful project management involves the coordination of tasks, people, organizations, and other resources to achieve a goal. Three major elements are the project manager, the project team, and the project management system.

The project manager has the responsibility to integrate the efforts of people from various functional areas to achieve specified project goals. Traditional organizational hierarchies tend to slow progress on projects because of a lack of communication, coordination, and sometimes motivation. A project manger can overcome these roadblocks to project completion. The project manager is responsible for establishing the project goals and providing the means to achieve them. The project manager must also specify how the work will be done and ensure that the appropriate hiring is done and any necessary training is conducted. The project manager must demonstrate leadership and provide the motivation necessary to accomplish the tasks required. Finally, the project manager evaluates progress and takes appropriate action when project schedules are in jeopardy.

Obviously, project managers must often cut across traditional functional lines in order to obtain the support necessary for the completion of a project. In most instances, this support is requested without formal authority. Thus the project manager must create a collaborative culture that relies heavily on social skills as well as technical expertise. Without the authority of a traditional functional manager and the associated system of rewards and punishments, project managers must earn their authority by building trust, respect, and credibility among project members, as well as by demonstrating sound decision making within a stimulating work environment.

The project team is a group of people, often representing different functional areas or organizations, led by the project manager. Most project management teams are multidisciplinary in nature, involving a wide variety of skills and organizational units. Often these teams include people from engineering, operations, auditing, and legal groups. Members of the project team may represent the suppliers of essential materials, components, or services and may be actively involved in the conduct of the project. The size and constituency of the team may fluctuate during the life of the projects, and the team will disband when the project has been completed.

The characteristics of a project team and its ultimate performance depend on many factors that involve both people and structural issues, although each organization has its own measures of performance. There is general agreement among project managers on which factors are necessary for the creation of a successful project team. These factors are divided into the following four categories:

- Task-related variables, which are direct measures of task performance, such as the ability to produce quality results on time and within budget, innovative performance, and the ability to change.
- People-related variables, which affect the inner workings of the team and include good communication, high involvement, the capacity to resolve conflict, and mutual trust and commitment to project objectives.
- Leadership variables, which are associated with the various leadership positions within the project team. These positions can be created formally, such as the appointment of project managers and task leaders, or emerge dynamically within the work process as a result of individually developed power based such as expertise, trust, respect, credibility, friendship, and empathy.
- Organizational variables, which include the overall organizational climate, command-control-authority structure, policies, procedures, regulation and regional cultures, values, and economic conditions.

Unit 8

The project management system consists of an organizational structure and information system. The organizational structure is specified by top management and defines the relationship of the project team members to the project manager. The traditional structure is the functional organization, whereby the project is housed in a specific functional area, presumably the one with the most interest in the project. The project manager must negotiate assistance from personnel in other functional areas. Under this structure, the project manager has minimal control over the timing of the project, but resource duplication across functional areas is minimized. At the other extreme is the pure project structure, whereby the team members work exclusively for the project manager on a particular project. Although this structure simplifies the lines of authority for the project manager, it could result in significant duplication of resources across functional areas. A compromise is the matrix structure, whereby each functional area maintains authority over who will work on the project and the technology to be used. In some cases, functional area managers also maintain the authority to prioritize the project work performed within their areas. Resource duplication is reduced relative to the pure project structure, but the project manager loses some control over the project because team members have two bosses. The project management system also provides for the integrative planning and control of the project and the accumulation of information related to performance, costs expressed in dollars or resource usage, the interrelated effects of schedule changes, and the projected times and costs of project completion.

New Words

finite ['fainait] *adj.* 有限的，限定的
interrelated [intəri'leitid] *adj.* 相关的
guideline ['gaidlain] *n.* 指导方针
definite ['definit] *adj.* 明确的，一定的
multiple ['mʌltipl] *adj.* 多样的，多重的
profession [prə'feʃən] *n.* 职业，专业
routine [ru:'ti:n] *n.* 常规；惯例；例行公事
advent ['ædvənt] *n.* 出现，到来
timing ['taimiŋ] *n.* 适时，时间选择
character ['kæriktə] *n.* 特性，性质，特征
temporary ['tempərəri] *adj.* 暂时的，临时的，临时性
assemble [ə'sembl] *vt.* 集合，聚集，装配 *vi.* 集合
wedding ['wediŋ] *n.* 婚礼，婚宴

remodel ['ri:'mɔdl] *vt.* 改建，改造，改变
pervasive [pə:'veisiv] *adj.* 弥漫的；遍布的；普遍的
audit ['ɔ:dit] *n.* 审计，稽核，查账
relocation [ˌri:ləu'keiʃən] *n.* 再定位；再布置，变换布置；再分配
roadblock ['rəudblɔk] *n.* 障碍，障碍物
jeopardy ['dʒepədi] *n.* 危险，危险
punishment ['pʌniʃmənt] *n.* 惩罚，处罚，惩处
earn [ə:n] *vt.* 赚，挣得，获得
credibility [ˌkredi'biliti] *n.* 可信性
multidisciplinary [ˌmʌlti'disiplinəri] *adj.* 包括各种学科的，多学科的

constituency [kən'stitjuənsi] n. 选民，顾客，支持者，赞助者	assistance [ə'sistəns] n. 帮助，协助，援助
disband [dis'bænd] v. 解散，裁减	duplication [ˌdju:pli'keiʃən] n. 重复；副本，复制
fluctuate ['flʌktjueit] vi. 变动，波动，涨落	exclusively [ik'sklu:sivli] adv. 排外地，专有地
appointment [ə'pɔintmənt] n. 任命，选派；约会，约定，预约	prioritize [prai'ɔritaiz] vt. 把……区分优先次序
dynamically [dai'næmikəli] adv. 动态地；动力地，动力学地	accumulation [əkju:mju'leiʃən] n. 积累，积聚
climate ['klaimit] n. 气候，风气	
negotiate [ni'gəuʃieit] v. 商议，谈判，磋商	

Phrases and Expressions

Winter Olympics 冬季奥运会	top management 高层管理
cut across 超越；取捷径；走近路	team member 队员
term paper 学期报告	motion picture 电影
surprise party 惊喜聚会	disaster relief 灾难救济，灾难救援
project manager 项目管理人	in jeopardy 在危险中
project team 项目研究小组，攻关队伍	in most instances 在大部分情况下
project management system 项目管理系统	

Notes

1 A project is an interrelated set of activities that has a definite starting and ending point and that results in a unique product or service.

本句中，that has a definite starting and ending point 和 that results in a unique product or service 是由 and 连接的两个并列的定语从句，修饰和限定表语 an interrelated set of activities。result in 的意思是 "结果；致使；导致"。请看下例：

Acting before thinking always results in failure.
做事不先考虑总会导致失败。

Unit 8

The accident resulted in the death of two people.
这场意外事故造成两人死亡。

英语中还有一个动词短语 result in，它的意思是"由……而造成，起于，由于"。请看下例：
Nothing has resulted from his efforts.
他的努力终成泡影。

2 The project manager must also specify how the work will be done and ensure that the appropriate hiring is done and any necessary training is conducted.

本句中，第一个并列连词 and 连接了两个并列谓语 specify 和 ensure。ensure 前面省略了情态动词 must。how the work will be done 是一个宾语从句，作 specify 的宾语。that the appropriate hiring is done 和 any necessary training is conducted 是由第二个并列连词 and 连接的名词性从句，作 ensure 的宾语。and 和 any necessary training 之间省略了引导词 that。

3 Without the authority of a traditional functional manager and the associated system of rewards and punishments, project managers must earn their authority by building trust, respect, and credibility among project members, as well as by demonstrating sound decision making within a stimulating work environment.

本句中，Without the authority of a traditional functional manager and the associated system of rewards and punishments 是一个介词短语，作条件状语；两个 by 引导的短语作方式状语，修饰谓语 must earn their authority。as well as 连接了两个方式状语，意思是"除了……之外，也，又"。请看下例：
He gave me money as well as advice.
他除了给我建议还给我钱。
She speaks English as well French.
她既会说英语还会说法语。

4 The characteristics of a project team and its ultimate performance depend on many factors that involve both people and structural issues, although each organization has its own measures of performance.

本句中，that involve both people and structural issues 是一个定语从句，修饰和限定 factors。although each organization has its own measures of performance 是一个让步状语从句，修饰谓语 depend on，depend on 的意思是"决定于；依靠，依赖"。请看下例：
It all depends on how you tackle the problem.
那要看你如何应付这问题而定。
Children must depend on their parents.
孩子们必须依赖他们的父母。

5 The traditional structure is the functional organization, whereby the project is housed in a specific functional area, presumably the one with the most interest in the project.

本句中，whereby the project is housed in a specific functional area 是一个非限定性定语从句，修饰 the functional organization。presumably the one with the most interest in the project 对 a specific functional area 作进一步补充说明。whereby 的意思是"借此,凭这个",等于 by or through which。house 在这里是一个动词,它本身的意思是"提供住处;供给房子用",这里用其引申意。请看下例:

He devised a plan whereby he might escape.

他设计了一个可以借以逃走的办法。

He is trying hard to feed and house his family.

他努力设法赡养和安置他的家属。

The personal picture exhibition is housed in that building.

个人画展设在那所房子里。

EX. 1 根据课文内容,回答以下问题。

1. What is a project?
2. Why do projects often cut across organizational lines?
3. Can you list some small projects and some large projects?
4. What do successful project management involve? What are the three major elements?
5. What responsibility does the project manager have?
6. What is the project team?
7. What may members of the project team represent?
8. What are the necessary factors that project managers agree on for the creation of a successful project team?
9. What does the project management system consist of? What does it also provide?
10. Who specifies the organizational structure? And What does the organizational structure define?

EX. 2 根据下面的英文释义,写出相应的英文词汇(使用本单元所学的单词、词组或缩略语)。

英文释义	词 汇
an occupation requiring considerable training and specialized study	
to cease to function as an organization; disperse	
risk of loss or injury; peril or danger	
to make over in structure or style; reconstruct	
the coming or arrival, especially of something extremely important	

a penalty imposed for wrongdoing	
to cause to rise and fall or vary irregularly	
the act of appointing or designating for an office or position.	
aid; help	
to arrange or deal with in order of importance	

EX. 3 把下列句子翻译为中文。

1. The design, development, and introduction of a new product or service are viewed as a one-of-kind type activity that is often referred to as a project.
2. Project management can be defined as planning, directing, and controlling resources to meet the technical, cost, and time constraints of the project.
3. A working knowledge of general management and familiarity with the special knowledge domain related to the project are indispensable.
4. There are some distinct differences between managing ongoing process and managing projects.
5. Because project teams are often newly formed group, it can take time for these groups to be effective.
6. Since projects are by definition not repetitive, flexibility is an important element in successful project management.
7. Effective project management requires continuous monitoring, updating, and replanning throughout the life of the project.
8. Project managers typically have a unique role within the traditional organization structure.
9. Typical leadership characteristics include the ability to organize and direct tasks, facilitate group decision-making, and assist in conflict and problem resolutions.
10. A high-performing project team not only focuses on task-related skills for producing technical results on time and within budget, but also on team members and leadership qualities.

EX. 4 把下面的短文翻译成中文。

Generally, project management is distinguished from the general management of corporations by the mission-oriented nature of a project. A project organization will generally be terminated when the mission is accomplished. According to the Project Management Institute, the discipline of project management can be defined as follows: Project management is the art of directing and coordinating human and material resources throughout the life of a project by using modern management techniques to achieve predetermined objectives of scope, cost, time, and quality and participation satisfaction.

Text B

Behavioral Aspect of Project Management

Project management differs from management of more traditional activities mainly because of its limited time framework and the unique set of activities involved, which gives rise to a host of rather unique problems. The following describes more fully the nature of projects and their behavioral implications.

1. The Nature of Projects

Projects go through a series of stages—a life cycle—which include project planning, execution of major activities, and project phase-out. During this life cycle, a variety of skill requirements are involved. An analogous set of circumstances exists in constructing a house. Initially a site must be found, and plans must be drawn up and approved by the owner and possibly a town building commission or other regulatory agency. Then a succession of activities occur, each with its own skill requirements, starting with the site preparation, then laying the foundation, erecting the frame, roofing, constructing exterior walls, wiring and plumbing, installing kitchen and bathroom fixtures and appliances, interior finishing work, and painting and carpeting work. Similar sequences are found on large construction projects, in R&D work, in the aerospace industry, and in virtually every other instance where projects are being carried out.

In effect, projects bring together personnel with diverse knowledge and skills, most of whom remain associated with the project for less than its full life. Some personnel go from project to project as their contributions become needed, and others are "on loan", either on a full-time or part-time basis, from their regular jobs. The latter is usually the case when a special project exists within the framework of a more traditional organization. Certain kinds of organizations tend to be involved with projects on a regular basis; examples include consulting firms, architects, writers and publishers, and construction firms. In those organizations, it is not uncommon for some individuals to spend virtually all of their time with projects.

Some organizations use a matrix organization that allows them to integrate the activities of a variety of specialists within a functional framework. For instance, they have certain people who prepare proposals, others who concentrate exclusively on engineering, others who devote their efforts to marketing, and so on.

2. The Project Manager

The central figure in a project is the project manager. He or she bears the ultimate responsibility for the success or failure of the project. The role of the project manager is one of an organizer—a person who is capable of working through others to accomplish the objectives of the project.

Once the project is underway, the project manager is responsible for effectively managing each of the following:
- The work, so that all of the necessary activities are accomplished in the desired sequence.
- The human resources, so that those working on the project have direction and motivation.
- Communication, so that everybody has the information they need to do their work.
- Quality, so that performance objectives are realized.
- Time, so that the project can be completed on a time.
- Costs, so that the project is completed within budget.

The job of project manager can be both difficult and rewarding. The manager must coordinate and motivate people who sometimes owe their allegiance to other mangers in their functional areas. In addition, the people who work on a project frequently possess specialized knowledge and skills that the project manager lacks. Nevertheless, the manager is expected to guide and evaluate their efforts. Project managers must often function in an environment that is beset with uncertainties. Even so, budgets and time constraints are usually imposed, which can create additional pressures on project personnel. Finally, the project manager may not have the authority needed to accomplish all the objectives of the project. Instead, the manager must sometimes rely on persuasion and the cooperation of others to realize project goals.

The reward of the job of project manager come from the challenges of the job, the benefits of being associated with a successful project, and the personal satisfaction of seeing it through to its conclusion.

3. The Pros and Cons of Working on Projects

People are selected to work on special projects because the knowledge or abilities they possess are needed. In some instances, however, their supervisors may be reluctant to allow them to interrupt their regular jobs, even on a part-time basis, because it may require training a new person to do a job that will be temporary. Moreover, managers don't want to lose the output of good workers. The workers themselves are not always eager to participate in projects because it may mean working for two bosses who impose differing demands, and may cause disruption of friendships and daily routines, and the risk of being replaced on the current job. Furthermore, there may be fear of being associated with an unsuccessful project because of the adverse effect it might have on career advancement. In too many instances, when a project is phased out and the project team disbanded, team members tend to drift away from the organization for lack of a new project and the difficulty of returning to former jobs. This tendency is more pronounced after lengthy projects and is less likely to occur when a team member works on a part-time basis.

In spite of the potential risks of being involved in a project, people are attracted by the potential rewards. One is the dynamic environment that surrounds a project, often a marked contrast to the more staid environment in which some may feel trapped. Some individuals seem to thrive in more dynamic environment; they welcome the challenge of working under pressure and solving new problems. Then, too, projects may present opportunities to meet new people and to increase future job opportunities, especially if the project is successful. In addition, association with a project can be a source of status among fellow workers. Finally, working on projects frequently inspires a team spirit, increasing morale and motivation to achieve successful completion of project goals.

New Words

behavioral [bi'heivjərl] *adj.* 行为的, 动作的
circumstance ['sə:kəmstəns] *n.* 环境, 详情, 境况
execution [,eksi'kju:ʃən] *n.* 实行, 完成, 执行
phase-out [feiz-aut] *n.* 逐步淘汰
analogous [ə'næləgəs] *adj.* 类似的, 相似的
approve [ə'pru:v] *vt.* 批准, 通过 *vi.* 赞成, 满意
succession [sək'seʃən] *n.* 连续, 继承, 继任
foundation [faun'deiʃən] *n.* 基础, 根本, 建立
erect [i'rekt] *vt.* 盖, 使竖立, 使直立 *adj.* 直立的, 竖立的, 笔直的
frame [freim] *n.* 框, 框架, 架子; 骨架
exterior [eks'tiəriə] *adj.* 外部的, 外在的
fixture ['fikstʃə] *n.* 固定设备
appliance [ə'plaiəns] *n.* 用具, 器具
aerospace ['ɛərəuspeis] *n.* 航空宇宙
consulting [kən'sʌltiŋ] *adj.* 商议的, 咨询的

architect ['ɑ:kitekt] *n.* 建筑师
publisher ['pʌbliʃə] *n.* 出版者, 发行人
construction [kən'strʌkʃən] *n.* 建筑, 建筑物
virtually ['vɜ:tjuəli] *adv.* 事实上, 实质上
matrix ['meitriks] *n.* 矩阵
proposal [prə'pəuzəl] *n.* 提议, 建议
engineering [,endʒi'niəriŋ] *n.* 工程(学)
bear [bɛə] *v.* 负担, 忍受, 带给
organizer ['ɔ:gənaizə] *n.* 组织者, 建立者
underway ['ʌndə'wei] *adj.* 起步的, 进行中的
rewarding [ri'wɔ:diŋ] *adj.* 报答的, 有益的, 值得的
allegiance [ə'li:dʒəns] *n.* 忠贞, 效忠
pro [prəu] *adv.* 正面地 *adj.* 肯定的, 支持的
con [kɔn] *adv.* 反面地
eager ['i:gə] *adj.* 热心于, 渴望着
impose [im'pəuz] *vt.* 强加; 征税
staid [steid] *adj.* 沉静的
trapped [træpt] *adj.* 捕集的, 捕获的
status ['steitəs] *n.* 身份, 地位, 情形

Unit 8

Phrases and Expressions

give rise to 引起，发生
draw up 草拟；写
regulatory agency 管理机构
a succession of 一连串，一系列
lay foundation 奠基；打基础
interior finishing 内部修饰
aerospace industry 航空和航天工业
in effect 有效

bring together 集合
on loan 借贷
matrix organization 矩阵制组织
be capable of 能够
be beset with 被……包围
adverse effect 反作用
drift away 渐渐离开
team spirit 团队精神

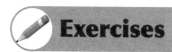

Exercises

EX. 5 根据文章所提供的信息填空。

1. Projects go through a series of stages, which include _____, _____, and _____ _____.
2. Some organizations use a matrix organization that allows them to _____ the activities of a variety of _____ within a _____ framework.
3. The central figure in a project is _____. He or she bears the ultimate responsibility for _____ of the project.
4. The job of project manager can be both _____ and _____.
5. The workers are not always eager to participate in projects because it may mean _____, and may cause disruption of friendships and daily routines, and _____.

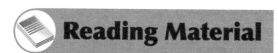

Reading Material

Text	Notes
Project Management Tiers	
Funny how organizations start off doing projects pretty well and then get progressively[1] worse at it. We see five tiers[2] of PM development, driven by:	[1] *adv.* 日益增多地 [2] *n.* 列，行，排，层，等级

- The proportion[3] of people working on multiple projects.
- The proportion of projects that are judged a strategic business success.
- The strength of the organization's PM protocol[4] (methodology[5] for approving, prioritizing and managing projects).

During this downward spiral[6], the "Mother of all Battles" between cross-functional projects and functional silos takes place. When executive pain over repeated project failure becomes excruciating[7], the organization acts to accommodate[8] cross-functional projects in the hierarchy. In more detail, the tiers we have identified are:

1. Alpha[9] Organizations

Executive, "Wow, let's put a team together to fix this!" project team member, "Wow! I get to be on a project team!" In the Alpha organization, projects are novel and sheer[10] enthusiasm often overcomes woeful[11] PM techniques and the total absence of an organizational protocol for PM. What makes things work is that there are only a few projects and relatively few people are working on multiple projects. This combination keeps enthusiasm high and resource contention[12] low. However, this success soon moves the organization up to the Beta tier.

2. Beta[13] Organizations

Project member, "What's more important, these high priority projects or my real job?" Executive, "This is a high priority project and so is that one!"

In the Beta organization, the density of projects has increased and the lack of an organizational protocol for PM begins to cause problems. No one explicitly approves or budgets all projects and soon resource contention begins. In addition, unclear accountability[14] and authority relationships now adversely[15] affect project performance. We see the opening skirmish[16] between cross-functional projects and departmental "silos." The silos win in a bloodbath[17] of failed projects and confused employees.

3. Omega[18] Organizations

Project team member, "Oh, another project, now I have three full time jobs." Executive, "Great, here's another 78 page project plan that will delight the customers and make us a world-class something or other!"

[3]	n. 比例, 均衡, 面积
[4]	n. 草案, 协议
[5]	n. 方法学, 方法论
[6]	n. 螺旋
[7]	adj. 极痛苦的, 折磨人的
[8]	vt. 供应, 供给, 使适应
[9]	n. 希腊字母的第一个字母, 第一个
[10]	adj. 全然的, 纯粹的, 绝对的
[11]	adj. 悲伤的, 悲哀的
[12]	n. 争夺, 争论
[13]	n. 希腊字母中的第二个字母, 第二个
[14]	n. 有责任, 有义务, 可说明性
[15]	adv. 逆地; 相反地
[16]	n. 小冲突
[17]	n. 大屠杀
[18]	n. 欧米加 (希腊字母的最后一个字)

The Omega organization has a high project density with many people working on multiple projects. There is now a project approval and funding mechanism[19] but executives have little ability to actually uncover what each particular project will yield[20]. Budgets and completion dates mean nothing as executives set them based on wants rather than by data based decision-making. Micro-management becomes a religion as executives and PMs confuse highly detailed plans with good control. The result is that people engage in a mountain of activity and achieve very little. The "Mother of all Battles" between departmental silos[21] and cross-functional projects continues, with the silos sucking in new functions so they encompass entire projects. Meanwhile, project size and duration expand to the point where they become departments.

4. Theta[22] Organizations

Project team member, "I am working 67 hours a week for the privilege[23] of spending 3 hours in weekly status meetings, listening to people I dislike try to decide what this project is all about." Executive, "Stop whining[24] about resources, budgets and lack of cooperation. It'll be your job if this isn't done by November 30 (and maybe mine too)."

The Theta organization is in crisis, projects are not reliable vehicles for meeting competitive threats or improving performance. Here is where we see the same massive[25] project started over and over again. When we suggest that less than a third of the projects produce a strategically significant result, no one disagrees. People learn to keep their heads down and do only what they are told to do. In the cross functional project versus[26] silo battle, the exhausted[27] combatants[28] take only occasional pot shots at each other because no one cares anymore.

5. Delta[29] Organizations

Project team member, "What's my job, title and department, you ask? Actually, it's easier to tell you about the achievements I'm aiming for—that's what people around here care about." Executive, "Okay, I understand the tradeoffs[30]. Two months sooner will cost me either $675,000 more or an 8% smaller increase in market share."

The Delta organization's executives manage portfolios[31] of projects as if they were investments. They judge performance against objectively measured outcomes, and they control the trade-offs between a project's MOS, budget, duration and risk using data, not mushy opinions. Executives hold PMs accountable for the MOS. As a result, people at each level in a project's hierarchy are accountable and rewarded for their individual measured achievement; and they have the authority to assign measured achievements to those under them.

[19] *n.* 机械装置，机构，机制
[20] *v.* 出产，生长，生产
[21] *n.* 筒仓，地窖
[22] *n.* 希腊字母的第八个字
[23] *n.* 特权，特别待遇
[24] *n.* 抱怨，牢骚，哀鸣
[25] *adj.* 大规模的，宏伟的
[26] *prep.* 对（指诉讼，比赛等中），与……相对
[27] *adj.* 耗尽的，疲惫的
[28] *n.* 战士，战斗员
[29] *n.* 三角洲，德耳塔（希腊字母的第四个字）
[30] *n.*（公平）交易，折中，权衡
[31] *n.* 一组投资

项目管理

　　1998年冬季奥运会是一个典型的限定了时间跨度的项目运作。一般而言，许多相互关联的活动必须在一个严格的时间、成本、绩效指标范围内进行规划和监控。一个项目就是一系列相关联的活动，它具备一个明确的起点和终点，并产出一个特定的产品或服务。因为需要组织和众多专业人员的多样化技能，项目常常要涉及组织的各个层面。此外，即使是常规性的项目，每一个也都是独特的。不确定性，例如新技术的出现或某个事件的时机选择，都能够改变项目的特征。最后，项目是临时性的活动，人员、物料和设备被组合起来在一个特定的时间期限内完成一个目标，然后终止。

　　项目在日常生活中很普遍。规划婚礼、重建浴室、撰写学期论文、组织令人惊喜的生日晚会都是小型项目的例子。在商业领域，项目也非常普遍。进行公司审计、重新规划公司布置、策划广告活动、购买公司、开发新产品、生产电影、提供灾难安慰都是大型项目的例子。无论项目大或小，它都影响着每一个人。

　　成功的项目管理涉及为实现目标协调任务、人员、组织和其他资源，其中三个主要因素是项目经理、项目团队和项目管理系统。

　　项目经理有责任整合来自不同职能领域的人员的努力以实现特定的项目目标。因为缺乏沟通、协调和激励，传统的组织层级会使项目的进度变慢。一个项目经理能够克服这些障碍帮助项目完成。项目经理有责任建立项目目标和提供实现目标的方法。项目经理必须描述工作如何完成，确保进行恰当的招聘和必要的培训。项目经理必须体现其领导力，为实现任务提供必要的激励。最后，项目经理必须评价项目进度，并在项目进程处于危险时采取恰当的行动。

　　显然，项目经理必须常常地跨越职能边界以获得完成项目的必要支持。在多数情形下，项目经理是在没有正式的权力要求下获得这些支持的。因此，项目经理必须营造一种依靠社会以及技术专家技能建立的合作性文化。没有传统的职能经理的权威以及相应的奖励和惩罚体制，项目经理必须通过在项目成员中建立信任、尊重和可信度，以及在激励性的工作氛围中证明其决策的明智来树立其权威。

　　项目团队是一群人的集合，常常表现为由项目经理领导的不同职能部门和不同组织。大多数项目管理团队本质上是多学科性的，涉及大量多样性的技能和组织单元，通常这些团队包括来自工程、运作、审计和法律方面的人员。这些项目团队的成员可能代表了基本原料、组件或服务的供应商，他们可能被积极地纳入到项目的运作中来。在项目生命周期中团队的规模和参与者可能波动，当项目完成时团队将被解散。

　　一个项目团队的特征及其最终绩效取决于许多因素，它包括人员与结构两方面的问题。尽管每个组织都有其自己的绩效指标，但是项目经理们对于那些影响项目团队成功的必要因素持一致意见。这些因素被划分为四类：

- 任务相关因素是任务绩效的直接指标，例如按时在预算范围内生产高质量结果的能力、创新绩效以及变革能力。

- 与人相关的因素影响团队内部的工作方式，包括良好的沟通、高参与度、解决冲突的能力，相互信任和对项目目标的承诺。
- 领导方面的变量与项目团队内的各种领导职位相关。这些职位可能是被正式设立的，例如项目经理和任务组长，或是在工作的过程中基于个体发展的专业知识、信任、尊重、可信度、友谊和感情投入而动态出现的。
- 组织变量包括整体的组织氛围、命令—控制—权力结构、政策、程序、规则和地区的文化、价值观与经济条件。

项目管理系统由一个组织结构和信息系统构成。高层管理者明确组织的结构，定义项目团队成员与项目经理的关系。传统结构是职能型组织，项目在一个特定的职能部门内展开，可能它是对项目最感兴趣的领域。来自其他职能部门的人员帮助必须由项目经理进行协调。在这种项目结构下，项目经理对项目时间安排的控制力最小，但是跨职能领域的资源重复也得以最小化。另一种极端情况是单纯的项目结构，团队成员为了一个特定的项目完全独自和专门地为项目经理工作。尽管这种结构简化了项目经理的权力链，但它可能导致跨职能领域的资源重复。一种折中的办法是采用矩阵制结构，每个职能领域对于谁从事该项目和使用什么技术拥有决策权力。在某些情形下，职能部门经理也拥有确定权力决定项目工作在其职能部门开展的优先次序。与单纯的项目结构相比，矩阵制结构的资源重复减少了，但是，因为团队成员拥有两个上级，项目经理失去了部分控制项目的权力。项目管理系统也提供对项目的整合规划和控制、积累与绩效相关的信息、用美元或资源使用体现的成本支出、进度改变带来的相关影响、项目完成的计划时间和成本。

Unit 9

Text A

Financial Management

To survive and prosper, a company must satisfy its customers. It must also produce and sell products and services at a profit. To carry on business, companies need an almost endless variety of real assets. Many of these assets are tangible, such as machinery, factories, and offices; others are intangible, such as technical expertise, trademark, and patents. All of them must be paid for.

To obtain the necessary money, the company sells financial assets, or securities. These pieces of paper have value because they are claims on the firm's real assets and the cash that those assets will produce. For example, if the company borrows money from the bank, the bank has a financial asset. That financial asset gives it a claim to a stream of interest payments and to repayment of the loan. The company's real assets need to produce enough cash to satisfy these claims.

Financial managers stand between the firm's real assets and the financial markets in which the firm raises cash. Usually, financial manager faces two basic problems. First, how much money should the firm invest, and what specific assets should the firm invest in? This is the firm's investment decision. Second, how should the cash required for an investment be raised? This is the financing decision. Thus, financial management is concerned with the acquisition, financing, and management of assets with some overall goal in mind. Thus, the decision function of financial management can be broken down into three major areas: the investment, financing, and asset management decisions.

The investment decision is the most important of the firm's three major decisions. It begins with a determination of the total amount of assets needed to be held by the firm. Picture the firm's balance sheet in your mind for a moment. Imagine liabilities and owner's equity being listed on the right side of the firm's balance sheet and its assets on the left. The financial manager needs to determine the dollar amount that appears above the double lines on the left-hand side of the balance sheet—that is, the size of the firm. Even when this number is known, the composition of the assets must still be decided. For example, how much of the firm's total assets should be devoted to cash or to inventory? Assets that can no longer be economically justified may need to be reduced, eliminated, or replaced.

Today's investments provide benefits in the future. Thus the financial manger is concerned not solely with the size of the benefits but also with how long the firm must wait for them. The sooner the profits come in, the better. In addition, these benefits are rarely certain; a new project may be a great success—but then again it could be a dismal failure. The financial manager needs a way to place a value on these uncertain future benefits.

The second major decision of the firm is the financing decision. Here the financial manager is concerned with the makeup of the right-hand side of the balance sheet. If you look at the mix of financing for firms across industries, you will see marked differences. Some firms have relatively large amount of debt, while others are almost debt free.

Once the mix of financing has been decided, the financial manager must still determine how best to physically acquire the needed funds. When a company needs financing, it can invite investors to put up cash in return for a share of profits or it can promise investors a series of fixed payments. In the first case, the investor receives newly issued shares of stock and becomes a shareholder, a part-owner of the firm. In the second, the investor becomes a lender who must one day be repaid. The choice of the long-term financing mix is often called the capital structure decision, since capital refers to the firm's sources of long-term financing, and the markets for long-term financing are called capital markets.

Within the basic distinction—issuing new shares of stock versus borrowing money—there are endless variations. Suppose the company decides to borrow. Should it go to capital markets for long-term debt financing or should it borrow from a bank? Should it borrow in Paris, receiving and promising to repay euros, or should it borrow dollars in New York? Should it demand the right to pay off the debt early if future interest rates fall?

In addition, dividend policy must be viewed as an integral part of the firm's financing decision. The dividend-payout ratio determines the amount of earnings that can be retained in the firm. Retaining a greater amount of current earnings in the firm means that fewer dollars will be available for current dividend payments. The value of the dividends paid to stockholders must therefore be balanced against the opportunity cost of retained earnings lost as a means of equity financing.

The third important decision of the firm is the asset management decision. Once assets have been acquired and appropriate financing provided, these assets must still be managed efficiently. The financial manager is charged with varying degrees of operating responsibility over existing assets. These responsibilities require that the financial manager be more concerned with the management of current assets than with that of fixed assets. A large share of the responsibility for the management of fixed assets would reside with the operating managers who employ these assets.

Unit 9

New Words

prosper ['prɔspə] v. 成功，兴隆，昌盛
tangible ['tændʒəbl] adj. 有形的，切实的
intangible [in'tændʒəbl] adj. 无形的，难以明了的
expertise [,ekspə'ti:z] n. 专家的意见，专门技术
trademark ['treidmɑ:k] n. 商标
patent ['peitənt] n. 专利权，执照
security [si'kjuəriti] n. 证券，债券
claim [kleim] n. (根据权利提出)要求，要求权
raise [reiz] vt. 筹集
financing [fai'nænsiŋ] n. 筹措资金，理财
liability [,laiə'biliti] n. 债务，负债
solely ['səuli] adv. 只是；独自；完全；单独
dismal ['dizməl] adj. 可怕的，灾难性的；阴沉的，凄凉
makeup ['meikʌp] n. 组成，结构
marked [mɑ:kt] adj. 有记号的，显著的
debt [det] n. 债，债务
part-owner [pɑ:t-'əunə] n. 共有者
variation [,vɛəri'eiʃən] n. 变更，变化，变异
euro ['juərəu] n. 欧元
investor [in'vestə] n. 投资者
lender ['lendə] n. 出借人，贷方
dividend ['dividend] n. 股息，红利
earnings ['ɜ:niŋs] n. 收益；工资，收入
retain [ri'tein] vt. 保持，保留
reside [ri'zaid] vi. 归于，居住

Phrases and Expressions

financial management 财务管理
at a profit 赚钱，有利润
carry on 继续开展，坚持
real assets 不动产
tangible assets 有形资产
intangible assets 无形资产
financial assets 金融资产
financial manager 财务经理
investment decision 投资决策
financing decision 融资决策
asset management decision 资产管理决策
owner's equity 所有者权益
interest rate 利率
balance sheet 资产负债表
put up 提供
capital structure decision 资本构成决策
capital market 资本市场
pay off 还清，付清
dividend policy 股息分配方针
opportunity cost 机会成本
equity financing 产权融资
be charged with 承担
fixed assets 固定资产

Notes

1. Financial managers stand between the firm's real assets and the financial markets in which the firm raises cash.

   本句中，in which the firm raises cash 是一个介词前置的定语从句，修饰和限定 the financial markets。

2. The financial manager needs to determine the dollar amount that appears above the double lines on the left-hand side of the balance sheet—that is, the size of the firm.

   本句中，that appears above the double lines on the left-hand side of the balance sheet 是一个定语从句，修饰和限定 the dollar amount。that is 的意思是"即，也就是说"，the size of the firm 的意思是"公司的规模"。

3. Some firms have relatively large amount of debt, while others are almost debt free.

   本句中，while 是一个连词，等于 whereas。表示对比，意思是"然而；而"。请看下例：
   Some people like coffee, while others like tea.
   有些人喜欢咖啡，而有些人喜欢茶。

4. These responsibilities require that the financial manager be more concerned with the management of current assets than with that of fixed assets.

   本句中，that the financial manager be more concerned with the management of current assets than with that of fixed assets 是一个宾语从句，作 require 的宾语。在该从句中，be 前面省略了 should。第二个 that 指代 the management。

EX. 1　根据课文内容，回答以下问题。

1. How many kinds of real assets are mentioned in the passage? What are they? Can you give examples of each kind?
2. Why do financial assets or securities have value?
3. How many basic problems do the financial manager face? What are they?
4. What is financial management concerned with?
5. How many major areas can the decision function of financial management be broken down into? What are they?
6. Which is the most important of the firm's three major decisions? What does it begin with?
7. What is the financial manger concerned with in investment decision?
8. What is the financial manager concerned with in financing decision?
9. What is the financial manager charged with in the asset management decision?
10. What do these responsibilities mentioned in the last paragraph require?

Unit 9

EX. 2 根据下面的英文释义，写出相应的英文词汇（使用本单元所学的单词、词组或缩略语）。

英文释义	词　汇
a name, symbol, or other device identifying a product, officially registered and legally restricted to the use of the owner or manufacturer	
something for which one is liable; an obligation, a responsibility, or a debt	
to be vested, as a power or right; to live in a place permanently or for an extended period	
person who puts money in	
a share of profits received by a stockholder or by a policyholder in a mutual insurance society	
a document indicating ownership or creditorship; a stock certificate or bond	
incapable of being perceived by the senses	
a demand for something as rightful or due	
a grant made by a government that confers upon the creator of an invention the sole right to make, use, and sell that invention for a set period of time	
to gather together; collect	

EX. 3 把下列句子翻译为中文。

1. Efficient financial management requires the existence of some objectives or goal.
2. Shareholders who are dissatisfied with management performance may sell their shares and invest in another company.
3. Although various objectives are possible, the fundamental goal of a firm is to maximize the wealth of the firm's present owners.
4. Maximizing shareholder wealth does not imply that management should ignore social responsibility such as protecting the consumer.
5. Some people suggest that the primary monitoring of managers comes not from the owners but from the managerial labor market.
6. A major facet of financial management involves providing the financing necessary to support assets.
7. If you become a financial manger, your ability to adapt to change, raise funds, invest in assets, and manage wisely will affect the success of your firm.
8. Decisions regarding the management of assets must be made in accordance with the underlying objectives of the firm.
9. A company will be more or less risky depending upon the amount of debt in relation to equity

in its capital structure.

10. Financial managers are supposed to make financial decisions that serve shareholders' interests.

EX. 4 把下面的短文翻译成中文。

A smart and effective financial manager makes decisions which increase the current value of the company's shares and the wealth of its stockholders. That increased wealth can then be put to whatever purposes the shareholders want. They can give their money to charity or spend it in glitzy nightclubs; they can save it or spend it now. Whatever their personal tastes or objectives, they can all do more when their shares are worth more.

Text B

Financial Accounting and Managerial Accounting

In a broad sense, accounting is the process of identifying, measuring, and communicating economic information about an organization for the purpose of making decisions and informed judgments.

Who makes these decisions and informed judgments? Users of accounting information include the management of the entity or organization; the owners of the organization; potential investors and creditors of the organization; employees; and various federal, state, and local governmental agencies that are concerned with regulatory and tax matters.

Accounting information must be provided for just about every kind of organization. Accounting for business firms is what many people initially think of, but not-for-profit social service organizations, governmental units, educational institutions, social clubs, political committees, and other groups all require accounting for their economic activities.

1. Financial Accounting

Financial accounting generally refers to the process that results in the preparation and reporting of financial statements for an entity. The financial statements present the financial position of an entity at a point in time, the results of the entity's operations for some period of time, the cash flow activities for the same period of time, and other information about the entity's financial resources, obligations, owner's interests, and operations.

Financial accounting is primarily externally oriented. The financial statements are directed to individuals who are not in a position to be aware of the day-to-day financial and operating activities of the entity. Financial accounting is also primarily concerned with the historical results of an entity's performance. Financial statements reflect what has happened in the past, and although reader may want to project past activities and their results into future performance, financial statements are not a clear crystal ball. Many corporate annual reports make reference to the historical nature of financial accounting information to emphasize its importance to users.

2. Managerial Accounting

Managerial accounting is concerned with the use of economic and financial information to plan and control many of the activities of the entity and to support the management decision-making process. Managerial accounting has an internal orientation, as opposed to the primarily external orientation of financial accounting. The transactions generated by the accounting information system and used for financial reporting purposes are also used in managerial accounting, but the latter are more likely to have a future orientation, such as in the preparation of budgets.

3. Managerial Accounting Contrasted to Financial Accounting

Managerial accounting supports the internal planning future-oriented decisions made by management. Financial accounting has more of a scorekeeping, historical orientation, although data produced by the financial accounting process form some of the foundation on which plans are based. Planning is the key part of the management process, and although there are many descriptions of that process, a generally acceptable definition would include reference to the process of planning, organizing, and controlling an entity's activities so that the organization can accomplish its purpose.

Not all of a firm's objectives are stated in financial terms by any means. For example, market share, employee morale, absence of layoffs, and responsible corporate citizenship are all appropriate objectives that are expressed in non-financial terms. However, many of the firm's goals will be financial in nature. The accountant plays a major role in identifying these goals, in helping to achieve them, and in measuring the degree to which they have been accomplished.

Emphasis on the future is a principal characteristic that makes managerial accounting different from financial accounting. Anticipating what revenues will be and forecasting the expenses that will be incurred to achieve those revenues are critical activities of the budgeting process. Another difference between managerial accounting and financial accounting that is emphasized in planning is the breath of focus. Financial accounting deals primarily with the financial statements for the organization as a whole; managerial accounting is more concerned with units within the organization. Thus, even though an overall company ROI objective is established, effective planning requires that the planned impact of the activities and results of each unit of the organization be considered.

Measuring results involves using the historical data of financial accounting, and because of the time required to perform financial accounting and auditing procedures, there is usually a time lag of weeks or months between the end of an accounting period and the issuance of financial statements. However, for performance feedback to be most effective, it should be provided as quickly as possible after action has been completed. Management accounting is not constrained by generally accepted accounting principles, so approximate results can be quickly generated for use in the control process. In other words, relevant data, even though not absolutely accurate in a financial accounting sense, are useful for evaluating performance soon after an activity has been completed.

If time and effort have been devoted to develop a plan, it is appropriate to attempt to control the activities of the organization so that the goals of the plan are accomplished. Many of the activities of the managerial accountant are related to cost control; this control emphasis will be seen in most of the managerial accounting ideas.

Another management concept relevant to the control process is that if an individual is to be held accountable, or responsible, for the results of an activity, that individual must also have the authority to influence those results. If a manager is to be held responsible for costs incurred by a unit of the organization, the financial results reported for that unit should not include costs incurred by other units that have been arbitrarily assigned to the unit being evaluated. In other words, the results should not reflect costs that the manager being held responsible cannot control.

Management accountants work extensively with people in other functional areas of the organization. For example, industrial engineers and management accountants work together to develop production standards, which are the expected or allowed times and costs to make a product or perform an activity. Management accountants help production people interpret performance reports, which compare actual and planned production and costs. Sales personnel, the marketing staff, and management accountants are involved in estimating a future period's sales. Personnel professionals and management accountants work together to determine the cost effect of compensation changes. And the management accountant will play a significant role in the firm's systems development life cycle process by providing key insight to the planning, analysis, design, and implementation phases of an organization's information systems projects. These few key examples illustrate the need for management accountants to have a breadth of knowledge and interest about the organization and its operating environment. The examples also suggest that it is appropriate for persons in other functional areas to have a general understanding of managerial accounting.

New Words

informed [in'fɔːmd] *adj.* 见多识广的
judgment ['dʒʌdʒmənt] *n.* 判断
entity ['entiti] *n.* 实体；组织，机构，团体
creditor ['kreditə] *n.* 债权人
obligation [ˌɔbli'geiʃən] *n.* 义务，职责，债务

federal ['fedərəl] *adj.* 联邦的，联合的
governmental [ˌɡʌvən'mentl] *adj.* 政府的
agency ['eidʒənsi] *n.* 机构；代理处，行销处，代理，中介
regulatory ['reɡjulətəri] *adj.* 规章的；制定规章的；受规章限制的

Unit 9

tax [tæks] n. 税, 税款, 税金
oriented ['ɔ:rientid] adj. 导向的
crystal ['kristl] adj. 结晶状的
morale [mɔ'rɑ:l] n. 道德, 士气, 民心
layoff ['lei,ɔ:f] n. 临时解雇, 操作停止
citizenship ['sitizənʃip] n. 公民的身份, 公民的职责和权利
accountant [ə'kauntənt] n. 会计 (员), 会计师
revenue ['revinju:] n. 收入, (国家的) 岁入; 税收
issuance ['iʃuəns] n. 发行, 发布
absolutely ['æbsəlu:tli] adv. 完全地, 绝对地
constrain [kən'strein] vt. 强迫, 抑制, 拘束

approximate [ə'prɔksimeit] adj. 近似的, 大约的
accountable [ə'kauntəbl] adj. 应负责的, 有责任的
arbitrarily ['ɑ:bitrərili] adv. 武断地, 任意地, 专横地
interpret [in'tə:prit] v. 解释, 说明
extensively [iks'tensivli] adv. 广阔地
compensation [kɔmpen'seiʃən] n. 补偿, 赔偿
insight ['insait] n. 洞察力, 见识
illustrate ['iləstreit] vt. 解释, 举例说明, 图解
breadth [bredθ] n. 宽度, 幅宽

Phrases and Expressions

financial accounting 财务会计
managerial accounting 管理会计
in a broad sense 广义地说
for the purpose of 为了
educational institution 教育机构
financial statements 财务决算
financial position 财务状况
cash flow 现金流转

annual report 年度报告
make reference to 提及, 涉及
market share 市场份额
cost control 成本控制
time lag 时滞
play a significant role in... 在……起重要作用

Abbreviations

ROI (Return on Investment) 投资回报率

Exercises

EX. 5 根据文章所提供的信息回答问题。

1. What is accounting in a broad sense?
2. What does Financial accounting generally refer to?
3. What do the financial statements present?
4. What is managerial accounting concerned with?
5. Which has an external orientation, managerial accounting or financial accounting?
6. What is the difference between managerial accounting and financial accounting?
7. What is a principal characteristic that makes managerial accounting different from financial accounting?
8. What does financial accounting deal primarily with? What about managerial accounting?
9. What should people do if time and effort have been devoted to develop a plan?
10. Do management accountants work extensively with people in other functional areas of the organization? Give examples.

Reading Material

Text	Notes
The Six Most Important Ideas in Finance What would you say if you were asked to name the six most important ideas in finance? Here is our list. **1. Net Present Value** When you wish to know the value of a used car, you look at prices in the secondhand[1] car market. Similarly, when you wish to know the value of a future cash flow, you look at prices quoted[2] in the capital markets[3], where claims to future cash flows are traded. If you can buy cash flows for your shareholders at a cheaper price than they would have to pay in the capital market, you have increased the value of their investment. This is the simple idea behind net present value[4]. When we calculate a project's NPV, we are asking whether the project is worth more than it cost. We are estimating its value by calculating what its cash flows would be worth if a claim on them were offered separately to investors and traded in the capital markets.	[1] *adj.* 间接获得的,旧的,二手的 [2] *vt.* 报(价) [3] *n.* 资本市场 [4] *n.* 净现值

This is why we calculate NPV by discounting[5] future cash flows at the opportunity cost of capital—that is, at the expected rate of return offered by securities[6] having the same degree of risk as the project. In well-functioning[7] capital markets, all equivalent[8] risk assets are priced to offer the same expected return. By discounting at the opportunity cost of capital, we calculate the price at which investors in the project could expect to earn that rate of return.

Like most good ideas, the net present value rule is obvious when you think about it. But notice what an important idea it is. The NPV rule allows thousands of shareholders, who may have vastly different levels of wealth and attitudes toward risk, to participate in the same enterprise and to delegate[9] its operation to a professional manager. They give the manager one simple instruction[10]: "Maximize net present value."

2. Risk and Return

Some people say that modern finance is all about the capital asset pricing model. That's nonsense[11]. If the capital asset pricing model had never been invented, our advice to financial managers would be essentially the same. The attraction of the model is that it gives us a manageable way of thinking about the required return on a risky investment.

Again, it is an attractively simple idea. There are two kinds of risks—those that you can diversify[12] away and those that you can't. The only risks people care about are the ones that they can't get rid of—the non-diversifiable ones.

You can measure the non-diversifiable, or market, risk of an investment by the extent to which the value of the investment is affected by a change in the aggregate[13] value of all the assets in the economy. This is called the beta of the investment. The required return on an asset increases in line with its beta.

Many people are worried by some of the rather strong assumptions[14] behind the capital asset pricing model, or they are concerned about the difficulties of estimating a project's beta. They are right to be worried about these things. One day, we will have much better theories than we do now, but we are prepared to bet that these more sophisticated[15] theories will retain[16] the two crucial ideas behind the capital asset pricing model: investors don't like risk and require a higher return to compensate; the risk that matters is the risk that investors cannot get rid of.

[5] v. 减少,打折
[6] n. 有价证券
[7] adj. 运转良好的
[8] adj. 相等的,相当的
[9] vt. 委派……为代表
[10] n. 指示,用法说明
[11] n. 胡说,废话
[12] v. 使多样化,作多样性的投资
[13] n. 总计,合计
[14] n. 假定,设想
[15] adj. 复杂的,诡辩的
[16] vt. 保持,保留

3. Efficient Capital Markets

The third fundamental idea is that security prices accurately reflect available information and respond rapidly to new information as soon as it becomes available. This efficient-market theory comes in three flavors[17], corresponding to different definitions of "available information". The weak form[18] says that prices reflect all the information in past prices, the semistrong[19] form says that prices reflect all publicly available information, and the strong form holds that prices reflect all acquirable[20] information.

Don't misunderstand the efficient-market idea. It doesn't say that there are no taxes or costs; it doesn't say that there aren't some clever people and some stupid ones. It merely implies that competition in capital markets is very tough—there are no money machines, and security prices reflect the true underlying values of assets based on the best information available to investors.

4. MM's Irrelevance Propositions

The irrelevance[21] propositions of Modigliani and Miller (MM) imply that you can't increase value through financing policies unless these policies also increase the total cash flow[22] available to investors. Financing decisions that simply repackage[23] the same cash flows don't add value.

Financial managers often ask how much their company should borrow. MM's response is that as long as borrowing does not alter the total cash flow generated by the firm's assets, it does not affect firm value.

Miller and Modigliani used a similar argument[24] to show that dividend policy does not affect value unless it affects the total cash flow available to present and future shareholders. A firm that pays you an increased dividend and gets the cash back by selling more shares is simply putting cash in one of your pockets and taking it out of another.

The same ideas can be run in reverse. Just as splitting up[25] the cash flows doesn't add value, neither does combining different cash-flow streams. This implies that you can't increase value by putting two whole companies together unless you thereby increase total cash flow. Thus there are no benefits to mergers[26] solely for diversification.

5. Option Theory

In everyday conversation we often use the word option as synonymous[27] with choice or alternative; thus we speak of someone as having a number of options. In finance an option refers specifically to the opportunity to trade in the future on terms that are fixed today. Smart mangers know that it is often worth paying today for the option to buy or sell an asset tomorrow.

---

[17] *n.* 情味，风味
[18] 弱式
[19] 半强式
[20] *adj.* 可获得的
[21] *n.* 不相关，枝节问题
[22] 流动现金
[23] *vt.* 重新包装
[24] *n.* 论点
[25] 分裂，分散转移
[26] *n.* 合并，归并
[27] *adj.* 同义的

Companies are willing to pay extra for capital projects that give them future flexibility. Also, many securities provide the company or the investor with options. For example, a convertible[28] bond[29] gives the owner an option to exchange the bond for shares.

Managers spend much more time thinking about options that they used to. This is partly because they increasingly use options to help limit risk. Also, managers and economists are more aware that many assets contain disguised[30] real options.

6. Agency Theory

A modern corporation is a team effort involving many player, including management, employees, shareholders, and bondholders[31]. The members of this corporate team are bound together by a series of formal and informal contracts to ensure that they pull together.

For a long time economists assumed that all players acted for the common good. But in the last 20 years we have learned a lot about the possible conflicts of interest and how companies try to overcome such conflicts. These ideas are collectively known as agency theory.

[28] *adj.* 可改变的，自由兑换的

[29] *n.* 公债，债券，合同

[30] *v.* 假装，伪装，掩饰

[31] *n.* 债券持有人，公司债所有者

财务管理

为了生存与繁荣，企业必须满足顾客的需要，同时企业也必须在盈利的情况下生产和销售产品与服务。为了运作业务，企业需要几乎无止境的多样化资产。其中许多是有形的，如机器、工厂和办公室；有些则是无形的，如技术诀窍、商标、专利。所有这些资产都是要付费的。

为了获得必要的资金，企业出售其金融资产或有价证券。这些商业证券都是有价值的，它们是企业资产以及资产产生的现金的凭证。例如，如果企业从银行借款，银行就有了金融资产。这种资产使银行有权要求企业对该贷款及其利息进行偿付。企业的资产需要产生足够的现金以满足这些偿付要求。

财务经理站在公司资产与公司获取现金的金融市场之间，面临着两个基本的问题。第一，企业应该投资多少资金？企业应该将资金投资于哪些特定的资产？这是企业的投资决策。第二，企业进行投资的现金从何而来？这是融资决策。因此，财务管理关注的是为了实现某些整体目标而进行的资产获取、融资和管理活动。由此，财务管理的决策功能可以被分解为三个主要方面：投资决策、融资决策和资产管理决策。

投资决策是企业三个主要决策中最重要的。投资决策首先从决定企业整体所需要的资本数量开始。试想一下公司的资产负债表，负债和所有者权益列在资产负债表的右边，资产列在左边。财务经理需要决定在资产负债表的左侧两条线上出现的美元数字，即企业的规模。即使这个数据已明确，财务经理还需要决定资产的构成。例如，企业的总资产是如

何分配给现金或存货的？那些不再能带来效益的资产可能需要被减少、停止或替代。

今天的投资将受益于将来。因此财务经理不仅考虑利益的范围，也关注企业等待利益回报的时间周期。利益越早回报对企业越有利。此外，未来的回报利益很少是明确的，一个新项目可能获得巨大成功，但之后也可能是一个可怕的失败。财务经理必须有方法让这些不确定的未来收益带来价值。

融资决策是第二个主要的决策。此时财务经理关注的是资产负债表右侧的构成。当你观察跨行业的融资组合时，你会发现存在着明显差异。一些企业拥有相对较大数量的债务，而其他企业则几乎没有债务。

当财务经理决定了融资组合后，他必须决定如何最优地获得所需要的资金。当一家企业需要融资时，它能够邀请投资者提供现金以享受回报，或者它能够承诺一系列的固定回报。在第一种情形下，投资者接受最新发行的股份，成为股东，即企业的部分所有者。在第二种情况下，投资者成为债权人，要求某天得到偿还。长期的融资组合选择通常被称为资本结构决策，因为资本指的是企业长期融资的来源，而长期融资的市场则被称为资本市场。

在发行新股份与借债之间存在的基本差异中，还存在着无尽的变化。假设企业决定借债，那么它应该是到资本市场上获得长期的债务融资，还是向银行借款？企业应该是从巴黎借到欧元，并承诺用欧元偿还呢，还是在纽约借美元？如果远期利率下降，企业是否应该要求早些偿还债务？

此外，股息分配政策是企业融资决策的重要组成部分。股息支付比率决定了企业能够将收益留存于企业的数量。当前收益越多地留存于企业意味着当前越少的股息可偿付资金数量。因此财务经理必须平衡偿付给股东的股息价值与作为产权融资的手段失去的留存收益而导致的机会成本。

公司的第三个重要的决策是资产管理决策。一旦企业获得了资产，并提供了恰当的融资，还需要对这些资产进行有效的管理。财务经理承担着不同程度的运作现有资产的职责。这些职责要求财务经理除关注固定资产，应更多地考虑对现有资产的管理。固定资产的管理职责主要由使用这些资产的运营经理承担。

Unit 10

Text A

MIS

Short for management information system, and pronounced as separate letters, MIS refers broadly to a computer-based system that provides managers with the tools for organizing, evaluating and efficiently running their departments. In order to provide past, present and prediction information, an MIS can include software that helps in decision making, data resources such as databases, the hardware resources of a system, decision support systems, people management and project management applications, and any computerized processes that enable the department to run efficiently.

Within companies and large organizations, the department responsible for computer systems is sometimes called the MIS department.

1. Software

Computer instructions or data. Anything that can be stored electronically is software. The storage devices and display devices are hardware.

The terms software and hardware are used as both nouns and adjectives. For example, you can say: "The problem lies in the software," meaning that there is a problem with the program or data, not with the computer itself. You can also say: "It's a software problem."

The distinction between software and hardware is sometimes confusing because they are so integrally linked. Clearly, when you purchase a program, you are buying software. But to buy the software, you need to buy the disk (hardware) on which the software is recorded.

Software is often divided into two categories:

Systems software: Includes the operating system and all the utilities that enable the computer to function.

Applications software: Includes programs that do real work for users. For example, word processors, spreadsheets, and database management systems fall under the category of applications software.

2. Database

Often abbreviated DB. A collection of information organized in such a way that a computer program can quickly select desired pieces of data. You can think of a database as an electronic filing system.

Traditional databases are organized by fields, records, and files. A field is a single piece of information; a record is one complete set of fields; and a file is a collection of records. For example, a telephone book is analogous to a file. It contains a list of records, each of which consists of three fields: name, address, and telephone number.

An alternative concept in database design is known as Hypertext. In a Hypertext database, any object, whether it be a piece of text, a picture, or a film, can be linked to any other object. Hypertext databases are particularly useful for organizing large amounts of disparate information, but they are not designed for numerical analysis.

To access information from a database, you need a database management system (DBMS). This is a collection of programs that enables you to enter, organize, and select data in a database.

Increasingly, the term database is used as shorthand for database management system.

3. Hardware

Refers to objects that you can actually touch, like disks, disk drives, display screens, keyboards, printers, boards, and chips. In contrast, software is untouchable. Software exists as ideas, concepts, and symbols, but it has no substance.

Books provide a useful analogy. The pages and the ink are the hardware, while the words, sentences, paragraphs, and the overall meaning are the software. A computer without software is like a book full of blank pages—you need software to make the computer useful just as you need words to make a book meaningful.

4. Decision Support System

Abbreviated DSS, the term refers to an interactive computerized system that gathers and presents data from a wide range of sources, typically for business purposes. DSS applications are systems and subsystems that help people make decisions based on data that is culled from a wide range of sources.

For example: a national on-line book seller wants to begin selling its products internationally but first needs to determine if that will be a wise business decision. The vendor can use a DSS to gather information from its own resources to determine if the company has the ability or potential ability to expand its business and also from external resources, such as industry data, to determine if there is indeed a demand to meet. The DSS will collect and analyze the data and then present it in a way that can be interpreted by humans. Some decision support systems come very close to acting as artificial intelligence agents.

Unit 10

DSS applications are not single information resources, such as a database or a program that graphically represents sales figures, but the combination of integrated resources working together.

5. Applications

A program or group of programs designed for end users. Software can be divided into two general classes: systems software and applications software. Systems software consists of low-level programs that interact with the computer at a very basic level. This includes operating systems, compilers, and utilities for managing computer resources.

In contrast, applications software (also called end-user programs) includes database programs, word processors, and spreadsheets. Figuratively speaking, applications software sits on top of systems software because it is unable to run without the operating system and system utilities.

New Words

pronounce [prəˈnauns] vt. 发音；发出……音
broadly [brɔːd] adj. 广泛的，广博的
evaluate [iˈvæljueit] vt. 评价,估计,求……的值
prediction [priˈdikʃən] n. 预言，预报
computerize [kəmˈpjuːtəraiz] vt. 用计算机处理，使计算机化
instruction [inˈstrʌkʃən] n. 指令，指示
software [ˈsɔftwɛə] n. 软件
distinction [disˈtiŋkʃən] n. 区别, 差别, 级别
confuse [kənˈfjuːz] vt. 搞乱，使糊涂
category [ˈkætigəri] n. 种类，类别
utility [juːˈtiliti] n. 应用程序
spreadsheet [ˈspredʃiːt] n. 电子制表软件，电子数据表
piece [piːs] n. 块，件，片
data [ˈdeitə] n. 数据

field [fiːld] n. 域
record [ˈrekɔːd] n. 记录
file [fail] n. 文件，档案
hypertext [ˈhaipətekst] n. 超文本
particularly [pəˈtikjuləli] adv. 独特地，显著地
disparate [ˈdispərət] adj. 异类的，不同的
increasingly [inˈkriːsiŋli] adv. 越来越多地，逐渐增加地，日益地
disk [disk] n. 磁盘
keyboard [ˈkiːbɔːd] n. 键盘
board [bɔːd] n. 电路板
chip [tʃip] n. 芯片
substance [ˈsʌbstəns] n. 物质
cull [kʌl] vt. 挑选，拣出，采集
resource [riˈsɔːs] n. 资源
compiler [kəmˈpailə] n. 编译器，编译程序

Phrases and Expressions

in order to … 为了……
storage device 存储设备
display device 显示设备
divide into 分成
operating system 操作系统
word processor 文字处理程序

in such a way 以这样的一种方式
disk drive 磁盘驱动器
gather information 采集信息
end user 终端用户
applications software 应用软件

Abbreviations

MIS (Management Information System) 管理信息系统
DB (DataBase) 数据库
DBMS (DataBase Management System) 数据库管理系统
DSS (Decision Support System) 决策支持系统

Notes

1 Short for management information system, and pronounced as separate letters, MIS refers broadly to a computer-based system that provides managers with the tools for organizing, evaluating and efficiently running their departments.

　　本句中，Short for management information system, and pronounced as separate letters 是对主语 MIS 的补充说明。that provides managers with the tools for organizing, evaluating and efficiently running their departments 是一个定语从句，修饰和限定 a computer-based system。介词短语 for organizing, evaluating and efficiently running their departments 作 the tools 的定语，表示用途。

2 In order to provide past, present and prediction information, an MIS can include software that helps in decision making, data resources such as databases, the hardware resources of a system, decision support systems, people management and project management applications, and any computerized processes that enable the department to run efficiently.

　　本句中，主语是 an MIS，谓语是 can include，In order to provide past, present and prediction information 是目的状语，修饰谓语。that helps in decision making, data resources such as databases 是一个定语从句，修饰和限定 software。that enable the

Unit 10

department to run efficiently 也是一个定语从句，修饰和限定 any computerized processes。

❸ In a Hypertext database, any object, whether it be a piece of text, a picture, or a film, can be linked to any other object.

本句中，whether it be a piece of text, a picture, or a film 是一个条件状语从句，意思是"无论它是文本块、图片还是电影"。

❹ The vendor can use a DSS to gather information from its own resources to determine if the company has the ability or potential ability to expand its business and also from external resources, such as industry data, to determine if there is indeed a demand to meet.

本句中，动词不定式短语 to gather information from its own resources 作目的状语。if the company has the ability or potential ability to expand its business 和 if there is indeed a demand to meet 是宾语从句，作 determine 的宾语。

EX. 1 根据课文内容，回答以下问题。

1. What is software? What is hardware?
2. How many categories can software be divided into? What are they?
3. What is a field? What is a record? What is a file? Give an example to illustrate it.
4. What do you need when you want to access information from a database?
5. What does DSS stand for? What does the term refer to?

EX. 2 根据下面的英文释义，写出相应的英文词汇（使用本单元所学的单词、词组或缩略语）。

英文释义	词 汇
something foretold or predicted; a prophecy	
to examine and judge carefully; appraise	
an authoritative direction to be obeyed; an order	
the programs, routines, and symbolic languages that control the functioning of the hardware and direct its operation	
a computer and the associated physical equipment directly involved in the performance of data-processing or communications functions	
a distinguishing factor, attribute, or characteristic	
to set down for preservation in writing or other permanent form	

a collection of related data or program records	
fundamentally distinct or different in kind; entirely dissimilar	
a program that translates another program written in a high-level language into machine language so that it can be executed	

EX. 3 把下列句子翻译为中文。

1. The research project has only been under way for three months, so it's too early to evaluate its success.
2. The firm decided to computerize its wages department.
3. The boss gave me so many instructions at one time that I got muddled up.
4. He isn't particularly clever but industrious.
5. New settlers came in increasing numbers.
6. The local library is a valuable resource.
7. The committee discussed strategic marketing factors.
8. These difficulties are caused by natural disasters.
9. There are three options open to us in that matter.
10. This information will be less confusing if it's produced in tabular form.

EX. 4 把下面的短文翻译成中文。

Today MIS are becoming more flexible by providing access to information whenever needed (rather than prespecified reports on a periodic basis). Users can often generate more customized reports by selecting subsets of data (such as listing the products with 2% increase in sales over the past month), using different sorting options (by sales region, by salesperson, by highest volume of sales) and different display choices (graphical, tabular).

Text B

Components of Information System

One definition of an information system is the following: an information system is an integrated, computer-user system for providing undistorted information to support the operations, management, and decision-making functions of an organization. The components of an information system are its purpose, people, procedures, information, and information technology.

1. Purpose

The purpose is the reason for having the system; it is something we are attempting to accomplish. As we know, a major goal of most organizations is survival. When we look at information system, it is usually possible and desirable to identify narrower, more specific objectives and purposes. For example, one goal of the order entry system for a mail order company might be to provide more personalized customer service, and a specific way of doing that is to retrieve customer order history data for the customer representative using the system within five seconds of the request being made. Let's assume for a moment that the system uses telephone numbers to identify customers. The service representative keys in the telephone number, which they have obtained from the customer, and the information system searches through a database and retrieves a record of sales transactions that match the customer telephone number.

Every information system should be designed for one or more purpose. This seems like a relatively simple concept, but it is interesting to note that for many I/S development efforts that have run into difficulty, the purpose was not clearly specified up front. Also, unless the purpose can be clearly identified and described in measurable terms, there is no way to evaluate the effectiveness of the information system.

2. People

People are an integral part of information systems. Sooner or later people are involved in using the information generated by the system. Therefore, we will always define information systems as having a "people component", though sometimes it may not be obvious.

To illustrate, consider an information system designed to facilitate inventory control. At a low level, we could identify computer software that runs on some type of computer hardware. The program accepts as input the amount of a particular item sold, calculates the quantity of the item on hand, compares this to a predetermined reorder level, and produces as output a line indicating the quantity of the item that should be reordered. This line is stored in a file, which will later be printed onto a low-stock report.

3. Procedures

Procedures, or work practices, are the human activities required to interact with other components of the information system. Procedures describe how the people involved with the information system should interact with the information technology. For example, when you remove cash from your bank account using an automated teller machine (ATM), you follow a set of procedures. You need to insert your bank card, enter your personal information number, and so on. If you don't follow the procedures properly, the information system will function and it will not accomplish its purpose.

4. Data and Information

One important function of mangers, acting as components of an organizational system, is making decisions. In organization, managers seldom make decisions by themselves. They collect information from a variety of sources, analyze that information with other, and then transmit the information in order to coordinate their actions. Organizational decision-making can be viewed as a transformation process requiring information as an input, and providing a decision as an output. Viewed in this way, it is easy to see that without good information, it will be difficult to reach a good decision.

Data is the term applied to unstructured facts which are gathered about some entity, event, or observation. Data can be generated, stored, retrieved, filed, updated, and deleted. It is also important to keep in mind that there are costs associated with capturing, storing, and manipulating data. In addition to obvious costs for physical items such as computer storage media and input forms, there are usually very expensive human costs of employees required for tasks such as data entry. Data can become a marketable commodity, one that can be bought and sold.

Information, on the other hand, implies (1) that some structure has been imposed on the data, (2) that the data have been evaluated for a certain purpose by a decision maker or a computer, and (3) that uncertainty as to what action to take has been reduced. This latter point is critical. Information can be defined as a message or signal that changes, in the mind of the receiver, the probability that a given alternative will occur in a given situation. That is, the message reduces the receiver's uncertainty about how to act.

5. Information Technology

Information technology includes the hardware and software used to store, retrieve, process, and transmit data. This could include computer hardware, telecommunications hardware, software, networking hardware and software, and so on.

Keep in mind that information technology cannot accomplish any goals by itself. The technology is simply a tool to be used for accomplishing a specific business goal. Information technology enables a vision—it does not provide it.

Information technology is the means to reduce overload and minimize distortion. There are four specific technologies that are particularly helpful in that role if used selectively and with discretion. These are (1) networking: the ability to interconnect different computers to exchange data no matter where the computers are; (2) database management: the ability to centrally store large amounts of data, images, and sounds and then provide decentralized access to anyone in the organization with the proper clearance; (3) telecommunications: the ability to transmit with high levels of speed, integrity, accuracy, and security large amounts of data, images, and sounds; and (4) personal computing: the ability for individuals to work on desktop and portable computes powerful enough to be independent of a central computer and therefore able to provide customized support.

undistorted [ˌʌndɪsˈtɔːtɪd] *adj.* 未失真的，不偏激的

procedure [prəˈsiːdʒə] *n.* 程序，进程

survival [səˈvaɪvəl] *n.* 生存，幸存

Unit 10

remove [ri'mu:v] vt. 移动，开除
insert [in'sə:t] vt. 插入，嵌入
update [ʌp'deit] n. 更新，现代化
delete [di'li:t] vt. 删除
manipulate [mə'nipjuleit] vt. (熟练地)操作，巧妙地处理
marketable ['mɑ:kitəbl] adj. 适于销售的
commodity [kə'mɔditi] n. 商品，日用品
probability [,prɔbə'biliti] n. 可能性，或然性，概率
receiver [ri'si:və] n. 接受者，接收器，收信机
retrieve [ri'tri:v] v. 重新得到，找回
transmit [trænz'mit] vt. 传输，转送，传达
hardware ['hɑ:dwɛə] n. 硬件，(电子仪器的)部件

network ['netwə:k] n. 网络，网状物
overload ['əuvə'ləud] n. 超载，负荷过多
distortion [dis'tɔ:ʃən] n. 扭曲，变形，曲解
selectively [si'lektivli] adj. 选择的，选择性的
interconnect [,intəkə'nekt] vt. 使互相连接
clearance ['kliərəns] n. 清除
accuracy ['ækjurəsi] n. 精确性，正确度
desktop ['desktɔp] n. 桌面桌上型电脑
portable ['pɔ:təbl] adj. 轻便的，手提(式)的

Phrases and Expressions

bank account 银行存款
data entry 数据登记项，数据输入

be independent of 与……无关；不依赖；不取决于

Exercises

EX. 5 根据文章所提供的信息回答问题。

1. What is the definition of an information system?
2. What are the components of an information system?
3. What is the purpose?
4. What is a major goal of most organizations?
5. Why will we always define information systems as having a "people component", though sometimes it may not be obvious?
6. What are procures? What do they describe?

7. What is one important function of mangers? What do they do?
8. What can organizational decision-making be viewed as?
9. What does information technology include?
10. How many specific technologies are there that are particularly helpful in that role of reducing overload and minimizing distortion if used selectively and with discretion? What are they?

Text	Notes
Information Management and Society The increased use of information system impacts almost everyone and everything, from individuals to society as a whole. Businesses must be very careful to protect their data, its integrity[1] and privacy[2], and the way it is used. While technology is presumed[3] to increase employment in general, those workers displaced[4] by technology must be retrained. They must learn new skills to find a new position or to operate the technology that now performs their old job. Governments have long been involved in collecting large amounts of data. Technology has enabled them to collect and operate on this data more efficiently. Lower prices, improved capabilities, and more user-friendly[5] features have made technology available to many more people. An important social issue is providing access to technology for everyone. Increasing dependence on technology brings new issues and risks to an organization and a society. These include data control issues from workers, consultants, and business partners. Ways to minimize data threats including training, oversight[6] committees[7], audits[8], and the separation of duties. Threats also come from the outside. These can be minimized by software and hardware techniques including the encryption[9] of data, dial-back modems[10], or access controls. Working in today's technological environment brings business ethics[11] increasingly to the forefront[12], not only for companies as a whole, but also for individual workers. People's lives can be impacted by technology mishaps[13] such as inaccurate[14] data, the abuse[15] of information, or defective[16] or poorly designed software or hardware.	[1] *n.* 完整，完全，完整性 [2] *n.* 秘密，隐私 [3] *vt.* 假设，假定 [4] *vt.* 移置，转移，取代，置换 [5] *adj.* 用户界面友好的，用户容易掌握使用的 [6] *n.* 勘漏，失察，疏忽 [7] *n.* 委员会 [8] *n.* 审计，稽核，查账 [9] *n.* 编密码 [10] *n.* 调制解调器 [11] *n.* 道德，伦理 [12] *n.* 最前部，最前线 [13] *n.* 灾祸 [14] *adj.* 错误的，不准确的 [15] *n.* 滥用 [16] *adj.* 有缺陷的

1. Effect of Technology on the Privacy of Individuals

The ease with which information regarding individuals can be acquired is astonishing. Basic and statistical[17] data can be purchased from sources such as the government, universities, clubs, mail-order[18] firms, and the Internet[19].

Employee privacy is another issue. Computers can be used to monitor employees and what they do while they are working on the computer. Some employers read their employees' electronic mail[20] or evaluate their performance using the computer. Ways to protect yourself include asking the company not to distribute your personal data, why they need the data, and what data are optional to give. You can also ask the company not to distribute your personal data. You have the right to check any data that refers to you and to ask to have it changed if you feel the data is inaccurate. Some people find the increased use of technology dehumanizing[21], since companies can know increasing amounts of information about their employees and their work habits.

2. Jobs

It is generally believed that technology increases jobs overall and improves the standard of living. However, as technology replaces more jobs of less skilled workers, those workers will have a more difficult time finding other jobs unless they are retrained. The new jobs provided by technology tend to be better paying[22], physically safer, and less repetitive[23]. To remain competitive, everyone must continuously learn new skills to stay ahead in a rapidly changing marketplace. It is important to carefully study technology trends to predict correctly in which skills to invest for the future. Technology offers people with disabilities[24] the opportunity to work in ways never previously thought possible.

3. Telecommuting

As the percentage of service versus manufacturing jobs increases, the opportunities to telecommute[25], or work from home, increase. Service jobs tend to be less dependent on a worker's physical location. Cities with long commute times such as New York are experimenting with telecommuting. The organization gains because of decreased costs for office space and flexibility in hiring additional workers. Evaluating and managing telecommuting employees are difficult tasks, however. The worker gains the time and expense of commuting to work, but loses because of a loss of personal contact, decreased motivation, and a home environment that can be more comfortable and more distracting[26].

[17] *adj.* 统计的, 统计学的
[18] *n.* 邮购
[19] *n.* 因特网, 国际互联网络
[20] *n.* 电子邮件
[21] *v.* 使机械化, 使失掉人性
[22] *adj.* 支付的, 有利的
[23] *adj.* 重复的, 反复性的
[24] *n.* 无力, 无能, 残疾
[25] *vi.* (在家里通过使用与工作单位连接的计算机终端) 远距离工作
[26] *adj.* 娱乐的, 消遣的

4. Education

The effects of technology on education have not been as marked as in other areas of society. Some internet teaching is occurring, but this phenomenon is not widespread due to the high cost of development and lack of interaction. Problems with using technology to educate include its expense, the fact that developing lessons through technology is time intensive, and the limited evidence that teaching through technology is the same or better than traditional methods.

5. Access to Technology

The gap between the haves and the have-nots can easily be widened through the abuse of technology. This occurs most readily through the control of access to technology. Many suggest that as companies get new hardware and software, the old equipment should be donated[27] to poor schools or poor countries. Although this technology might be completely outdated, the recipients might otherwise not have received anything. On the other hand, rapid advances in technology and decreasing costs of hardware sometimes cost the nonprofit organization more than the outdated equipment is worth.

[27] *v.* 捐赠，赠予

6. Threats to Information

The biggest threat to information comes from authorized users who make mistakes such as deleting wanted data, designing flaws[28] into programs, or who input the wrong information. Through careful design, testing, and training, some of these problems can be minimized internally.

[28] *n.* 缺点，裂纹

As technology changes, external threats change and so do the criminals. For example, robbers are now more likely to hold up customers at an ATM rather than trying to hold up a bank. Threats to information can come from such places as employees and consultants, outside hackers[29], links to business partners, and viruses[30].

[29] *n.* 电脑黑客
[30] *n.* 病毒

7. Threats from Employees

While a company must trust its employees, it also faces a threat from them. Careful screening and monitoring of potential and current employees can minimize risks. Especially complicated issues can arise with IS employees. Since these employees provide programs and support, they must be given greater access to technology than other employees. This access provides them with a greater capability to harm information. There are also ways to diminish this risk, such as the separation of duties. Teamwork in technological endeavors[31] can help to keep workers honest without impinging[32] on their individual privacy. Consultants can also provide input on employee honesty.

[31] *n.* 努力，尽力
[32] *n.* 碰撞

Unit 10

管理信息系统

MIS是管理信息系统的缩写,要按字母读音分开读,广义指的是基于计算机的,为管理人员提供组织、评价和管理自己部门工具的系统。为了提供过去、现在和将来的信息,MIS包括辅助决策软件、数据库一类数据资源、系统硬件资源、决策支持系统、人力管理和项目管理应用软件,以及任何能够使部门更有效运行的计算机化的处理过程。

在公司或大的组织中,负责计算机系统的部门有时也叫作"MIS部"。

1. 软件

软件就是计算机指令或数据。任何可以电子化存储的东西都是软件。存储设备和显示设备是硬件。

术语"软件"和"硬件"通常既用作名词也用作形容词。例如,可以说:"问题在软件上,"意思是问题在程序或数据上,而不在计算机本身。也可以说:"这是一个软件问题。"

有时人们会混淆软件与硬件之间的区别,因为它们的联系十分紧密。很明显,当购买一个程序时,是在购买软件。但是要购买该软件,就必须买记录软件的磁盘(硬件)。

软件可以分为以下两类:

系统软件:包括操作系统和其他所有能使计算机运行的实用程序。

应用软件:包括用户用来做实际工作的程序。例如,字处理器、电子表格和数据库管理系统,这些都属于应用软件。

2. 数据库

数据库(Database)经常缩写为DB。数据库是一个信息的集合,这些信息的组织方式使计算机程序能够快速挑选所期望的数据。也可以把数据库看作一个电子文件系统。

传统的数据库是以字段、记录和文件组织起来的。一个字段就是一个单独的信息;一个记录就是所有字段的集合;一个文件就是一些记录的集合。例如,电话号码本就像文件,它包括记录表,每一个记录由三个域组成:姓名、地址及电话号码。

数据库设计中另外一个可选择的概念叫作"超文本"。在超文本数据库中,任何一个对象(无论是文本块、图片还是电影)都可以链接到另外一个对象。超文本数据库在组织大量的异型信息时特别有用,但它们并不适用于数值分析。

要从数据库中访问信息,需要数据库管理系统(DBMS)。这是一些可以让用户输入、组织和选择数据的程序。

术语"数据库"越来越多地用作数据库管理系统的缩写。

3. 硬件

硬件就是可以触摸的物体,如磁盘、磁盘驱动器、显示屏、键盘、打印机、电路板和芯片。相对应的,软件是不可触摸的。软件以思想、概念和符号形式存在,而不是以物理实体形式存在。

这与图书很相似。纸张和墨是硬件，而文字、句子、图形及它们的含义是软件。一个没有软件的计算机，就像全是白纸的书——软件对计算机的作用就像文字对书的作用一样。

4. 决策支持系统

决策支持系统缩写为DSS，这个术语涉及一个交互式的计算机化的系统，该系统从非常广泛的领域（特别是商业领域）收集和表现数据。DSS是一个系统，并且是一个帮助人们依据数据做决策的子系统，这些数据是从广泛领域精选的。

例如，一个国家在线图书销售商要开始在国际上销售它的产品，首先要确定这是否是一个明智的商业决策。该经销商可以使用DSS从自己的资源中收集信息以确定该公司是否有能力或潜在的能力来扩大自己的业务，它也可以从外部资源（如行业数据）收集信息来决定这样做是否合适。DSS将收集和分析这些数据，并以某种可以为人所理解的方式表现数据。某些决策支持系统的作用与人工智能工具很接近。

DSS不只用于单一的系统资源（如数据库或销售数据图形化表示的工具软件），而是综合使用各种相关资源。

5. 应用软件

应用软件是为终端用户设计的一个或一组程序。软件一般可以分为两类：系统软件和应用软件。系统软件包括可以与计算机底层进行交互的低级程序，包括操作系统、编译程序、管理计算机资源的实用程序。

相对应的，应用软件（也叫作"终端用户程序"）包括数据库程序、字处理器及电子表格。比方说，应用软件坐在系统软件上，因为没有操作系统和系统工具软件应用软件就无法运行。

附录 词汇总表

单 词 表

A

absence ['æbsəns] *n.* 缺乏，没有；不在，缺席（1B）[1]

absolutely ['æbsəlu:tli] *adv.* 完全地，绝对地（9B）

absorb [əb'sɔ:b] *vt.* 吸收（5B）

abundance [ə'bʌndəns] *n.* 丰富，充裕，丰富充裕（4A）

accelerated [ək'seləreitid] *adj.* 加速的（6B）

accommodate [ə'kɔmədeit] *vt.* 供应，供给，使适应（6B）

accomplish [ə'kɔmpliʃ] *vt.* 完成，达到，实现（1A）

accountable [ə'kauntəbl] *adj.* 应负责的，有责任的（9B）

accountant [ə'kauntənt] *n.* 会计（员），会计师（9B）

accounting [ə'kauntiŋ] *n.* 会计；会计学；清算账目（1B）

accumulate [ə'kju:mjuleit] *v.* 积聚，堆积（6B）

accumulation [əkju:mju'leiʃən] *n.* 积累，积聚（8A）

accuracy ['ækjurəsi] *n.* 精确性，正确度（10B）

acknowledge [ək'nɔlidʒ] *vt.* 承认，公认（4A）

acquire [ə'kwaiə] *vt.* 获得，学到（1B）

acquisition [ˌækwi'ziʃən] *n.* 获得，获得物（3A）

activity [æk'tiviti] *n.* 行动，行为（1A）

actualize ['æktjuəlaiz] *vt.* 实现，实施（4A）

adaptation [ˌædæp'teiʃən] *n.* 适应，改编（7B）

additional [ə'diʃənl] *adj.* 另外的，附加的，额外的（3A）

adequacy ['ædikwəsi] *n.* 适当，足够（3A）

adjusting [ə'dʒʌstiŋ] *n.* 调整，调制（1A）

adjustment [ə'dʒʌstmənt] *n.* 调整，调节（5A）

administer [əd'ministə] *v.* 管理；给予，执行（1B）

administration [ədminis'treiʃən] *n.* 管理，经营（6A）

advance [əd'va:ns] *n.* 前进；提升（5B）

advantage [əd'va:ntidʒ] *n.* 优势，有利条件，利益（1B）

advent ['ædvənt] *n.* 出现，到来（8A）

adversarial [ˌædvə'seəriəl] *adj.* 敌手的，对手的，对抗(性)的（7A）

advertise ['ædvətaiz] *v.* 做广告，登广告（6B）

aerospace ['ɛərəuspeis] *n.* 航空宇宙（8B）

aesthetic [i:s'θetik] *adj.* 美学的，审美的，有审美感的（1B）

affect [ə'fekt] *vt.* 影响（5A）

affordable [ə'fɔ:dəbl] *vt.* 提供，给予，供应得起（4A）

aftermarket ['a:ftə,ma:kit] *n.* 配件市场（6B）

aftermath ['a:ftəmæθ] *n.* 结果，后果（1A）

agency ['eidʒənsi] *n.* 机构；代理处，行销处，代理，中介（9B）

allegiance [ə'li:dʒəns] *n.* 忠贞，效忠（8B）

alliance [ə'laiəns] *n.* 联盟，联合（1A）

allocation [ˌæləu'keiʃən] *n.* 分配，安置（6A）

alter ['ɔ:ltə] *v.* 改变（1B）

alternative [ɔ:l'tə:nətiv] *adj.* 选择性的，二中择一的（4A）

analogous [ə'næləgəs] *adj.* 类似的，相似的（8B）

---

[1] 括号里的数字代表单元，字母代表文章。例如，1B 表示本单词出自 Unit 1 的 Text B。

analysis [ə'næləsis] n. 分析；分解（3A）
analyze ['ænəlaiz] vt. 分析；分解（3A）
announcement [ə'naunsmənt] n. 宣告，发表，一项公告（1A）
anticipate [æn'tisipeit] vt. 预期，期望；占先，抢先（3A）
appliance [ə'plaiəns] n. 用具，器具（8B）
applicant ['æplikənt] n. 申请者，请求者（3A）
apply [ə'plai] vt. 应用；实施；运用；使用（5B）
appointment [ə'pɔintmənt] n. 任命，选派；约会，约定，预约（8A）
appraisal [ə'preizəl] n. 评定；鉴定；评价，估价（3A）
approach [ə'prəutʃ] n. 方法，步骤，途径，通路（5A）
approve [ə'pru:v] vt. 批准，通过 vi. 赞成，满意（8B）
approximate [ə'prɔksimeit] adj. 近似的，大约的（9B）
aptitude ['æptitju:d] n. 天资，才能，聪颖（3A）
arbitrarily ['ɑ:bitrərili] adv. 武断地，任意地，专横地（9B）
architect ['ɑ:kitekt] n. 建筑师（8B）
aspect ['æspekt] n.（问题等的）方面（3A）
aspire [əs'paiə] vi. 热望，立志（2B）
assemble [ə'sembl] vt. 集合，聚集，装配 vi. 集合（8A）
assembly [ə'sembli] n. 组装，装配；集合（6A）
assign [ə'sain] vt. 分配，指派（1A）
assign [ə'sain] vt. 分配，指派（5A）
assistance [ə'sistəns] n. 帮助，协助，援助（8B）
associated [ə'səuʃieitid] adj. 伴随的，有关的（6B）
assortment [ə'sɔ:tmənt] n. 分类（6A）
assume [ə'sju:m] vt. 承担（7A）
assumption [ə'sʌmpʃən] n. 假定，设想（4B）
attachment [ə'tætʃmənt] n. 附件（2A）
attainable [ə'teinəbl] adj. 可到达的，可得到的（2A）
attend [ə'tend] vt. 出席，参加；照顾，护理；注意（1B）

attention [ə'tenʃən] n. 注意，关心，关注，注意力（7B）
attractive [ə'træktiv] adj. 吸引人的，有魅力的（1B）
audit ['ɔ:dit] n. 审计，稽核，查账（8A）
auditor ['ɔ:ditə] n. 审计员，查账员（1A）
authority [ɔ:'θɔriti] n. 权力，职权（1A）
automatically [ɔ:tə'mætikli] adv. 自动地；机械地（5B）
automation [ɔ:tə'meiʃən] n. 自动化操作；自动控制；自动操作（5B）
availability [ə,veilə'biliti] n. 可用性，有效性，实用性（6A）
available [ə'veiləbəl] adj. 可得到的；可利用的（4A）
await [ə'weit] vt. 等候，准备（2B）
awaken [ə'weikən] v. 唤醒，醒来，唤起（2A）
award [ə'wɔ:d] n. 奖，奖品 vt. 授予，判给（7B）

B

background ['bækgraund] n. 背景，后台（2A）
bear [bɛə] v. 负担，忍受，带给（8B）
behavior [bi'heivjə] n. 举止，行为（1A）
behavioral [bi'heivjərl] adj. 行为的，动作的（8B）
benchmark ['bentʃmɑ:k] n. 衡量标准，基准（2A）
beverage ['bevəridʒ] n. 饮料（6B）
blaze [bleiz] vi. 燃烧，照耀，激发（7B）
blue-chip [blu:tʃip] adj. 独特的；值钱的（4A）
blur [blə:] vt. 使模糊；使看不清（5B）
board [bɔ:d] n. 电路板（10A）
bond [bɔnd] n. 公债，债券，合同，联结（1B）
bonus ['bəunəs] n. 奖金，红利（3A）
bookkeeping ['buk,ki:piŋ] n. 簿记（1B）
boundary ['baundəri] n. 边缘；界线；边界；境界（5B）
branding [brænd] n. 品牌定位，品牌化（2A）
breach [bri:tʃ] n. 违背，破坏 vt. 打破，突破（1A）
breadth [bredθ] n. 宽度，幅宽（9B）
broaden ['brɔ:dn] vt. 加宽，使扩大，加阔（5A）
broadly [brɔ:d] adj. 广泛的，广博的（10A）
budget ['bʌdʒit] n. 预算 vi. 做预算，编入预算（1A）
budget ['bʌdʒit] n. 预算 vi. 做预算，编入预算（1B）

buffer ['bʌfə] vt. 减轻；缓冲；保护（5B）
bully ['buli] n. 欺凌弱小者；恶棍 vt. 威吓，威逼（2B）

C

calculator ['kælkjuleitə] n. 计算器（4B）
candidate ['kændidit] n. 候选人，投考者（3A）
candor ['kændə] n. 直截了当，坦白，直率（2A）
capability [ˌkeipə'biliti] n.(实际)能力，性能，容量（5A）
capable ['keipəbl] adj. 有能力的，能干的（3A）
capitalist ['kæpitəlist] n. 资本家（2A）
capitalize [kə'pitəlaiz] vt. 变成资本，以大写字母写（1B）
career [kə'riə] n. 事业，生涯（1A）
category ['kætigəri] n. 种类，类别（10A）
challenge ['tʃælindʒ] n. 挑战 vt. 向……挑战（3B）
channel ['tʃænl] n. 渠道；途径（6A）
character ['kæriktə] n. 特性，性质，特征（8A）
characterize ['kæriktəraiz] vt. 表……特点，具有……特征；描绘，刻画，形容（人或物）（4A）
chip [tʃip] n. 芯片（10A）
church [tʃə:tʃ] n. 教堂，礼拜堂（5A）
circumstance ['sə:kəmstəns] n. 环境，详情，境况（8B）
citizenship ['sitizənʃip] n. 公民的身份，公民的职责和权利（9B）
claim [kleim] n. (根据权利提出)要求，要求权（9A）
classify ['klæsifai] v. 分类（1A）
cleanliness ['klenlinis] n. 干净，清洁（2B）
clearance ['kliərəns] n. 清除（10B）
climate ['klaimit] n. 气候，风气（8A）
coax [kəuks] v. 哄，用好话相劝；诱出（4B）
coercion [kəu'ə:ʃən] n. 强迫，威压（4A）
cohesive [kəu'hi:siv] adj. 有黏着力的，凝聚性的（1B）
commercialize [kə'mə:ʃəlaiz] v. 使商业化，使商品化（6A）
commitment [kə'mitmənt] n. 许诺，承担义务（7A）

commodity [kə'mɔditi] n. 商品，日用品（10B）
communicate [kə'mju:nikeit] v. 沟通，通信（1B）
communication [kəˌmju:ni'keiʃn] n. 沟通，传达（1A）
compensation [kɔmpen'seiʃən] n. 补偿，赔偿（9B）
compete [kəm'pi:t] vi. 比赛，竞争（1A）
compile [kəm'pail] vt. 编译，编辑，汇编（6A）
compiler [kəm'pailə] n. 编译器，编译程序（10A）
complaint [kəm'pleint] n. 诉苦；抱怨；牢骚（5B）
complement ['kɔmplimənt] vt. 补助，补足（3A）
computerize [kəm'pju:təraiz] vt. 用计算机处理，使计算机化（10A）
con [kɔn] adv. 反面地
concept ['kɔnsept] n. 观念，概念（1A）
concept ['kɔnsept] n. 观念，概念（2B）
conceptual [kən'septjuəl] adj. 概念上的（1B）
conduct ['kɔndʌkt] v. 实施，处理；经营；引导（4B）
confidential [kɔnfi'denʃəl] adj. 秘密的，机密的（2A）
conflict ['kɔnflikt] n. 冲突，斗争（4B）
conformance [kɔn'fɔ:məns] n. 一致性，适应性（7A）
confront [kən'frʌnt] vt. 使面临，对抗（1B）
confuse [kən'fju:z] vt. 搞乱，使糊涂（10A）
confused [kən'fju:zd] adj. 混乱的；困惑的（4B）
conquest ['kɔnkwest] n. 征服（4B）
consciously ['kɔnʃəsli] adv. 有意识地，自觉地（2B）
consequently ['kɔnsikwəntli] adv. 从而；所以；因此（5B）
consistency [kən'sistənsi] n. 一致性，连贯性（2B）
consolidation [kənˌsɔli'deiʃən] n. 巩固，合并；整理；调整（6B）
constantly ['kɔnstəntli] adv. 经常地，不断地，坚持不懈地（1B）
constituency [kən'stitjuənsi] n. 选民，顾客，支持者，赞助者（8A）

constitute ['kɔnstitjuːt] vt. 组成，构成，任命（6A）
constrain [kən'strein] vt. 强迫，抑制，拘束（9B）
constrained [kən'streind] adj. 被强迫的，拘泥的（1A）
constraint [kən'streint] n. 约束，强制，局促（5A）
construction [kən'strʌkʃən] n. 建筑，建筑物（8B）
consulting [kən'sʌltiŋ] adj. 商议的，咨询的（8B）
consumption [kən'sʌmpʃən] n. 消费，消费量（6A）
container [kən'teinə] n. 容器，集装箱（6B）
contaminated [kən'tæmineitid] adj. 被污染的（6B）
context ['kɔntekst] n. 背景，上下文（2B）
continuity [,kɔnti'njuiti] n. 连续性，连贯性（6A）
continuously [kən'tinjuəsli] adv. 不断地；连续地（5B）
contract ['kɔntrækt] n. 合同 v. 订约（1A）
contribution [,kɔntri'bjuːʃən] n. 文献；贡献，捐赠（1B）
control [kən'trol] n.&vt. 控制，支配，管理（1A）
convert [kən'vəːt] vt. 使转变，转换，使……改变信仰（5A）
convince [kən'vins] vt. 使确信，使信服；说服（4B）
coordinate [kəu'ɔːdinit] vt. 调整，整理（1A）
coordination [kəu,ɔːdi'neiʃən] n. 协调，调和（1A）
cornerstone ['kɔːnəstəun] n. 墙角石；基础（7A）
corporate ['kɔːpərit] adj. 社团的，法人的，公司的（1B）
credibility [,kredi'biliti] n. 可信性（8A）
credible ['kredəbl] adj. 可信的，可靠的（2A）
creditor ['kreditə] n. 债权人（9B）
crucial ['kruːʃəl] adj. 极重要的；有决定性的（5A）
crystal ['kristl] adj. 结晶状的（9B）
cull [kʌl] vt. 挑选，拣出，采集（10A）
customer ['kʌstəmə] n. 消费者（2A）
customize [kʌstəmaiz] v. 定制；用户化（5B）
cycle ['saikl] n. 周期，循环（5A）

D

data ['deitə] n. 数据（10A）
debt [det] n. 债，债务（9A）
decentralize [diː'sentrəlaiz] n. 分散（3A）

decision [di'siʒən] n. 决策，决定（1A）
deem [diːm] v. 认为，相信（3A）
default [di'fɔːlt] n. 食言，不履行责任（2A）
defect [di'fekt] n. 过失，缺点（7B）
defective [di'fektiv] adj. 有缺陷的（6B）
define [di'fain] vt. 定义，详细说明（1A）
definite ['definit] adj. 明确的，一定的（8A）
definitely ['definitli] adv. 明确地，干脆地（7B）
delete [di'liːt] vt. 删除（10B）
deliberate [di'libərət] adj. 周密计划的；深思熟虑的（2B）
demanding [di'mɑːndiŋ] adj. 需要技能的；要求高的；过分要求的，苛求的（1B）
demonstrate ['demənstreit] vt. 示范，证明，论证（4A）
demonstration [,deməns'treiʃən] n. 示范，实证（2A）
demotion [,diː'məuʃən] n. 降级（3A）
dependence [di'pendəns] n. 依靠；依赖；信任（5B）
deploy [di'plɔi] v. 展开，配置（6B）
deployment [di'plɔimənt] n. 展开，部署，调度（3A）
designate ['dezigneit] vt. 指明，指出，任命，指派（1B）
desktop ['desktɔp] n. 桌面桌上型电脑（10B）
despite [dis'pait] prep. 不管，不论；尽管（2B）
destination [desti'neiʃ(ə)n] n. 目的地，终点（3A）
detect [di'tekt] vt. 察觉，发觉，侦查（7A）
determine [di'təːmin] v. 决定，确定（1A）
detrimental [,detri'mentl] adj. 有害的（6B）
development [di'veləpmənt] n. 开发；发展（2A）
deviation [,diːvi'eiʃən] n. 背离，偏离（7B）
devote [di'vəut] vt. 投入于，献身（4B）
diagnose ['daiəgnəuz] v. 诊断（1A）
diagnose ['daiəgnəuz] v. 诊断（1B）
diagnostic [,daiəg'nɔstik] adj. 诊断的（1A）
differential [difə'renʃ(ə)l] n. 差别，差异 adj. 有差别的，有区别的（6A）
diluted [dai'ljuːtid] adj. 无力的；冲淡的（6A）

dimension [di'menʃən] *n.* 范围；尺寸；尺度；维；规模（5B）
disappointment [,disə'pɔintmənt] *n.* 失望（4B）
disaster [di'zɑ:stə] *n.* 灾难，天灾，灾祸（5A）
disband [dis'bænd] *v.* 解散；裁减（8A）
discharge [dis'tʃɑ:dʒ] *n.* 解雇，遣走（3A）
discomfort [dis'kʌmfət] *n.* 不便之处，不适（4A）
discount ['diskaunt] *n.* 折扣；贴现（3A）
discourage [dis'kʌridʒ] *vt.* 使气馁，阻碍（2B）
discretion [dis'kreʃən] *n.* 判断力（1B）
disk [disk] *n.* 磁盘（10A）
dismal ['dizməl] *adj.* 可怕的，灾难性的；阴沉的，凄凉（9A）
disparate ['dispərət] *adj.* 异类的，不同的（10A）
disposal [dis'pəuzəl] *n.* 处理，处置，清除（6B）
disruption [dis'rʌpʃən] *n.* 中断，分裂，瓦解，破坏（6B）
disseminate [di'semineit] *v.* 散布，传播，宣传（1A）
disseminator [di'semineitə] *n.* 传播者（1A）
distinction [dis'tiŋkʃən] *n.* 区别，差异，级别（10A）
distinguish [dis'tiŋgwiʃ] *v.* 区别，辨别（1B）
distortion [dis'tɔ:ʃən] *n.* 扭曲，变形，曲解（10B）
distribution [,distri'bju:ʃən] *n.* 分销（4A）
distributor [dis'tribjutə] *n.* 发行人；销售者；批发商（5B）
disturbing [di'stɜ:biŋ] *adj.* 烦扰的（5B）
diversity [dai'və:siti] *n.* 多样，不同，千变万化，差异（4A）
dividend ['dividend] *n.* 股息，红利（9A）
dizzying ['diziiŋ] *adj.* 令人昏乱的，灿烂的（4A）
document ['dɔkjumənt] *vt.* 用文件证明；为……提供文件（3A）
domain [dəu'mein] *n.* 范围，领域（2B）
dominate ['dɔmineit] *v.* 支配；控制；占优势（5B）
dramatically [drə'mætikəli] *adv.* 戏剧地，引人注目地（1A）
duplication [,dju:pli'keiʃən] *n.* 重复；副本，复制（8A）

duty ['dju:ti] *n.* 义务，责任，职责，职务（1A）
dynamically [dai'næmikəli] *adv.* 动态地；动力地，动力学地（8A）

E

eager ['i:gə] *adj.* 热心于，渴望着（8B）
earn [ə:n] *vt.* 赚，挣得，获得（8A）
earnings ['ɜ:niŋs] *n.* 收益；工资，收入（9A）
ecological [,ekə'lɔdʒikəl] *adj.* 生态学的，社会生态学的（2B）
economic [,i:kə'nɔmik] *adj.* 经济（上）的（2B）
economical [,i:kə'nɔmikəl] *adj.* 节约的，经济的（6A）
effectively [i'fektivli] *adv.* 有效地，有力地（1A）
efficiently [i'fiʃəntli] *adv.* 有效率地，有效地（1A）
eliminate [i'limineit] *vt.* 排除，消除（7A）
elimination [i,limi'neiʃən] *n.* 排除，除去，消除（6B）
emergence [i'mə:dʒəns] *n.* 浮现，露出，出现（2A）
emergence [i'mə:dʒəns] *n.* 显露；出现；发生（5B）
empathize ['empəθaiz] *v.* 移情，神会（1B）
emphasis ['emfəsis] *n.* 强调；重点（5B）
emphasize ['emfəsaiz] *vt.* 强调，着重（1A）
employ [im'plɔi] *v.* 使用，运用（5A）
employment [im'plɔimənt] *n.* 雇用，使用，利用（3A）
empower [im'pauə] *v.* 授权与，使能够（3A）
enable [i'neibl] *vt.* 使能够，使成为可能，使实现（5A）
encyclopedia [en,saiklə u'pi:diə] *n.* 百科全书（4B）
endeavor [in'devə] *n.&vi.* 尽力，努力（1A）
engineering [,endʒi'niəriŋ] *n.* 工程（学）（8B）
enhance [in'hɑ:ns] *vt.* 提高，增强（3A）
ensure [in'ʃuə] *vt.* 确保，确保，保证（3A）
enterprise ['entəpraiz] *n.* 企业，事业，计划，事业心，进取心（1A）
entity ['entiti] *n.* 实体；组织，机构，团体（9B）
environment [in'vaiərənmənt] *n.* 环境，周围环境（1B）

167

equipment [i'kwipmənt] n. 装备，设备，器材，装置（3A）
equivalent [i'kwivələnt] adj. 相等的，相当的（7B）
erect [i'rekt] vt. 盖，使竖立，使直立 adj. 直立的，竖立的，笔直的（8B）
erratic [i'rætik] adj. 无确定路线，不稳定的（6A）
essential [i'senʃəl] adj. 本质的，实质的，基本的（1A）
establish [i'stæbliʃ] vt. 成立，建立（6A）
establishment [is'tæbliʃmənt] n. 确立，制定（6A）
euro ['juərəu] n. 欧元（9A）
evaluate [i'væljueit] vt. 评价，估计，求……的值（10A）
excel [ik'sel] vt.&vi. 优于；胜过（5B）
excellence ['eksələns] n. 优秀，卓越（4A）
excessive [ik'sesiv] adj. 过多的，过分的，额外（4A）
exclusively [ik'sklu:sivli] adv. 排外地，专有地（8A）
execution [,eksi'kju:ʃən] n. 实行，完成，执行（8B）
executive [ig'zekjutiv] n. 执行者，经理主管人员，决策人，董事会；行政官 adj. 决策和执行的，实行的，执行的，行政的（4A）
expectation [,ekspek'teiʃən] n. 期望，期待，预料，指望，展望（6A）
expend [iks'pend] vt. 花费，消耗，支出（6B）
expenditure [iks'penditʃə] n. 支出，花费（6A）
expertise [,ekspə'ti:z] n. 专家的意见，专门技术（9A）
expiration [,ekspaiə'reiʃən] n. 满期，终止（6B）
explicit [iks'plisit] adj. 外在的，清楚的（2B）
explode [iks'pləud] vi. 爆炸，爆发，破除，激发（4A）
explosive [iks'pləusiv] adj. 爆炸（性）的；爆发（性）的（5B）
extend [iks'tend] vi. 延伸，延续，继续扩张（6A）
extensively [iks'tensivli] adv. 广阔地（9B）
exterior [eks'tiəriə] adj. 外部的，外在的（8B）
exterminate [iks'tə:mineit] v. 消除（4B）

F

facet ['fæsit] n.（多面体的）面，层（6B）
facilitate [fə'siliteit] vt. 使容易，使便利，推动（3A）
facility [fə'siliti] n. 设施，设备（5A）
factor ['fæktə] n. 因素，要素（2A）
fantastic [fæn'tæstik] adj. 极好的，极妙的；幻想的，奇异的（4B）
favor ['feivə] vt. 喜欢，支持，赞成 n. 喜爱，好感，宠爱（4A）
feasibility [,fi:zə'biləti] n. 可行性，可能性（2A）
federal ['fedərəl] adj. 联邦的，联合的（9B）
feedback ['fi:dbæk] n. 反馈（1B）
fiduciary [fi'dju:ʃəri] adj. 基于信用的，信托的，受信托的 n. 被信托者，受托人（1A）
field [fi:ld] n. 域（10A）
fierce [fiəs] adj. 凶猛的，猛烈的，热烈的（4A）
figment ['figmənt] n. 臆造的事物，虚构的事（2B）
figurehead ['figəhed] n. 名头，有名无实的领导（1A）
file [fail] n. 文件，档案（10A）
finance [fai'næns] n. 财政，金融；财政学（1B）
financing [fai'nænsiŋ] n. 筹措资金，理财（9A）
finite ['fainait] adj. 有限的，限定的（8A）
firm [fə:m] n. 公司，商行，（合伙）商号（3A）
firsthand [fə:st'hænd] adv. 第一手地；直接地 adj. 直接的；直接得来的；直接采购的（5B）
fixture ['fikstʃə] n. 固定设备（8B）
fluctuate ['flʌktjueit] vi. 变动，波动，涨落（8A）
foolproof ['fu:lpru:f] n. 安全装置 adj. 十分简单的，十分安全的（7A）
forecast ['fɔ:ka:st] vt. 预想，预测，预报（6A）
forecasting ['fɔ:ka:stiŋ] n. 预测，预报（3A）
formal ['fɔ:məl] adj. 正式的，形式的（2A）
format ['fɔ:mæt] n. 形式，格式 vt. 安排……的格局或规格（2A）
foundation [faun'deiʃən] n. 基础，根本，建立（8B）
frame [freim] n. 框，框架，架子；骨架（8B）
framework ['freimwə:k] n. 构架，框架，结构（1A）

framework ['freimwə:k] n. 构架，框架，结构（2A）
frontier ['frʌntjə] n. 国境，边疆，边境（1A）
fulfillment [ful'filmənt] n. 履行，实行（6B）

G

geographical [,dʒiə'græfikəl] adj. 地理学的，地理的（6A）
global ['gləub(ə)l] adj. 全球的，全世界的（1B）
governmental [,gʌvən'mentl] adj. 政府的（9B）
graduate ['grædjueit] n.（大学）毕业生，研究生（1B）
graph [grɑ:f] n. 图表，曲线图（2A）
guarantee [,gærən'ti:] n. 保证，保证书，担保，抵押品 vt. 保证，担保（2A）
guidance ['gaidəns] n. 指导，领导（1A）
guide [gaid] vt. 指导，支配，管理 n. 领路人，导游者，向导；引导者；指南（4A）
guideline ['gaidlain] n. 指导方针（8A）

H

handler ['hændlə] n. 处理者，管理者（1A）
hardware ['hɑ:dwɛə] n. 硬件，（电子仪器的）部件（10B）
hazardous ['hæzədəs] adj. 危险的，冒险的（6B）
hierarchy ['haiərɑ:ki] n. 层次，层级（1A）
hypertext ['haipətekst] n. 超文本（10A）

I

identification [ai,dentifi'keiʃən] n. 辨认，鉴定，证明，视为同一（6A）
ideology [aidi'ɔlədʒi] n. 意识形态（2B）
illustrate ['iləstreit] vt. 解释，举例说明，图解（9B）
image ['imidʒ] n. 形象；肖像；图像（4A）
implement ['implimənt] vt. 贯彻，实现（1B）
implicitly [im'plisitli] adv. 含蓄地，暗中地（2B）
imply [im'plai] vt. 暗示，意味（1A）
impose [im'pəuz] vt. 强加；征税（8B）
improve [im'pru:v] v. 改善，改进（1A）
inappropriate [,inə'prəupriit] adj. 不适当的，不相称的（3A）
incentive [in'sentiv] n. 动机 adj. 激励的（7B）

inconsistent [,inkən'sistənt] adj. 不一致的，不协调的，矛盾的（2B）
increasingly [in'kri:siŋli] adv. 越来越多地，逐渐增加地，日益地（10A）
indicator ['indikeitə] n. 指标（1A）
inevitably [in'evitəbli] adv. 不可避免地；必然地（5B）
infer [in'fə:] v. 推断（2B）
inflexibility [in'fleksəbliti] n. 不屈性；顽固；不变性（5B）
informality [,infɔ:'mæliti] n. 非正式（2A）
informational [,infə'meiʃənəl] adj. 报告的，情报的（5A）
informed [in'fɔ:md] adj. 见多识广的（9B）
ingrained [in'greind] adj. 彻底的，根深蒂固的（2B）
inherent [in'hiərənt] adj. 固有的；内在的（5B）
innovative ['inəuveitiv] adj. 创新的，革新的（6B）
insert [in'sə:t] vt. 插入，嵌入（10B）
inside-out ['in'saidaut] adv. 彻底地，里面翻到外面（4B）
insight ['insait] n. 洞察力，见识（9B）
inspect [in'spekt] vt. 检查，视察（7A）
institution [,insti'tju:ʃən] n. 公共机构，协会，制度（5A）
instruction [in'strʌkʃən] n. 指令，指示（10A）
instructor [in'strʌktə] n. 教师（7B）
insurance [in'ʃuərəns] n. 保险，保险单（4B）
intangible [in'tændʒəbl] adj. 无形的，难以明了的（9A）
integral ['intigrəl] adj. 主要的，必备的；完整的，整体的（6A）
integration [,inti'greiʃən] n. 整合；综合（5B）
intensify [in'tensifai] vt. 加强（4A）
intensive [in'tensiv] adj. 精深的，透彻的，强烈的（1B）
interconnect [,intəkə'nekt] vt. 使互相连接（10B）
interest ['intrist] n. 利益，利害；兴趣，关心；利息（3A）
interlock [intə'lɔk] vt.&vi. 连锁；连串（5B）

intermediate [,intə'mi:djət] adj. 中间的（5A）
internally [in'tənəli] adv. 在内，在中心（7B）
interpersonal [,intə'pə:snəl] adj. 人与人之间的（1B）
interpersonal [,intə'pə:snəl] adj. 人与人之间的；人际的；涉及人与人之间的关系的（1A）
interpret [in'tə:prit] v. 解释，说明（9B）
interrelated [intəri'leitid] adj. 相关的（8A）
interview ['intəvju:] vt. 访问，采访；接见；会见（4A）
introduce [,intrə'dju:s] vt. 引起；介绍，传入，引进，提出（6A）
intruder [in'tru:də] n. 入侵者（2B）
invasion [in'veiʒən] n. 入侵（4A）
inventory ['invəntri] n. 商品目录；清单；存货，库存量（5A）
invest [in'vest] vt.&vi. 投资（1B）
investment [in'vestmənt] n. 投资（1A）
investor [in'vestə] n. 投资者（1A）
investor [in'vestə] n. 投资者（9A）
invite [in'vait] vt. 邀请（5B）
involvement [in'vɔlvmənt] n. 参与；包含（7A）
isolate ['aisəleit] vt. 使隔离；使孤立（5B）
issuance ['iʃuəns] n. 发行，发布（9B）

J
jeopardy ['dʒepədi] n. 危险，危险（8A）
judgment ['dʒʌdʒmənt] n. 判断（9B）

K
keen [ki:n] adj. 敏锐的，敏捷的，热心的（4A）
keyboard ['ki:bɔ:d] n. 键盘（10A）

L
lag [læg] vi. 落后；滞后；跟不上；落伍 n. 落后（5B）
landscape ['lændskeip] n. 风景；景观；庭园；山水（5B）
layoff ['lei,ɔ:f] n. 临时解雇，操作停止（9B）
legally ['li:gəli] adv. 法律上，合法地（3A）
lender ['lendə] n. 出借人，贷方（9A）
liability [,laiə'biliti] n. 债务，负债（9A）
liable ['laiəbl] adj. 有责任的，有义务的（1A）
liaison [li(:)'eizɑ:n] n. 联络（1A）

likelihood ['laiklihud] n. 可能，可能性（3A）
literally ['litərəli] adv. 照字面意义；逐字地（5B）
loan [ləun] n.（借出的）贷款，借出 v. 借给（2A）
locate [ləu'keit] vt. 确定，找出，找到（3A）
location [ləu'keiʃən] n. 位置，场所，特定区域（6A）
locational [ləu'keiʃənəl] adj. 位置上的（5A）
logistic [ləu'dʒistik] adj. 后勤学的，后勤的，物流的（6A）
logistical [ləu'dʒistikəl] adj. 后勤学的，后勤的，物流的（6A）
logistics [lə'dʒistiks] n. 物流；后勤学，后勤（6A）

M
magnify ['mægnifai] vt. 放大，扩大，赞美（6B）
makeup ['meikʌp] n. 组成，结构（9A）
management ['mænidʒmənt] n. 管理，处理，经营（1A）
maneuver [mə'nu:və] n. 运用，操作（2B）
manipulate [mə'nipjuleit] vt.（熟练地）操作，巧妙地处理（10B）
manipulation [mə,nipju'leiʃən] n. 处理，操作，操纵（1A）
manufacturer [,mænju'fæktʃərə] n. 制造业者，厂商（4B）
manufacturing [,mænju'fæktʃəriŋ] n. 制造业 adj. 制造业的（5A）
marked [mɑ:kt] adj. 有记号的，显著的（9A）
marketable ['mɑ:kitəbl] adj. 适于销售的（10B）
marketer ['mɑ:kitə] n. 市场商人（4A）
marketing ['mɑ:kitiŋ] n. 行销，买卖（1B）
matrix ['meitriks] n. 矩阵（8B）
maximize ['mæksmaiz] vt. 使……最大化，使……达到最大（程度）（3A）
mean [mi:n] vt. 意为，想要 adj. 低劣的，卑鄙的；吝啬的；普通的，简陋的（4A）
means [mi:nz] n. 手段，方法（4A）
measure ['meʒə] n. 方法，测量，措施（1A）
measurement ['meʒəmənt] n. 测量，度量（1A）
mediate ['mi:diit] v. 仲裁，调停，作为引起……的媒介（2B）
mentor ['mentɔ:] n. 良师益友，导师，指导者（7B）

merge [mə:dʒ] v. 合并，并入（2B）
merger ['mə:dʒə] n. 合并，归并（1A）
methodology [meθə'dɔlədʒi] n. 方法学，方法论（7B）
milestone ['mailstəun] n. 里程碑，重要事件，转折点（2A）
mission ['miʃən] n. 使命，任务（1A）
mitigate ['mitigeit] v. 减轻（2A）
mobilization [,məubilai'zeiʃən] n. 动员（1A）
mobilize ['məubilaiz] v. 动员（1B）
mold [məuld] vt. 浇铸，塑造（1B）
monitor ['mɔnitə] n. 监管人员 vt. 监控（1A）
morale [mɔ'rɑ:l] n. 道德，士气，民心（9B）
mousetrap ['mausətræp] n. 捕鼠器（4B）
multidisciplinary [,mʌlti'disiplinəri] adj. 包括各种学科的，多学科的（8A）
multiform ['mʌltifɔ:m] adj. 多种形式的（6B）
multiple ['mʌltipl] adj. 多样的，多重的（8A）

N

neglected [ni'glektid] adj. 被忽视的（4B）
negotiate [ni'gəuʃieit] v. 与某人商议，谈判，磋商（1A）
negotiate [ni'gəuʃieit] v. 商议，谈判，磋商（8A）
negotiator [ni'gəuʃieitə] n. 磋商者，交涉者，出售者，交易者（1A）
network ['netwə:k] n. 网络，网状物（10B）
niche [nitʃ] n. 小生境，合适的环境（2B）
nonhuman ['nɔn'hju:mən] adj. 非人类的（3A）
non-profit [nɔn'prɔfit] adj. 非盈利的（2A）
norm [nɔ:m] n. 标准；规范（5B）
normality [nɔ:'mæliti] n. 常态（7B）
notion ['nəuʃən] n. 概念，观念，想法（7B）

O

objective [əb'dʒektiv] n. 目标，目的 adj. 客观的，公正的，无偏见的（4A）
obligation [,ɔbli'geiʃən] n. 义务，职责，债务（9B）
obtainable [əb'teinəbl] adj. 能得到的，可到手的（4A）
occur [ə'kə:] vi. 发生，出现（4A）
odds [ɔdz] n. 机会，可能性（2A）
offer ['ɔfə] n. 出价，提议（4A）

opening ['əupniŋ] n. 空缺，机会（3A）
operate ['ɔpəreit] v. 运营，运转，起作用（1A）
operationalize [,ɔpə'reiʃənlaiz] vt. 使用于操作，使开始运转，实施（6A）
opponent [ə'pəunənt] n. 对手，反对者（2B）
opportunity [,ɔpə'tju:niti] n. 机会，时机（1B）
optional ['ɔpʃənəl] adj. 可选择的,随意的（6A）
order ['ɔ:də] n. 订单；定购（5B）
orderly ['ɔ:dəli] adv. 依次地，顺序地（6A）
organizer ['ɔ:gənaizə] n. 组织者,建立者（8B）
orientation [,ɔrien'teiʃən] n. 方向，方位，定位（4A）
oriented ['ɔ:rientid] adj. 导向的（9B）
origin ['ɔridʒin] n. 起源，由来，起因（4A）
outcome ['autkʌm] n. 结果，成果（1A）
outside-in ['aut'saidin] adv. 里面翻到外面，彻底地（4B）
outwit [aut'wit] vt. 以智取胜；瞒骗（2B）
overall [əuvər'ɔ:l] adj. 全部的，总的（3A）
overcapacity [,əuvəkə'pæsiti] n. 生产能力过剩（4B）
overhaul [,əuvə'hɔ:l] v. 检查（7A）
overlap ['əuvə'læp] v. （与……）交叠，重叠；部分相同，在特性或功能上相似，相当（6A）
overload ['əuvə'ləud] n. 超载，负荷过多（10B）
overlook [,əuvə'luk] vt. 忽略；没注意；俯瞰，俯视（4B）
oversee [,əuvə'si:] v. 俯瞰，监视，检查（7B）
overtime ['əuvətaim] adv. 超时；加班 n. 超时；加班；加班费（5A）

P

paradigm ['pærədaim] n. 范例（7B）
paraphrase ['pærəfreiz] vt. 解释，释义；意译（2B）
particularly [pə'tikjuləli] adv. 独特地，显著地（10A）
part-owner [pɑ:t-'əunə] n. 共有者（9A）
patent ['peitənt] n. 专利权，执照（2A）
patent ['peitənt] n. 专利权，执照（9A）
pattern ['pætən] n. 模式（2B）
payroll ['peirəul] n. 薪水册，职工工资册，（公司）应付工资总额（1B）

peer [piə] n. 同等的人，贵族（1B）
penetrate ['penitreit] vt. 穿透；渗透；看穿（5B）
percentage [pə'sentidʒ] n. 百分率；百分比（7B）
perception [pə'sepʃən] n. 理解，感知，感觉（7A）
perfect [pə'fikt] vt. 使完美无瑕 adj. 完美的，全然的，理想的（4B）
performance [pə'fɔ:məns] n. 履行，执行，成绩（1A）
permit [pə(:)'mit] v. 许可；允许；准许 n. 通行证；许可证；执照（5B）
personality [,pə:sə'næliti] n. 个性，人格，人物（2B）
perspective [pə'spektiv] n. 远景，前途，观点，看法，观察（1A）
perspective [pə'spektiv] n. 设想，洞察力（2B）
pervasive [pə:'veisiv] adj. 弥漫的；遍布的；普遍的（8A）
phase [feiz] n. 阶段，状态（3A）
phase-out [feiz-aut] n. 逐步淘汰（8B）
philosophy [fi'lɔsəfi] n. 基本原理，观点，哲学，哲学体系（4A）
physiological [,fiziə'lɔdʒikəl] adj. 生理学的，生理学上的（5A）
Picasso ['pikɑ:sou] n. 毕加索（2B）
piece [pi:s] n. 块，件，片（10A）
pioneer [paiə'niə] n. 先驱，倡导者，先遣兵（7B）
ploy [plɔi] n. 策略，计谋（2B）
policy ['pɔlisi] n. 政策，方针；手段；计谋；策略（3A）
popular ['pɔpjulə] adj. 通俗的，流行的，受欢迎的（4A）
population [,pɔpju'leiʃən] n. 人口（4B）
portable ['pɔ:təbl] adj. 轻便的，手提（式）的（10B）
portion ['pɔ:ʃən] n. 一部分，一份（1B）
position [pə'ziʃən] n. 位置，职位（1B）
possess [pə'zes] vt. 占有，拥有，持有（1B）
postpone [pəust'pəun] v. 推迟，延期，缓办（6B）
potential [pə'tenʃ(ə)l] adj. 可能的，潜在的（4A）
preceding [pre'si:diŋ] adj. 在前的，前述的（2B）

preconception [pri:kən'sepʃən] n. 成见，偏见；先入为主的概念（2B）
predetermine ['pri:di'tə:mi] v. 预定，预先确定（6A）
prediction [pri'dikʃən] n. 预言，预报（10A）
preference ['prefərəns] n. 偏爱，优先选择（4A）
preferred [pri'fə:d] v. 提出，提升，建议；选择某事物（1A）
premium ['primjəm] n. 额外费用；奖金；奖赏；保险费（6B）
presentation [,prezen'teiʃən] n. 报告，介绍，陈述（1A）
presumably [pri'zju:məbəli] adv. 可能，大概，推测起来（4A）
prevalent ['prevələnt] adj. 普遍的，流行的（7A）
pricing ['praisiŋ] n. 定价（4A）
principal ['prinsəpəl] adj. 主要的，首要的（1B）
principle ['prinsəpl] n. 法则，原则，原理（4A）
prioritize [prai'ɔritaiz] vt. 把……区分优先次序（8A）
priority [prai'ɔriti] n. 优先，优先权（5A）
pro [prəu] adv. 正面地 adj. 肯定的，支持的
probability [,prɔbə'biliti] n. 可能性，或然性，概率（10B）
procedure [prə'si:dʒə] n. 程序，进程（10B）
procurement [prə'kjuəmənt] n. 采购，获得，取得（6A）
profession [prə'feʃən] n. 职业，专业（8A）
profit ['prɔfit] n. 利润，益处，得益 vi. 得益，利用 vt. 有益于，有利于（1A）
profitable [,prɔfitə'bl] adj. 有利可图的（4A）
progress ['prəugres] n. 前进，进步（1A）
promotion [prə'məuʃən] n. 促销；促进（4A）
promotional [prəu'məuʃənel] adj. 促进的；促销的；奖励的（6A）
pronounce [prə'nauns] vt. 发音；发出……音（10A）
propel [prə'pel] vt. 推进，驱使（3A）
properly ['prɔpəli] adv. 适当地，完全地（3A）
proposal [prə'pəuzəl] n. 提议，建议（8B）

propose [prə'pəuz] vt. 计划，建议（2B）
prospective [prə'spektiv] adj. 未来的；盼望中的，预期的（1B）
prosper ['prɔspə] v. 成功，兴隆，昌盛（9A）
provide [prə'vaid] vt. 供应，供给（1B）
publisher ['pʌbliʃə] n. 出版者，发行人（8B）
punishment ['pʌniʃmənt] n. 惩罚，处罚，惩处（8A）
purpose ['pə:pəs] n. 目的，意图，用途，效果，决心，意志 vt. 打算，企图，决心（3A）
purposefully ['pə:pəsfuli] adj. 有目的的，自觉的（2B）
pyramid ['pirəmid] n. 金字塔 v. （使）成金字塔状，（使）渐增，（使）上涨（1A）

Q

qualification [ˌkwɔlifi'keiʃən] n. 资格，条件（3A）
qualified ['kwɔlifaid] adj. 有资格的（3A）
qualify ['kwɔlifai] vt. 限制，限定（2A）
quantitatively ['kwɔntitətivli] adv. 数量上（7B）
quantity ['kwɔntiti] n. 量，数量（6A）
quotation [kwəu'teiʃən] n. 引用语，价格，报价单，行情表（2B）

R

raise [reiz] vt. 筹集（9A）
random ['rændəm] adj. 任意的，随便的，胡乱的（5A）
range [reindʒ] vi. （在一定范围内）变化，变动 n. 范围（5A）
rapid ['ræpid] adj. 迅速的，快的（4B）
realize ['riəlaiz] vt. 认识到，了解；实现，实行（1B）
realm [relm] n. 领域（2B）
reasonable ['ri:znəbl] adj. 合理的，有道理的（4A）
recall [ri'kɔ:l] n. 收回，召回（6B）
receipt [ri'si:t] n. 收条，收据（1B）
receiver [ri'si:və] n. 接受者，接收器，收信机（10B）
reclaim [ri'kleim] vt. 收回，要求归还（6B）
recognition [rekəg'niʃ(ə)n] n. 承认；认可（2B）
recognize ['rekəgnaiz] vt. 承认，认可；认出（1B）
recommend [rekə'mend] vt. 推荐，介绍（7A）

recommendation [ˌrekəmen'deiʃən] n. 劝告，建议（1A）
reconcile ['rekənsail] vt. 使和解，使和谐，使顺从（6A）
record ['rekɔ:d] n. 记录（10A）
recruit [ri'kru:t] vt. 征募，使恢复，补充（1B）
recruitment [ri'kru:tmənt] n. 补充，征募新兵（3A）
redesign [ˌri:di'zain] v. 重新设计（7A）
reduce [ri'dju:s] vt. 减少，缩减；降低（4B）
refinement [ri'fainmənt] n. 提炼，改进（7B）
refurbish [ri:'fə:biʃ] vt. 翻新，刷新（2A）
regulatory ['regjulətəri] adj. 规章的；制定规章的；受规章限制的（9B）
related [ri'leitid] adj. 相关的，有关系的（1B）
relationship [ri'leiʃənʃip] n. 关系，关联（1A）
reliability [riˌlaiə'biliti] n. 可靠性，安全性；可信赖性（4B）
reliable [ri'laiəbl] adj. 可靠的，可信赖的（7A）
relocation ['ri:ləu'keiʃən] n. 再定位；再布置，变换布置；再分配（8A）
remodel ['ri:'mɔdl] vt. 改建，改造，改变（8A）
remove [ri'mu:v] vt. 移动，开除（10B）
rent [rent] n. 租金（2B）
repay [ri(:)'pei] v. 偿还，报答（2A）
replace [ri(:)'pleis] vt. 取代；替换；代替（5B）
replenish [ri'pleniʃ] v. 补充（5B）
replenishment [ri'pleniʃmənt] n. 补给，补充（6A）
represent [ˌri:pri'zent] vt. 代表；表现（3A）
requirement [ri'kwaiəmənt] n. 需求；要求；必要条件（5B）
reservation [ˌrezə'veiʃən] n. 预定；预约（5B）
reside [ri'zaid] vi. 归于，居住（9A）
resolve [ri'zɔlv] vt. 解决（4A）
resource [ri'sɔ:s] n. 资源（10A）
respective [ri'spektiv] adj. 各自的；各个的（5B）
responsibility [risˌpɔnsə'biliti] n. 责任，职责（1A）
responsible [ris'pɔnsəbl] adj. 有责任的，可靠的，可依赖的，负责的（1A）
restructure [ri'strʌktʃə] vt. 重构，调整，改组（2A）

retailer [ri:'teilə] n. 零售商人（6A）
retailing ['ri:teiliŋ] n. 零售业（5A）
retain [ri'tein] vt. 保持，保留（9A）
retrieve [ri'tri:v] v. 重新得到，找回（10B）
reveal [ri'vi:l] vt. 展现，显示，揭示，暴露（1B）
revenue ['revinju:] n. 收入，（国家的）岁入；税收（9B）
reverse [ri'və:s] vt. 颠倒；反转；翻转；（使）倒退；改变 n. 相反，背面，反面，倒退 adj. 相反的，倒转的，颠倒的（6B）
reward [ri'wɔ:d] n. 报酬，奖金 vt. 酬劳，奖赏（3A）
rewarding [ri'wɔ:diŋ] adj. 报答的，有益的，值得的（8B）
rigid ['ridʒid] adj. 刚硬的，刚性的，严格的（6B）
roadblock ['rəudblɔk] n. 障碍，障碍物（8A）
robbery ['rɔbəri] n. 抢掠，抢夺（1A）
robotics [rəu'bɔtiks] n. 机器人技术；机器人学（5B）
role [rəul] n. 角色，任务（1A）
routine [ru:'ti:n] n. 例行公事，常规，日常事务（1A）
routine [ru:'ti:n] n. 常规；惯例；例行公事（8A）
rule [ru:l] n. 规则，准则，标准（1A）

S

sale [seil] n. 销路，销售额；出售，卖出；廉价出售（4A）
satisfaction [,sætis'fækʃən] n. 满意，满足（4A）
scan [skæn] v. 细看，审视，浏览，扫描（1B）
schedule ['ʃedju:l; 'skedʒul] n. 时间表，进度表 v. 确定时间（1A）
schedule ['ʃedju:l; 'skedʒul] vt. 预定，安排 n. 时间表，进度表（5A）
scope [skəup] n. 范围，范畴，领域（5A）
scrap [skræp] vt. 扔弃，敲碎，拆毁（6B）
screen [skri:n] v. 初选，遴选，选拔，筛选（3A）
seasonality ['si:zənliti] n. 季节的，季节性（5A）
security [si'kjuəriti] n. 证券，债券（9A）
seek [si:k] v. 寻找，探索，寻求（1B）
segment ['segmənt] n. 段，节，片断（7B）
selection [si'lekʃən] n. 选拔，挑选（3A）

selectively [si'lektivli] adj. 选择的，选择性的（10B）
semi-finished ['semi-'finiʃt] adj. 半完成的，半制的，半成品的（6A）
seminar ['seminɑ:] n. 研究会，讨论发表会（1B）
senior ['si:njə] adj. 年长的，地位较高的，高级的（1B）
sense [sens] vt. 感到，理解，认识（4B）
share [ʃɛə] n, 共享，参与，份额，参股 vt. 分享，均分，共有，分配（1A）
share [ʃɛə] v. 共享，共用；分摊；共有 n. 共享，参与（4A）
shift [ʃift] n. 轮班，轮班职工；轮班工作时间（5A）
shift [ʃift] n. 移动，轮班，移位，变化（7A）
shipment ['ʃipmənt] n. 装船，出货（6B）
signal ['signl] n. 信号（7A）
significant [sig'nifikənt] adj. 重大的，重要的（1A）
similarly ['siməli] adv. 同样地，类似于（1B）
simultaneously [siməl'teiniəsly] adv. 同时地（6B）
situation [,sitju'eiʃən] n. 情形，境遇（1A）
slide [slaid] n. 幻灯片（2A）
slip [slip] vi. 滑动；滑倒 n. 滑倒，事故，片，纸片（4A）
societal [sə'saiətəl] adj. 社会的（4A）
society [sə'saiəti] n. 群体，团体（5A）
software ['sɔftwɛə] n. 软件（10A）
solely ['səuli] adv. 只是；独自；完全；单独（9A）
solution [sə'lju:ʃən] n. 解答，解决办法（7A）
specification [,spesifi'keiʃən] n. 详述，规格，说明书，规范（6A）
specify ['spesifai] vt. 指定，详细说明（3A）
spire [in'spaiə] vt. 鼓舞，激发（1A）
spokesperson ['spəukspə:sn] n. 发言人，代言人（1A）
spreadsheet [spredʃi:t] n. 电子制表软件，电子数据表（10A）
staff [stɑ:f] vt. 在……工作；为……配备职员；任职于（1A）
staff [stɑ:f] vt. 供给人员，充当职员（3A）

staid [steid] adj. 沉静的（8B）
stakeholder ['steikhəuldə] n. 股东（2A）
stand-alone [stand-ə'ləun] n. 独立的（7A）
status ['steitəs] n. 身份，地位，情形（8B）
stimulate ['stimjuleit] vt. 刺激，激励；增强；增加活力（4A）
stockroom ['stɔkrum] n. 商品储藏室；仓库（5B）
storage ['stɔridʒ] n. 贮藏（量），贮藏库，存储（5A）
strategic [strə'ti:dʒik] adj. 战略的（1A）
strategic [strə'ti:dʒik] adj. 战略的，战略上的（3A）
strategy ['strætidʒi] n. 策略，战略（1A）
strictly ['striktli] adv. 严格地；严厉地；精确地（5B）
strive [straiv] v. 努力，奋斗（7B）
subdivide ['sʌbdi'vaid] v. 再分，细分（6A）
subdivision ['sʌbdi,viʒən] n. 细分，一部（6A）
subordinate [sə'bɔ:dinit] n. 下属 adj. 次要的，下级的（1B）
subplan ['sʌb,plæn] n. 子计划，辅助方案（2A）
substance ['sʌbstəns] n. 物质（10A）
substantial [səb'stænʃəl] adj. 坚固的，实质的（4A）
substantially [səb'stænʃəli] adv. 主要地；实质上地；重大地；相当大地（6A）
succession [sək'seʃən] n. 连续，继承，继任（8B）
suggestion [sə'dʒestʃən] n. 提议，意见，暗示（1A）
supervision [,sju:pə'viʒən] n. 监督，管理（6B）
supervisor ['sju:pəvaizə] n. 主管，监督人，管理人（1A）
supervisory [,sju:pə'vaizəri] adj. 管理的，监督的（1A）
supplier [sə'plaiə] n. 供应商，厂商（1A）
survival [sə'vaivəl] n. 生存，幸存（10B）
survive [sə'vaiv] v. 幸免于，幸存，生还（4A）
susceptible [sə'septəbl] adj. 易受影响的，易感动的（6B）
sustainable [sə'steinəbl] adj. 足可支撑的，可持续的（2A）
synthesize ['sinθisaiz] v. 综合，合成（6A）
systematic [,sisti'mætik] adj. 系统的，体系的（3A）

T

tactical ['tæktikəl] adj. 战术的（5A）
talented ['tæləntid] adj. 有才能的；能干的（3A）
tangible ['tændʒəbl] adj. 有形的，切实的（9A）
target ['tɑ:git] n. 目标，对象（2A）
taste [teist] n. 喜爱，爱好；味道，味觉 v. 品尝，辨味；领略；体验，感到（4A）
tax [tæks] n. 税，税款，税金（9B）
taxpayer ['tæks,peiə] n. 纳税人（2A）
team [ti:m] n. 队，组（5A）
technical ['teknikəl] adj. 技术的，技术上的，技巧方面的（1B）
telecommunication ['telikəmju:ni'keiʃən] n. 电信，长途通信，无线电通信（5A）
temporary ['tempərəri] adj. 暂时的，临时的，临时性（8A）
Texas ['teksəs] n. 得克萨斯州（美国州名）（5B）
theory ['θiəri] n. 理论，学说（1B）
threat [θret] n. 威胁（1A）
threaten ['θretn] vt. 恐吓，威胁（2B）
tighten ['taitən] v. 变紧，绷紧，拉紧（7B）
timing ['taimiŋ] n. 适时，时间选择（8A）
tolerance ['tɔlərəns] n. 公差，宽容，忍受（7B）
tour [tuə] n. 巡回展；旅行；游历；旅游 v. 旅行；游历；巡回（5B）
trademark ['treidmɑ:k] n. 商标（9A）
trail [treil] n. 踪迹，痕迹，形迹（7B）
transaction [træn'zækʃən] n. 交易，业务，事务，交易办理（4A）
transcend [træn'send] vt. 超越，胜过（7A）
transform [træns'fɔ:m] vt. 转换；改变；改造（5B）
transformation [,trænsfə'meiʃən] n. 变化，转化，改适（5A）
transmit [trænz'mit] vt. 传输，转送，传达（10B）
trapped [træpt] adj. 捕集的，捕获的（8B）
treatment ['tri:tmən] n. 待遇；处置,处理（3A）
trend [trend] n. 倾向；趋势（5B）
trickle ['trikl] v. 滴流，使淌下；慢慢地移动（1A）
trigger ['trigə] vt. 引发，引起，触发（2A）

U

ultimately ['ʌltimətli] adv. 最后，终于（3A）
unapparent [,ʌnə'pærent] adj. 不明显的，不清楚的，模糊的，不曾预料的（1A）
unapparent [ʌn'sə:tnti] n. 无常，不确定，不可靠，（6A）
undergo [,ʌndə'gəu] vt. 经历，遭受，忍受（4A）
undergraduate [,ʌndə'grædjuit] n.（尚未取得学位的）大学生（1B）
underlying ['ʌndə'laiiŋ] adj. 在下面的，根本的，潜在的（7A）
understandable [ʌndə'stændəbl] adj. 可以理解的，可懂的（2A）
underway ['ʌndə'wei] adj. 起步的，进行中的（8B）
undistorted ['ʌndis'tɔ:tid] adj. 未失真的，不偏激的（10B）
undoubtedly [ʌn'dautidli] adv. 毋庸置疑地，的确地（3A）
unexpected ['ʌniks'pektid] adj. 想不到的，意外的，未预料到（5A）
unfamiliar ['ʌnfə'miljə] adj. 新奇的，不熟悉的，没有经验的（2A）
unlimited [ʌn'limitid] adj. 无限的，无约束的（2A）
unplanned ['ʌn'plænd] adj. 无计划的，未筹划的（6B）
unsought ['ʌn'sɔ:t] adj. 未追求的，未寻求的（4B）
upcoming ['ʌp,kʌmiŋ] adj. 即将来临的，预定将要（3A）
update [ʌp'deit] n. 更新，现代化（10B）
usable ['ju:zəbl] adj. 可用的，合用的，便于使用的（6A）
utility [ju:'tiliti] n. 效用，有用（4A）
utility [ju:'tiliti] n. 应用程序（10A）
utilization [,ju:tilai'zeiʃən] n. 利用，使用，应用（3A）
utilize [ju:'tilaiz] vt. 利用（1B）

V

valuation [vælju'eiʃən] n. 估价，评价，计算（2A）

variance ['vɛəriəns] n. 不一致，变化，变异（6B）
variation [,vɛəri'eiʃən] n. 变更，变化，变异（9A）
vast [vɑ:st] adj. 巨大的，辽阔的，大量的（6A）
velocity [vi'lɔsiti] n. 速度，速率，迅速（6B）
vendor ['vendɔ] n. 卖方；卖主（5B）
venture ['ventʃə] n. 冒险，投机，风险（1B）
versatile ['və:sətail] adj. 通用的，万能的（6B）
viable ['vaiəbl] adj. 可行的（7A）
viewpoint ['vju:,pɔint] n. 观点，视点（1B）
vigorously ['vigərəsli] adv. 精神旺盛地（4B）
virtually ['və:tjuəli] adv. 事实上，实质上（8B）
vision ['viʒən] n. 愿景（1A）
voter ['vəutə] n. 投票者，有投票权者（4B）
vulnerable ['vʌlnərəbel] adj. 易受攻击的；易受……的攻击（5B）

W

warehouse ['wɛəhaus] n. 仓库，货栈，大商店（6A）
warehousing ['wɛəhauziŋ] n. 仓库费；入仓库，仓库贮存（5A）
wedding ['wediŋ] n. 婚礼，婚宴（8A）
welfare ['welfɛə] n. 福利，安宁，幸福（4B）
well-being [wel-'bi:iŋ] adj. 康乐，安宁，福利（4A）
Weltanschauung ['velt'ɑ:nʃauəŋ] n. 世界观，人生观（2B）
whereas [wɛər'æz] conj. 然而，反之（3A）
wholesaler ['həulseilə] n. 批发商（6A）
willingness ['wiliŋnis] n. 自动自发，积极肯干（1B）
workforce ['wə:kfɔ:s] n. 劳动力（5B）
worldwide ['wə:ldwaid] adj. 遍及全世界的，世界范围的；世界性的（4B）
worn [wɔ:n] adj. 用旧的；疲倦的（7A）
worthy ['wə:ði] adj. 有价值的，应……的，可敬的，值得的（7B）

Y

yield [ji:ld] n. 收益；收成；回收率；生产；生产量（7B）

词 组 表

A

a collection of 很多，一批，一组（2A）
a handful of 少数；一把（4A）
a host of 许多，一大群（1B）
a list of... ……的清单（2A）
a portion of 一部分（1B）
a succession of 一连串，一系列（8B）
academic year 学年（3A）
act as 担当（5A）
adverse effect 反作用（8B）
aerospace industry 航空和航天工业（8B）
all corners of the world 世界各地；世界每个角落（5B）
an abundance of 丰富，许多（4A）
annual report 年度报告（9B）
applications software 应用软件（10A）
apply to 将……应用于（7B）
aptitude test 能力倾向测验（3A）
as such 同样地，同量地（2B）
ask permission 得到允许（3B）
aspire to 渴望，追求（2B）
assembly plant 装配厂（6A）
asset management decision 资产管理决策（9A）
at a discount 打折扣（6B）
at a profit 赚钱，有利润（9A）
at hand 在手边，在附近，即将到来（1B）
at least 至少（4A）
at sb.'s discretion 由……随意决定（1B）
audit committee 审核委员会（1A）
automobile manufacturer 汽车制造厂（4A）

B

balance sheet 资产负债表（9A）
balanced scorecard 平衡记分卡（2A）
bank account 银行存款（10B）
be accountable to sb. 对某人负责（1A）
be beset with 被……包围（8B）
be bound up with 与……有密切关系（2B）
be capable of 能够（8B）
be charged with 承担（9A）

be compatible with 适合，一致（2B）
be concerned with 关心，注重（3B）
be grouped into ... 被分成……（1A）
be identified with 视……为一体，认同（4A）
be independent of 与……无关；不依赖；不取决于（10B）
be involved in 涉及，参与（1A）
be liable for 负责，承担责任，对……有责任（1A）
be likely to 可能（1A）
be likely to do sth. 可能做某事（3A）
be pushed to 被推到（1A）
be responsible for 负责（1A）
be similar to 类似于……（6A）
big picture 总体局势（1B）
black belt 黑腰带（7B）
board of directors 董事会（1A）
branch manager 分公司经理（1A）
bring down 降低（4B）
bring together 集合（8B）
brings sth. to the attention of sb. 使某人注意到某物/某事（4B）
business goal 商业目标（2A）
business model 商业模式（2A）
business plan 商业计划（2A）
Business Week《商业周刊》（1B）
by all accounts 据大家所说（1B）
by comparison 比较起来（5A）
by virtue of 依靠，由于（3A）

C

call center 呼叫中心（7B）
call for 要求，提倡（4B）
campus recruiting 校园招聘（3A）
capital market 资本市场（9A）
capital structure decision 资本构成决策（9A）
capitalize on 利用（1B）
capture market 争取市场（2B）
carry on 继续开展，坚持（9A）
cash flow 现金流转（9B）

cause and effect 因果（1B）
channel of distribution 分销渠道（4A）
chemical spray 化学喷雾（器）（4B）
churn out 艰苦地做出（7B）
come through 经历，成功（3A）
conceive of 想象（2B）
conceptual skill 概念技能（1B）
consist of 包括，由……组成（3A）
consumer durable 耐用消费品（6B）
contribute to 有助于，导致（1A）
control chart 控制图表（7A）
cope with 处理，对付，应付；克服（4A）
corporate strategy 公司战略（5A）
cost control 成本控制（9B）
coupled with 加上，外加（6B）
course of action 做法，行动过程（2B）
cradle-to-cradle logistics "从摇篮到摇篮"物流（6B）
customer service 客户服务（3B）
cut across 超越；取捷径；走近路（8A）

D

data entry 数据登记项，数据输入（10B）
deal with 对付，应付；对待（3A）
decision-making tool 决策工具（2A）
demand and supply 供与求，供求（3A）
demand management 需求的监督和调节（4A）
department manager 部门经理（1A）
depending on 根据，依据（1A）
develop strategic plans 制定战略计划（1A）
devote energy to 把精力投到（4B）
directors and officers liability insurance 公司董事及高级职员责任保险（1A）
disaster relief 灾难救济，灾难救援（8A）
disk drive 磁盘驱动器（10A）
display device 显示设备（10A）
disturbance handler 干扰处理者（1A）
divide into 分成（10A）
dividend policy 股息分配方针（9A）
Doberman pinscher 一种德国种的短毛猎犬（2B）
draw on 利用，凭借（2A）
draw up 草拟；写（8B）

drift away 渐渐离开（8B）

E

e-commerce 电子商务（6B）
economy of scale 规模经济（6B）
educational institution 教育机构（9B）
elementary school 小学（3B）
elevator pitch 电梯推销，电梯游说（2A）
empathize with 同情（1B）
end user 终端用户（10A）
engage in 使从事于，参加（4A）
enjoy doing sth. 喜爱，喜欢；享受……的乐趣（3B）
environmental problem 环境问题（4B）
equity financing 资本筹措，股本融资，发行股票筹资（2A）
equity financing 产权融资（9A）
executive directors 执行董事（1A）
external factor 外部因素（5A）

F

fall into 落入，陷于（7B）
fiduciary duty 受托责任、受信义务、信托义务（1A）
financial accounting 财务会计（9B）
financial assets 金融资产（9A）
financial management 财务管理（9A）
financial manager 财务经理（9A）
financial position 财务状况（9B）
financial statements 财务决算（9B）
financing decision 融资决策（9A）
finished goods 成品（5B）
first-line manager 初级管理者（1A）
fixed assets 固定资产（9A）
focus on 注视，关注（1B）
for the purpose of 为了（9B）
free will 自愿，自由意志（2B）
from ... point of view 从……的角度（1A）
from this perspective 从这个角度看（1A）

G

gather information 采集信息（10A）
get over 爬过，克服（2B）
give rise to 引起，发生（8B）
give thought to 留意，注意；考虑，深思（4A）

give up 放弃(念头、希望等)，停止（3B）
give weight to 重视；加强（4B）
global village 全球村（5B）
go along with 一起去，赞同（3B）
go through 经历，经受，仔细检查，参加，履行（3B）

H

hard sell 硬卖，强行推销（4B）
have a significant impact on... 对……有重大影响（5B）
health care 卫生保健（5A）
health insurance 健康保险（3A）
home and abroad 国内外（4A）
human capital 人力资本（1A）
human resource planning 人力资源规划（3A）
human skill 人际技能（1B）

I

in a broad sense 广义地说（9B）
in addition 另外（1B）
in advance of 在……前面，超过（2B）
in conformance with 与……一致（1A）
in conjunction with 与……联合，与……协力（2A）
in connection with 与……有关，连同（4A）
in effect 有效（8B）
in essence 本质上；大体上；其实（5A）
in high demand 需要量很大（3A）
in jeopardy 在危险中（8A）
in most instances 在大部分情况下（8A）
in nature 实际上，本质上（5A）
in order to ... 为了……（10A）
in search of 寻找，追求（1B）
in such a way 以这样的一种方式（10A）
in support of 支持，支援（6A）
in the absence of 没有（2B）
in the direction of 朝……方向（3A）
in the face of 面对，面向，面临（3B）
in the long run 最后（4B）
in turn 反过来；轮流地；挨个，依次（5A）
industrial society 工业社会（5A）
inform sb. of 告知某人（1A）

insist on 坚持，坚决要求，强调（2B）
intangible assets 无形资产（9A）
intellectual property 知识产权（2A）
interest rate 利率（9A）
interested party 有关的当事人（2B）
interior finishing 内部修饰（8B）
internal auditors 内审员（1A）
International Monetary Fund 国际货币基金组织（2A）
inventory reduction 减少库存（6B）
investment decision 投资决策（9A）
investment return 投资回报（2A）

J

job analysis 工作分析（3A）
just as 正像……，如同（3A）

K

keep in mind 谨记（1B）
keep track of 明了，了解；记录，保持联系；跟踪（1B）

L

labor relation 劳资关系（3A）
labor union 工会（3A）
lay foundation 奠基；打基础（8B）
lay the foundation for 给……打下基础，为……奠定基础（3A）
lead to 导致（1B）
leave off 停止（5B）
life cycle 生命周期（6B）
logistical operations 物流管理（6A）
logistical system 物流系统（6A）

M

make contributions to... 为……做贡献（3B）
make reference to 提及，涉及（9B）
Malcolm Baldrige National Quality Award 马尔科姆·巴里奇国家质量奖（7B）
managerial accounting 管理会计（9B）
map out 制订（3A）
market positioning 市场定位（4A）
market share 市场份额（9B）
material management 材料管理（6A）
matrix organization 矩阵制组织（8B）

middle level manager 中层经理（1A）
military base 军事基地（5A）
money market 金融市场，货币市场，短期资金市场（4A）
motion picture 电影（8A）
Motorola Corp. 摩托罗拉公司（7B）

N

natural disaster 自然灾害（5A）
no longer 不再（5B）
non-executive directors 非执行董事（1A）

O

on loan 借贷（8B）
on the principle of 根据……的原则（4A）
open source 开源，开放资源（2A）
operating principle 运作原则（4A）
operating system 操作系统（10A）
operational definition 操作性定义（7A）
operational plan 运营计划（2A）
operations management 运营管理（5A）
opportunity cost 机会成本（9A）
oral presentation 口头陈述（2A）
out of the ordinary 不平常的，非凡的（3B）
outside resource 外部资源（1A）
owner's equity 所有者权益（9A）

P

pay off 还清，付清（9A）
performance appraisal 绩效考核（3A）
physical distribution 物理分销（4A）
physical distribution management 货物流通管理（6A）
pitch deck 融资演讲稿（2A）
plant capacity 工厂设备(生产)能力（2B）
play a significant role in ... 在……起重要作用（9B）
product development 产品开发（4A）
product return 退货（6B）
production scheduling 生产调度（6A）
profit from 得益于（7B）
project management system 项目管理系统（8A）
project manager 项目管理人（8A）
project plan 项目计划（2A）
project team 项目研究小组，攻关队伍（8A）

provide guidance to 指导（1A）
put forth 放出，提出，发表（3B）
put up 提供（9A）

R

rack up 获胜，击倒（4A）
real assets 不动产（9A）
regardless of 不管，不顾（3B）
regulatory agency 管理机构（8B）
remove from 拿走；撤走，除去（6A）
resource allocator 资源分配者（1A）
resource shortage 资源短缺（4B）
reverse logistics 逆向物流（6B）
reward system 奖励制度（1A）
role model 行为榜样（7B）
run a risk 冒险（4B）

S

safeguard against 保护；防卫（6B）
satisfy sb's needs 满足某人的需要（4A）
section leader 部门领导（1A）
set a tone 定调子（1A）
Six Sigma 6 西格玛（7B）
snatch away 迅速拿走（3A）
specialize in 擅长于，专攻（4A）
stand for 代表（7B）
start up 启动，新兴公司（2A）
start with 以……开始（4B）
storage device 存储设备（10A）
strategic partner 战略伙伴（2A）
strategic plan 战略计划（2A）
succeed in 在……方面成功（4A）
supply chain 供应链（6B）
supply chain management 供应链管理（2A）
surprise party 惊喜聚会（8A）
sustainable competitive advantage 可持续发展的竞争优势（2A）

T

take... into account 考虑（7A）
take advantage of 利用（7A）
take pictures 照相（3B）
tangible assets 有形资产（9A）
target market 目标市场（4A）

team member 队员（8A）
team spirit 团队精神（8B）
technical skill 技术技能（1B）
term paper 学期报告（8A）
Texas Instruments 得州仪器公司（5B）
tie together 捆绑在一起；配合（6A）
time frame 期限，时帧（5A）
time horizon 时间范围（5A）
time lag 时滞（9B）
top management 高层管理（8A）
top manager 高层管理者，高管人员（1A）
top-down approach 由上至下的方法（5A）
Total Quality Management 全面质量管理（6B）
track down 追捕到（4B）
transportation cost 运输成本（6B）

U
under the control of 受……的控制（6A）

V
value chain 价值链（5B）
vantage point 有利位置，优越地位，优势（6A）
vice versa 反之亦然（7A）
view ... as 把……看作（1A）
virtual enterprise 虚拟企业（5B）

W
Winter Olympics 冬季奥运会（8A）
with respect to 关于（5A）
word processor 文字处理程序（10A）
work overtime （超出时间的工作）加班（5A）
World Bank 世界银行（2A）

Z
zero-defect 零缺陷（6B）

缩 写 表

ATM(Automated Teller Machine) 自动取款机（5B）
B2B(Business to Business) 企业对企业的电子商务（5B）
CEO(Chief Executive Officer) 执行总裁，首席执行官（1A）
CFO(Chief Financial Officer) 首席财务官（1A）
DB(DataBase) 数据库（10A）
DBMS(DataBase Management System) 数据库管理系统（10A）
DMADV(Define, Measure, Analyze, Design, Verify) 定义、测量、分析、设计、校验（7B）
DMAIC(Define, Measure, Analyze, Improve, Control) 定义、测量、分析、改进、控制（7B）
DSS(Decision Support System) 决策支持系统（10A）
GE(General Electric Co.) [美] 通用电气公司（7B）
HRM(Human Resource Management) 人力资源管理（3A）
IT(Information Technology) 信息技术（2A）
MBA(Master of Business Administration) 工商管理硕士（1B）
MIS(Management Information System) 管理信息系统（10A）
NPO(Non-Profitable Organization) 非营利组织（1A）
OM(Operations Management) 运营管理（5A）
QC(Quality Control) 质量控制（7A）
ROI(Return on Investment) 投资回报率（9B）
SPC(Statistical Process Control) 统计过程控制（7A）
SWOT(Strengths Weaknesses Opportunities Threats) 竞争优势、竞争劣势、机会和威胁（2A）
TQM(Total Quality Management) 全面质量管理（7A）

ATM(Automatic Teller Machine) 自动取款机（8B）
B2B(Business to Business) 企业对企业电子商务（7D）
CKO(Chief knowledge Officer) 知识总裁（1A）
CFO(Chief Financial Officer) 首席财务官（1A）
DB(Database) 数据库（10A）
DBMS(Database Management System) 数据库管理系统（10A）
DMADV(Define, Measure, Analyze, Design, Verify) 界定、测量、分析、设计、验证（7B）
DMAIC(Define, Measure, Analyze, Improve, Control) 界定、测量、分析、改进、控制（7B）
DSS(Decision Support System) 决策支持系统（10A）
GE(General Electric Co.) 通用电气公司（7B）

HRM(Human Resource Management) 人力资源管理（4A）
IT(Information technology) 信息技术（1A）
MBA(Master of Business Administration) 工商管理硕士（1B）
MIS(Management Information System) 管理信息系统（10A）
NPO(Non-Profitable Organization) 非营利组织（1A）
OM(Operations Management) 生产管理（5A）
QC(Quality Control) 质量控制（7A）
ROI(Return on Investment) 投资回报率（6B）
SPC(Statistical Process Control) 统计过程控制（7A）
SWOT(Strengths Weaknesses Opportunities Threats) 优势劣势机会威胁综合分析法（2A）
TQM(Total Quality Management) 全面质量管理（7A）

U
under the control of 受……的控制（6A）

V
value chain 价值链（3D）
vantage point 有利的观点、观察点（6A）
vice versa 反之亦然（7A）
view ... as ... 将……看作（1A）
virtual enterprise 虚拟企业（5B）

W
Winter Olympics 冬季奥运会（8A）
with respect to 关于（5A）
word processor 文字处理程序（10A）
work overtime（超额）加班工作；加班（5A）
World Bank 世界银行（2A）

X
xerochasy 干裂开（6B）